Recent Sociology Titles from W. W. Norton

Code of the Street by Elijah Anderson

Social Problems by Joel Best

You May Ask Yourself: An Introduction to Thinking Like a Sociologist by Dalton Conley

The Real World: An Introduction to Sociology, 2nd Edition by Kerry Ferris and Jill Stein

Introduction to Sociology, 7th Edition, by Anthony Giddens, Mitchell Duneier, Richard P. Appelbaum, and Deborah Carr

Essentials of Sociology, 2nd Edition, by Anthony Giddens, Mitchell Duneier, Richard P. Appelbaum, and Deborah Carr

The Contexts Reader edited by Jeff Goodwin and James M. Jasper

When Sex Goes to School by Kristin Luker

Inequality and Society by Jeff Manza and Michael Sauder

Readings for Sociology, 6th Edition, edited by Garth Massey

Families As They Really Are, edited by Barbara Risman

A Sociology of Globalization by Saskia Sassen

The Sociology of News by Michael Schudson

The Corrosion of Character by Richard Sennett

Biography and the Sociological Imagination by Michael J. Shanahan and Ross Macmillan

A Primer on Social Movements by David Snow and Sarah Soule

Six Degrees by Duncan J. Watts

More than Just Race by William Julius Wilson

Norton Critical Editions

The Souls of Black Folk by W. E. B. Du Bois. edited by Henry Louis Gates Jr. and Terri Hume Oliver

The Communist Manifesto by Karl Marx, edited by Frederic L. Bender

The Protestant Ethic and the Spirit of Capitalism by Max Weber, translated by Talcott Parsons and edited by Richard Swedberg

For more information on our publications in sociology, please visit wwnorton.com

mix it up

popular culture, mass media, and society

david grazian

University of Pennsylvania

W. W. Norton   New York   London

W·W·NORTON

NEW YORK · LONDON

W. W. Norton & Company has been independent since its founding in 1923, when William Warder Norton and Mary D. Herter Norton first published lectures delivered at the People's Institute, the adult education division of New York City's Cooper Union. The Nortons soon expanded their program beyond the Institute, publishing books by celebrated academics from America and abroad. By mid-century, the two major pillars of Norton's publishing program—trade books and college texts—were firmly established. In the 1950s, the Norton family transferred control of the company to its employees, and today—with a staff of four hundred and a comparable number of trade, college, and professional titles published each year—W. W. Norton & Company stands as the largest and oldest publishing house owned wholly by its employees.

Editor: Karl Bakeman
Managing editor, College: Marian Johnson
Project editor: Sarah Mann
Editorial assistants: Rebecca Charney and Sarah Johnson
Copyeditor: Patterson Lamb
Production Manager: Eric Pier-Hocking
Design Director: Rubina Yeh
Book Designer: Brian Sisco
Photo Researchers: Julie Tesser
Layout by Carole Desnoes
Composition by TexTech, Inc.
Manufacturing by the Courier Companies—Westford Division

Library of Congress Cataloging-in-Publication Data

Grazian, David.
    Mix it up : popular culture, mass media, and society / David Grazian. —1st ed.
        p. cm.
    Includes index

ISBN: 978-0-393-92952-2 (pbk.)

    1. Popular culture. 2.   Mass media—Social aspects. I.   Title.
    HM621.G73 2010
    306—dc22

                                                                                2009049573

W. W. Norton & Company, Inc., 500 Fifth Avenue, New York, NY 10110
www.wwnorton.com

W. W. Norton & Company, Ltd., Castle House, 75/76 Wells Street, London WIT3QT

1234567890

For Meredith and Nathaniel

Contents

Preface

SOME ARGUE THAT POP CULTURE IS DISPOSABLE; OTHERS FIND IT despicable. No matter: in one form or another, it is here to stay. As a sociologist, one of the fun aspects of my job is deciphering what it all means, in part by exploring what different kinds of popular culture—mystery novels, rock and rap recordings, animated films, reality television shows, video games, Internet networking sites—may have in common. What makes popular culture *popular*, exactly? How do its numerous creators bring popular culture into existence? How do media companies like Viacom, NBC Universal, Sony, and Paramount Pictures decide which products to develop and promote? Why do people seem to enjoy some genres of entertainment more than others?

Since you are reading this preface, perhaps these kinds of questions have occurred to you from time to time. The purpose of this book is to begin a sincere intellectual conversation about popular culture, admittedly a topic often mocked for being trivial, ephemeral, tacky, and lacking in scholarly and academic merit. To those naysayers who think pop culture is unworthy of study, I would offer the reminder that the Disney Corporation took in revenues of nearly $38 billion in 2008. In that same year, the Batman film *The Dark Knight* grossed over a billion dollars worldwide at the box office, and consumers downloaded just over a billion songs from the Internet. In 2009, over 98 million TV viewers tuned in to watch the Pittsburgh Steelers defeat the Arizona Cardinals in Super Bowl XLIII. Regardless of whether *Dancing with the Stars* shares the artistic integrity of the New York City Ballet, popular culture matters deeply, to its countless fans, its creative producers and champions, and especially to the global economy. As scholars and students of society and social life, it certainly ought to matter to us.

Like all popular culture, *Mix It Up* benefited greatly from the contributions of many collaborators, and I thank them here. First and foremost, an enthusiastic round of applause to my editor, Karl Bakeman, and the entire Norton staff for the industriousness they brought to this project. In particular, I would like to thank Sarah Mann and Eric Pier-Hocking for managing the book as it moved through production. Julie Tesser deserves credit for her brilliant photo research, as does Patterson Lamb for her copyediting prowess, and Becky Charney and Sarah Johnson for their editorial assistance. I am also grateful to a number of editorial reviewers who commented on earlier chapter drafts: they include Andrew Bark, Wayne Brekhus, Tori Barnes-Brus, Scott Barretta, Jennifer Lena, Omar Lizardo, Jonathan Mermis-Cava, Matthew Oware, Johanna Pabst, and Thomas Streeter. Tyson Smith, Julie Szymczak, and Junhow Wei all remarked on earlier chapter drafts as well; their insights tremendously improved this book. Additionally, Rosalie Siegel offered invaluable professional advice.

Mix It Up developed out of a course I have taught at Penn in various iterations since my arrival there in 2001, and I thank the many sociology graduate students who helped to shape its curriculum by heroically serving as my teaching assistants: Faye Allard, Claire Barshied, Keith Brown, Rachelle Brunn, Bridget Costello, Sabrina Danielsen, Benjamin DiCicco-Bloom, Fareeda McClinton Griffith, Jan Jaeger, Colette Joyce, Stefan Klusemann, Taryn Kudler, Catherine Mayer, Keri Monahan, Bridget Nolan, Laura Napolitano, Yetunde Afolabi Pillischer, Elizabeth Raleigh, Georges Reniers, Jessica Rubin, Mollie Rubin, Lindsay Taggart Rutherford, Regina Smardon, Julie Szymczak, Elizabeth Vaquera, Junhow Wei, Lijun Yang, and Yuping Zhang. Over the years Cyndi Butz, Michael Cimicata, Robert Felton, Shirley Halperin and Sara Sherr generously shared their expertise on the media and culture industries with me and my students.

I also thank my colleagues at Penn for their encouragement and good cheer through the duration of this project. The Penn Humanities Forum provided financial support through a Mellon Faculty Research Fellowship, while Van Pelt Library lent me hundreds of rock and pop CDs, and Karen Cook passed along issues of *Rolling Stone* and *US Weekly* from the Population Studies Center's secret magazine collection. My pop culture-savvy colleagues and friends from Penn and its campus neighbors, especially Jacques Bromberg, David Comberg, Richardson Dilworth, Scott Hanson, Kristen Harknett, Jerome Hodos, Grace Kao, Doug McKee, Jason Schnittker, Bryant Simon, and Matt Wray, always supply much lively discussion. From points north of Philadelphia, Eric Klinenberg and Jason Kaufman provided valuable suggestions regarding curricular matters. Finally, my gratitude goes to Wendy Griswold for introducing me to the sociology of culture. Indeed, her influence on this book will be readily apparent to those familiar with her scholarly work and disciplinary vision.

On a personal note: Many thanks to my parents, Solomon and Kathy Grazian, for introducing me to Frank Sinatra, Neil Diamond, Simon and Garfunkel, the Beatles, and the Marx Brothers; Jason Gottlieb and Greg Karzhevsky, for encouraging me to recognize the musical complexities of progressive rock music from Pink Floyd to Rush; Darryl Jefferson, for introducing me to psychedelic soul; Aimee Strasko Carlisle, for opening my eyes to the super-hip world of indie rock; Chad Broughton, who brought me to my first Chicago blues club; Jeff Morenoff, for guiding me through my introduction to jazz and old-time folk music; Mark Ashley, for introducing me to the Internet (yes, the Internet); Joe Carey, Rod Coover, Anne Sussman, and Jon Wotman for turning me on to the pleasures of art-house, foreign, and independent cinema; and Sean Davis, for decoding for me the strange world of online role-playing video games. I extend my special appreciation to Garth Bond, Mike Cimicata, Bethany Klein, and Elia Pelios for sharing an unreasonable degree of lively banter and habit-forming debate on all things related to popular culture, its significance and trivialities alike. Their obsessions are only equal to my own.

Finally, I must thank my patient and caring wife, Meredith Broussard, who introduced me to our favorite band, the Magnetic Fields, and our son Nathaniel, a curious and precocious boy who has reintroduced me to the timeless pleasures of Dr. Seuss, Curious George, and the whole *Sesame Street* gang, from Oscar the Grouch to Cookie Monster. This book is dedicated to them—to my wife and son, that is, not Oscar and Cookie. No disrespect, of course—after all, I believe it was the great Cookie Monster himself who once said, "C is for cookie," and that's good enough for me.

David Grazian
Philadelphia, PA

An audience listens to the Vandals playing at a club. Popular culture is produced, consumed, and experienced within a context of overlapping sets of social relationships.

the straight story

THE SOCIAL ORGANIZATION
OF POPULAR CULTURE

LIKE GREAT WORKS OF ART OR SCIENTIFIC PROGRESS, EVEN THE MOST imaginative popular culture owes its reality to the hard-earned achievements of the past. On May 13, 2006, Barbados-born singer Rihanna scored her first No. 1 single on the Billboard U.S. pop chart with the catchy dance hit "SOS (Rescue Me)." Rihanna completed the song for Def Jam Recordings after being signed by its then-president and CEO, rapper Jay-Z. The lead single off her sophomore effort *A Girl Like Me* (2006), "SOS." was produced by Jonathan "J. R." Rotem, and its lyrics and music were written by Rotem and Evan "Kidd" Bogart.

Actually, that is not entirely accurate, since one other songwriter is also credited with composing the music for the single, specifically its irresistible bass line and drum beat. That songwriter is Ed Cobb, who wrote "Tainted Love," a song released in the 1980s by the British new wave duo Soft Cell, from which Rihanna and her producers liberally sample as background rhythm for their recording of "SOS." A one-hit wonder, Soft Cell's "Tainted Love" slowly climbed the Billboard U.S. Hot 100 singles chart in 1981 to No. 8, and before the duo exited into oblivion the song managed to spend what was at the time a record-breaking 43 weeks on the pop charts, almost a year. Like other 1980s British invasion artists (Depeche Mode, the Human League, Joe Jackson, the Cure), Soft Cell incorporated depressing song lyrics of unrequited love with post-punk improvisation and synthesized sound effects. In their dance remix of "Tainted Love," Soft Cell accomplished all three by integrating the signature track with a second song, "Where Did Our Love Go?" with vocals accompanied only by a sparse synth-pop bass line and beat.

Rihanna pays homage to "Tainted Love" when she sings "You got me tossin' and turnin' and I can't sleep at night," the one "SOS" lyric borrowed from the 1980s classic. Of course, Soft Cell can't really take credit for the line either, since the northern soul and rhythm-and-blues (R&B) singer Gloria Jones actually performed the original version of Ed Cobb's "Tainted Love" in 1964, and later rerecorded it in the mid-1970s with her husband Marc Bolan of the English rock band T. Rex. In fact, "Where Did Our Love Go?" is also a cover, also recorded in 1964, by the all-female Motown group the Supremes. With its lead vocals sung by Diana Ross, "Where Did Our Love Go?" was the first of twelve No. 1 songs recorded by the Supremes; their other top-charting hits include "Baby Love," "You Can't Hurry Love," "Stop! In the Name of Love," and "You Keep Me Hanging On," the last of which Rihanna also pays homage to in "SOS": "I'm out with you / Ya got me head over heels / Boy you keep me hanging on / By the way you make me feel."

What does this discography tell us about popular culture? Perhaps the clearest lesson to be gleaned is that pop music, like Greek tragedy and Elizabethan drama,

FIGURE 1.1:
The Origins of "SOS (Rescue Me)"

1981

**Tainted Love/
Where Did Our Love Go?**

Performed by Soft Cell
Produced by Mike Thorne
Written by Ed Cobb

2006

SOS (Rescue Me)

Performed by Rihanna
Produced by Jonathan "JR" Rotem
Written by Rotem, Evan "Kidd"
Bogart, and Ed Cobb

1976

Tainted Love

Performed by Gloria Jones and
Marc Bolan
Produced by Marc Bolan
Written by Ed Cobb

1964

Where Did Our Love Go?

Performed by the Supremes
Written by Lamont Dozier, Brian
Holland, and Edward Holland, Jr.

1964

Tainted Love

Performed by Gloria Jones
Written by Ed Cobb

can transcend its historical moment to enjoy endless cycles of rediscovery and reinvention (Griswold 1986), just as "Tainted Love" began as a 1960s northern soul song, and found new life as an 1980s synth-pop classic, which two decades later would be sampled for inclusion on a 2006 R&B dance hit. (And lest readers forget, in 2001 Marilyn Manson released his own alternative heavy-metal version of "Tainted Love" for inclusion on the *Not Another Teen Movie* film soundtrack, and the Pussycat Dolls included their own version on their debut album, *PCD.*)

The creators of popular culture rely on an endless repository of past work to inform their development of new and future projects, from pop singles to animated cartoons to feature films. In such cases the first step to achieving success as a cultural *producer* is to be a savvy *consumer* of mass media and popular culture.

Moreover, the 42-year (and counting) history of "Tainted Love" spotlights a number of cultural producers whose combined efforts carried this song through its numerous incarnations (see fig. 1.1). Popular culture is never the product of a solitary artist but always emerges from the *collective activity* generated by interlocking networks of cultural creators. Of course, this is not to suggest that Rihanna would not have recorded "SOS" at all, if not for these many participants—only that without their cumulative input and influence, her song would have sounded different from the way it currently does (Becker 1982).

All this highlights the major argument of this book: *popular culture is produced, consumed, and experienced within a context of overlapping sets of social relationships.* Some of those relationships are forged out of a spirit of musicianship and camaraderie, as illustrated by the two members of Soft Cell. Many more are contractual relationships between artists and business firms built out of economic convenience, like the relationship between Rihanna and Def Jam Recordings, or between Def Jam and its parent company Universal Music Group. Still others represent the close bonds between cultural creators and their audiences, or among the members of a social group who maintain a shared sense of identity, whether on the basis of class, race, nationality, religiosity, gender, or sexuality. This opens up a range of interesting questions: how are pop music genres such as rap, rhythm and blues, country, and heavy metal socially organized by industry personnel and audiences on the basis of social status? How do existing copyright laws impact the distribution of digital media? How are global

TABLE 1.1
Definitions of Popular Culture

Definition	Example
Culture that is "popular" is *well liked,* best demonstrated in a market economy through *commercial success.*	Films such as *Star Wars* or *Indiana Jones and the Kingdom of the Crystal Skull*
Popular culture refers to icons or media products that are *well known* the world over.	Paris Hilton or Princess Diana
Popular culture refers to commercial media considered *mass culture*—trivial, tacky, and pitched to the lowest common denominator for general consumption.	Commercial pop stars who target teen audiences, such as "boy bands" or *American Idol* singers
Popular culture refers to culture considered to *belong to the people* under the guise of democratic populism and authenticity.	Recording artists who create music that speaks to the experiences of ordinary working-class people

pop cultural styles like Afro-Cuban jazz, Turkish hip-hop, Bhangra dance music, and Bollywood film shaped by the local and regional settings in which they are transplanted? These questions all point to the centrality of social relationships in the creation, consumption, and experience of popular culture.

What Makes Pop Culture Popular?

In common parlance, popular culture refers to the aesthetic products created and sold by profit-seeking firms operating in the global entertainment market—horror movies, reality television, dance music, fashion magazines, graphic novels, literary fiction, remote-controlled toys, fast-food hamburgers, online video games. But understanding popular culture sociologically first requires that we define exactly what we mean by these two words of subtle complexity: *popular* and *culture.* Let us begin at the beginning: What does it mean for pop culture to be *popular*? It sounds simple, but in fact the word *popular* carries several distinct (and at times contradictory) connotations. First, and perhaps most obviously, (1) culture that is "popular" is *well liked,* and in a market economy that popularity is often best demonstrated through *commercial success* as measured by Nielsen ratings, video rentals, album sales, or box-office revenue. In 2008, the top-grossing films included *The Dark Knight, Iron Man, The Chronicles of Narnia: Prince Caspian,* and *Indiana Jones and the Kingdom of the Crystal Skull.* That last film took in $150 million in U.S. box-office receipts in its first four days of release and starred the most successful film actor in the world, Harrison Ford, who typically earns $25 million per film in addition to a share of their profits. Having starred in recurring roles as Han Solo, Indiana Jones, and Jack Ryan in some of the biggest film franchises of all time, his movies have grossed nearly $6 billion worldwide. Other popular A-list actors who earn over $20 million per film include Tom Cruise, Johnny Depp, Leonardo DiCaprio, Tom Hanks, Reese Witherspoon, Angelina Jolie, Cameron Diaz, Adam Sandler, Will Smith, and Denzel Washington.

Of course, not all popular culture succeeds commercially, and much of it isn't particularly well liked by anyone, especially annoying TV advertisements or well-known celebrities who seem to be famous for, well, simply *being famous* despite an obvious lack of talent or achievement (or sometimes *because* of that lack of talent, as in the case of the weird 2004 novelty success of tone-deaf *American Idol* contestant William Hung). In this sense, (2) popular culture refers to icons or media products that are globally *ubiquitous* and easily *recognized* (if perhaps disliked or mocked) the world over (Gamson 1994; Gabler 2000). The most clarifying examples come from the diamond-encrusted world of high society, and in our contemporary culture, Exhibit A is hotel heiress Paris Hilton. While her fame seems quite strange, her celebrity is actually modeled after similarly ostentatious women of wealth from earlier generations, including serial divorcées Zsa Zsa Gabor and Ivana Trump. Of course, there are certainly more likable exemplars, as illustrated by the waves of loss felt worldwide after the widely reported deaths of John F. Kennedy, Jr. (born just after his father won the American presidency in November 1960), and Princess Diana, the former wife of Prince Charles of Wales.

Today, Diana's sons, William and Harry, represent the kind (if not degree) of celebrity enjoyed by their beloved late mother.

However, despite the differences between Paris Hilton and the members of the British royal family, many critics see these icons as two sides of the same coin of mainstream mass culture. According to their worldview, (3) popular culture refers to commercial media thought to be trivial, tacky, and pitched to the lowest common denominator as *mass culture* intended for general consumption, like canned soup or chewing gum (MacDonald 1957). In this context, popular culture—Kid Rock, Chicken McNuggets, *America's Funniest Home Videos*—is unfavorably compared to the fine arts as represented by Italian opera, French nouvelle cuisine, and *cinéma vérité*. In these instances, the *populations* implicated by the use of *pop* culture as a pejorative label tend to be socially marginalized by class, race, and often age—hence the critical panning of melodramatic "pop" stars who target preadolescent and teenage audiences such as boy bands, *American Idol* winners, and the cast of *High School Musical*. Of course, mass culture also has its many defenders, including those who argue for its intellectual complexity and depth, increasing innovativeness and social relevance, kitschy fun and contemporary cool, and similarities to past cultural touchstones now canonized as great art (Simon 1999; Johnson 2006).

Yet for another set of artists and audiences, (4) popular culture is associated with songs, dances, and other folk expressions *belonging to the people* under the guise of democratic populism and authenticity. This last connotation of popular culture refers to recording artists who create roots-oriented music such as blues, reggae, and certain strains of American rock, country, and rap, whose music is said to channel the traditional hopes and dreams of ordinary working-class people. They include legends such as Robert Johnson, Woody Guthrie, Hank Williams, Johnny Cash, Bob Dylan, Neil Young, and Bob Marley, while in recent decades musicians of this ilk have included rock singer-songwriters like Bruce Springsteen, and politically oriented hip-hop artists such as Public Enemy, Wyclef Jean, and the Roots.

Defining Culture

As if the multiple and contradictory connotations of the word *popular* were not confusing enough, defining *culture* can be equally frustrating, particularly since this complex term has finely differentiated meanings in a variety of dispersed intellectual traditions and academic disciplines. For example, in the humanities, culture represents what Raymond Williams (1983, p. 90) identifies as "the works and practices of intellectual and especially artistic activity," particularly those that lead toward "a general process of intellectual, spiritual and aesthetic development." The first part of this definition suggests the outward forms that culture takes in the humanities: great novels and concertos, classical architecture and painting, Wagnerian opera and contemporary experimental poetry. In the fields of literature, music, philosophy, and art history, culture represents the most revered expressions of the human condition—Shakespeare's *King Lear* and *Hamlet,* Dostoyevsky's *Crime and Punishment* and Melville's *Moby-Dick,*

Beethoven's Fifth Symphony and Bach's Toccata and Fugue in D Minor. As for culture's function, it is not merely one of entertainment, but "intellectual, spiritual and aesthetic development"; in other words, the purpose of culture is nothing less than the cultivation of the mind as a path toward greater enlightenment and epicurean pleasure. It is only through experiencing culture as such that an individual—and by extension, an entire human society—can truly come to be thought of as "civilized."

This humanist vision of culture suggests a high-minded and perhaps inaccessible world of challenging ideas communicated through complicated texts. In contrast, in the social sciences, culture refers to "a particular way of life, whether of a people, a period, a group, or humanity in general" (Williams 1983, p. 90). To the sociologist (or anthropologist, psychologist, economist, political scientist, or communication scholar, for that matter), culture refers to a mode of living in the world as a social being, as represented by the practices, rituals, behaviors, activities, and artifacts that make up the experience of everyday life. For example, culture can refer to the styles of cooking and eating enjoyed by a people—their cuisines, recipes, ingredients, spices, kitchen tools, and table manners. We can appreciate this fact even though it is hard to imagine our *own* modern culinary folkways—say, slurping down Froot Loops cereal for breakfast—as particularly cultural. After all, it would not be unusual to find the serving utensils of an ancient society (such as their clay pitchers, metal spoons, or drinking goblets) exhibited in an art museum, or in an archaeology textbook. The improvised games children play—Double Dutch, Red Rover, hopscotch, freeze tag, dodge ball—are also cultural, as are our dirty jokes, obscene gestures, and other locker-room antics.

To this end, sociologists of culture are interested in a wide spectrum of everyday rituals and social activities associated with public life, including sports participation and spectatorship, dating and courtship, retail shopping, beauty and cosmetic enhancement, casino gambling, and cigarette smoking. However, for some this anthropological conception of culture may seem to suggest an impossibly broad inventory of possible topics for analysis, as vast as human civilization itself. A helpful way to cut culture down to a manageable size is to focus on three properties common to both the humanist and social scientific understandings of culture. Culture is richly *symbolic,* invested with meaning and significance. The meanings attributed to culture are never simply given but are the product of human invention, *socially constructed* and agreed upon among a demonstrably large number of a society's members. Finally, for culture to be sensibly understood it must be *embodied* in some kind of recognizable form.

To best emphasize these three properties of culture, Wendy Griswold (1986, p. 5; 2004, p. 13), a sociologist at Northwestern University, characterizes the sociology of culture as the study of *cultural objects,* or "shared significance embodied in form." Cultural objects are social expressions of meaning that have been rendered into something tangible, like a Greek epic poem or a bronze sculpture. By the same token, cultural objects can be found in the world of popular

Why is Spider-Man an example of a popular cultural object?

culture as well as the fine arts—Homer's *Iliad* and Homer Simpson, John Milton's *Paradise Lost* and ABC's *Lost*. While sociologists of culture investigate and analyze "the works and practices of intellectual and especially artistic activity," these creative compositions not only include classical music and nineteenth-century Russian literature, but also mass media enjoyed in the contemporary world as a regular feature of everyday life: rock 'n roll and rhythm-and-blues music, celebrity magazines, animated cartoons, billboard advertising, network newscasts, comic books, reality television, Internet blogs, and Guitar Hero.

At the same time, a popular cultural object need not even be a traditional form of visual or aural media: it could be a meaningful nonverbal gesture, like a wide smile, a conspiratorial wink, an enthusiastic thumbs-up, or an aggressively pointed middle finger (Geertz 1973, pp. 6–7; Katz 1999, pp. 18–86). It could be an icon, like Abraham Lincoln (Schwartz 1996, 1998; Schwartz and Schuman 2005), or Cupid, or the Grand Canyon, or the Volkswagen logo. In this sense popular cultural objects operate at the level of language, with their articulated if complex meanings ready to be decoded among participants who inhabit a shared social environment.

Popular Culture as Collective Activity

Now that we have discussed a variety of meanings and exemplars associated with popular culture in the interests of developing as inclusive a definition as possible, the next step is to examine how popular culture can be best understood as an inherently social phenomenon. In his work on the social organization of culture and the arts, the sociologist Howard S. Becker (1982) observes that its production is first and foremost a *collective activity*. Whether a Jane Austen film adaption or a graphically violent video game, popular cultural objects are produced by collaborative webs of interconnected individuals working together toward a common goal and eventually consumed and experienced by audiences who attach shared meanings to them.

According to Becker (1982), media and popular culture are produced in the context of *art worlds,* or networks of participants whose combined efforts create movies, novels, musical compositions, comic books, advertising, and so forth. For some types of pop culture the collective nature of creative production is readily apparent, as anyone who has scanned the thousands of names listed in the closing credits at the end of a feature film surely knows (Becker 1982, pp. 7—9). Perhaps a less obvious example of the secondary creative workers or *support personnel* who labor in relative anonymity in the culture industries are those people necessary for recording music, since even compact discs (CDs) credited to a single artist like Beyoncé, Jack Johnson, or Justin Timberlake rely on teams of session musicians, studio engineers, and sound mixers. In the music industry, support personnel may also include the software developers responsible for the digital technology that enables the easy transfer of performed music into binary code and back into realized sound, and the record producer who matches the appropriate set of effects pedals to each guitarist. For most CDs, even the artwork materials (whether physical or digital) alone require the cooperative efforts of product managers, art directors, photographers, archivists, liner note writers, copyeditors, and other support staff (Becker 1982).

Given the collective nature of producing popular culture, it only makes sense that in a complex society like our own, networks of creative personnel are organized according to a highly segmented *division of labor,* as the aforementioned examples from recorded music and film suggest (Becker 1982, p. 7). The world of cinema alone could fill entire textbooks, given its limitless slate of specialized jobs: visual effects gaffer, gang boss painter, best boy, focus puller. A cursory look at university degree programs in fields of cultural production further highlights the emphasis toward specialization in the creative industries; for example, at New York University's Tisch School of the Arts students can earn graduate diplomas in Dramatic Writing, Interactive Telecommunications, and Moving Image Archiving and Preservation.

But while contemporary art worlds are notable for their high degree of segmentation, they are also known for their ability to efficiently organize *cooperative links* among a wildly diverse array of contributors who depend on one another when producing the stuff of pop culture and entertainment media (Becker 1982, pp. 24—28). Sometimes these participants collaborate regularly, like the four celebrity musicians who make up the Irish rock band U2, or the 107 members of the Chicago Symphony Orchestra, or the permanent editorial staff of *Rolling Stone*, or the thousands of compensated workers and unpaid interns employed by Walt Disney Pictures or Sony Music Entertainment. Other cultural producers work jointly with one another on a more ad hoc basis. For instance, television postproduction teams incorporate a range of creative workers (including video editors, sound engineers, and studio musicians) who work on clearly defined projects for a specified period of time, such as a single television season (Faulkner 1971). The installation of a chic boutique window display requires the cooperative but temporary efforts of stage set designers, visual artists, and mannequin handlers. A fashion magazine spread employs photographers, models, lighting technicians, makeup artists, copy writers, graphic designers, and other creative personnel, some of whom may work together for only a single day.

Why Support Personnel Matter

Some might argue that support personnel operate at the creative edges of art worlds rather than at their centers, although it certainly depends on one's perspective. After all, regardless of how well the lead singer of a recording can perform in the studio, the actual sound of a rock or dance track depends almost entirely on the ability of a sound engineer or producer to make smart and targeted choices likely considered arcane by almost any ordinary listener. For instance, Steve Albini is an independent rock musician whose bands include Big Black and Shellac, and as a music producer and engineer he has recorded albums for the Pixies, the Breeders, PJ Harvey, and Nirvana. As Albini (1997) points out in his essay "The Problem with Music," the expertise required of support personnel in the recording studio is not only extensive but integral to the production process in ways that are typically ignored by most lay audiences. According to Albini:

The minimum skills required to do an adequate job recording an album are:

••• **Working knowledge of all the microphones at hand and their properties and uses.** I mean something beyond knowing that you can drop an SM 57 without breaking it.

••• **Experience with every piece of equipment that might be of use and every function it might provide.** This means more than knowing what echo sounds like. Which equalizer has the least phase shift in neighbor bands? Which console has more headroom? Which mastering deck has the cleanest output electronics? . . .

••• **Ability to tune and maintain all the required instruments and electronics, so as to insure that everything is in proper working order.** This means more than plugging a guitar into a tuner. How should the drums be tuned to simulate a rising note on the decay? A falling note? A consonant note? Can a bassoon play a concert E-flat in key with a piano tuned to a reference A of 440 Hz? What percentage of varispeed is necessary to make a whole-tone pitch change? What degree of overbias gives you the most headroom at 10 Khz? What reference fluxivity gives you the lowest self-noise from biased, unrecorded tape? Which tape manufacturer closes every year in July, causing shortages of tape globally? What can be done for a shedding master tape? A sticky one?

••• **Knowledge of electronic circuits to an**

Producer Steve Albini.

extent that will allow selection of appropriate signal paths. This means more than knowing the difference between a delay line and an equalizer. Which has more headroom, a discrete class A microphone preamp with a transformer output or a differential circuit built with monolithics? Where is the best place in an unbalanced line to attenuate the signal? If you short the cold leg of a differential input to ground, what happens to the signal level? Which gain control device has the least distortion, a VCA, a printed plastic pot, a photoresistor, or a wire-wound stepped attenuator? Will putting an unbalanced line on a half-normalled jack unbalance the normal signal path? Will a transformer splitter load the input to a device parallel to it? Which will have less RF noise, a shielded unbalanced line or a balanced line with a floated shield? (pp. 168–69)

The Social Context of Popular Culture

The collaborative efforts of those who produce popular culture do not take place in a vacuum but in the context of lived social life, and that context matters in a variety of subtle and not so subtle ways. For instance, during the first half of the twentieth century the invention of discrete genre categories in the music industry reflected the widespread residential and market segregation of African American audiences from white consumers (Massey and Denton 1993; Peterson 1997). For this reason, otherwise indistinguishable music styles are often differently classified and subsequently advertised and sold on the basis of race—note the musical and lyrical similarities between 1950s blues, R&B, and rock 'n roll.

From an industry perspective rock 'n roll emerged as the most commercially viable of these genre categories, particularly among white teenagers—which is why even young readers have heard of Elvis Presley but few popular music fans remember the great African American blues artist Arthur "Big Boy" Crudup, who in 1946 wrote and recorded "That's All Right (Mama)," which Presley covered and released in 1954 as his very first single. Most pop music listeners have also never heard of the blues and R&B singer Big Mama Thornton, whose original 1952 recording of "Hound Dog" is today overshadowed (rightly or wrongly) by Presley's version, which *Rolling Stone* named one of the Top 20 rock 'n roll songs of all time.

The physical and social infrastructure of our cities and towns determines the fate of popular culture as well. For example, the development of privatized

How do social contexts affect the creation and consumption of popular culture? Consider the story of Elvis Presley (left), who covered "Hound Dog," which was originally recorded in 1952 by Big Mama Thornton (right).

suburbs and gated communities during the 1940s and 1950s contributed to an overall decline in urban nightlife and public leisure and a simultaneous rise in the popularity of home entertainment—particularly television. In 1953 two-thirds of family households in America owned at least one television set and by the mid-1960s that figure grew to a whopping 94 percent (Hannigan 1998; Cohen 2003, p. 302). As for the homegrown popular culture indigenous to the city, during the 1970s the interconnectedness and accessibility of New York's underground transit system facilitated the urban development of a citywide community of subway graffiti writers and muralists (Lachmann 1988). But by the 1980s, circumstances changed when increased police surveillance, the implementation of extreme security measures in the city's train yards (i.e., razor wire, guard dogs), and the tireless vigilance of transit cleaning crews all converged to weaken New York's subway graffiti subculture, perhaps forever (Lachmann 1988; Gladwell 2002, pp. 142−43).

This last example illustrates the highly influential role that government and the state play in the cultural production process. Through public funding agencies like the National Endowment for the Arts, the government directly contributes to certain kinds of cultural growth through its financial support of theaters, film festivals, museums, authors, and art studios. The Federal Communications Commission renders decisions on what sorts of socially defined "indecent" or "obscene" images or language may be permitted on the public airwaves and how many radio stations one company may own in a given regional market (Klinenberg 2007). Local and national laws also impact the context in which popular culture is manufactured and performed. In the 1920s, the early jazz music made famous by Louis Armstrong and Duke Ellington emerged during the era of Prohibition, which meant that some of the great music of that period was performed in illegal speakeasies and other clandestine haunts, its proprietors under constant threat of arrest. Similarly, U.S. federal laws surrounding the use of Ecstasy and other illegal drugs drove the hallucinogen-fueled electronic rave dance scene underground during the height of its popularity in the 1990s (Reynolds 1999); further anti-rave legislation and enforcement in cities across the country spelled the eventual death knell for this once vibrant subculture. Most recently, copyright laws and recent court rulings have constrained the use of sampling in popular music.

Likewise, we should be reminded that laws can also be designed to protect the freedoms of cultural producers as well. Thanks to the rigorous and continual defense of the U.S. Constitution and the First Amendment throughout our nation's history, American popular culture flourishes in a far more liberal political environment than in other countries. During the 1960s Uruguay's authoritative government banned, jailed, and pressured into exile a number of protest sing-ers for the lyrical content of their music (Milstein 2007). After the publication of Salman Rushdie's controversial 1988 novel *The Satanic Verses,* the book was banned in India; during the following year the Iranian Ayatollah Ruhollah Khomeini issued a *fatwa* against Rushdie, urging fellow Muslims to assassinate the author and his publishers. Meanwhile, China earns the shameful distinction of imprisoning more of its own journalists than any other country in the world, and the Chinese government regularly censors Internet sites to prevent the free dissemination of dissident speech (Meredith 2007, p. 152).

Audiences and the Consumption of Popular Culture

Is the 1957 Jerry Lee Lewis song title "Whole Lotta Shakin' Goin' On" a sexual reference? Does Tony die in the final scene of *The Sopranos*? In the 1994 movie *Pulp Fiction,* what's in the briefcase that John Travolta and Samuel L. Jackson retrieve for their mob boss? Is HBO's *The Wire* the best police drama in television history? For all of these examples, the answer depends on who is doing the responding, because questions of meaning, interpretation, and value are not ultimately decided by the creators of media and popular culture, but by its *consumers*. (This is not to say that the intentions or objectives of cultural creators do not matter a great deal; rather, it is to emphasize that they are hardly the *only* determinants of meaning that matter. Moreover, the multiple creators of a cultural object—say, the screenwriter, director, and leading or supporting actors of a movie or television show—may disagree among *themselves* as to the meaning or value of their collaborative work.) While in the world of cultural criticism all sorts of value judgments are rendered as if they were fact—*Walt Whitman is the center of the American literary canon* (Bloom 1994), *Bruce Springsteen is the mythos of rock 'n roll sprung to life* (Alterman 2001, p. 9), *Juno was the best movie*

How do social factors shape the meaning and value of popular culture? For instance, how do fans' and critics' arguments about Bruce Springsteen being "the mythos of rock 'n roll sprung to life" reflect the multivocal status of cultural objects?

According to JoEllen Shively, many Native American men are fans of classic Westerns in spite of the way the films portray American Indians. Why are these fans an example of an interpretive community?

of 2007 (Ebert 2007)—sociologists recognize that these arguments are simply claims to be argued and contested over by fans and detractors who attribute sometimes contradictory meanings to films, books, and music, meanings that are always up for grabs. In this sense, cultural objects are *multivocal* because they say different things to different audiences (Griswold 1987).

Of course, simply because audiences fabricate the meanings and interpretations attributed to popular culture, we should not necessarily infer that they do so randomly. For some cultural objects, certain assigned meanings are collectively held by vast numbers of people based on some overriding dominant ideology—those meanings are consequently able to hold sway in the world *as if* they were absolute and irrefutable. Various listeners may enjoy or dislike Bruce Springsteen's music, but almost no one disputes that he is a *rock* musician, even though music genres like "rock" are social inventions and industry labels that are always subject to debate and change. (As I suggest above, the stylistic differences between blues, 1950s rock 'n roll, and R&B are negligible at best. To emphasize the contestable nature of the rock genre category, try a thought experiment. How many music fans would identify Muddy Waters, Miles Davis, or Madonna as "rock 'n roll" performers? Perhaps not many, as it is likely that these artists are more popularly known as blues, jazz, and pop music legends, respectively—yet all three have been inducted into the Rock and Roll Hall of Fame.)

Since audiences draw on their own social circumstances when attributing meaning and value to popular culture, these meanings are often patterned according to persistent systems of social organization structured by differences in socioeconomic status, nationality, race, ethnicity, gender, sexuality, religion, or age. For example, in her study of Harlequin romance novels and their pre-dominantly female readers, Janice Radway (1991) discovers that Midwestern housewives enjoy romances for the independence and self-reliance typically assigned to their plucky heroines; their stories thus provide a much needed if temporary escape from the exhausting labor of child rearing and household management. In an analysis of audience reception of the 1956 motion picture *The Searchers,* a Hollywood Western, JoEllen Shively (1992) discovers that despite the frequently negative portrayal of American Indians in film, Native American men are enthusiastic fans of the genre, citing the beauty of the natural landscapes where Westerns are often set, and the free and independent cowboy lifestyle commonly celebrated in such movies. Meanwhile, since the cartoonish stereo-types of American Indians as heartless kidnappers and violent scalpers often depicted in traditional Westerns do not correspond to their own contemporary self-image, Native Americans simply ignore such slights, identifying more with the heroic cowboys featured in Hollywood cinema and portrayed by classic movie stars like John Wayne, Gary Cooper, and Clint Eastwood.

Audiences draw on their social identities and life experiences to make sense of media and popular culture, and those whose shared worldviews inform their understandings of culture in systematic ways are called *interpre-tive communities* (Radway 1991; also see Fish 1980). Yet as this last example illustrates, people's social circumstances not only influence the kinds of meanings they attribute to cultural objects, events, and experiences but also the kinds of pop culture they choose to consume in the first place. All things being equal, many African Americans (but not all, of course) are more likely to report listening to jazz, blues, soul, and rhythm-and-blues music than whites, who are more likely to attend classical music concerts, opera performances, and arts or crafts fairs (DiMaggio and Ostrower 1990). Urban professionals are more likely to appreciate abstract art than working-class suburbanites (Halle 1993). In the United States, women read for leisure more than men and are more likely to join book reading groups (Long 2003; Gris-wold 2008). According to the Pew Research Center's Internet & American Life Project, only 38 percent of senior citizens aged 65 and older go online or use computers, as opposed to 95 percent of teenagers.

Of course, many otherwise potential audiences are excluded from certain cultural pursuits due to their exorbitant costs, such as designer fashion, gourmet cuisine, nightclub bottle service, or exotic tourism. Likewise, some activities require excessive investments in time, like participating in U.S. Civil War reenactments or the annual Burning Man festival, a week-long radical arts event that takes place in the isolated Black Rock Desert, 120 miles north of Reno, Nevada. Other cultural pursuits, like reading the postmodern fiction of Thomas Pynchon or enjoying French New Wave cinema, may require an appropriately cosmopolitan upbringing or advanced educational background to successfully navigate. With regard to computer literacy and Internet usage, there is significant evidence that a "digital divide" endures that reflects class and racial inequalities persistent in American society.

Pop cultural consumer habits and experiences are not only shaped by one's specific social circumstances but also by the impact of outside social actors and structural forces. Successful touring bands and other traveling shows may not perform in small towns, preferring more populated cities and their affluent crowds. Political partisans, religious groups, and other community organizations may protest the final edit of a made-for-television movie, scaring away sponsors and thus blocking its dissemination on the airwaves. Media gatekeepers like TV celebrity Oprah Winfrey may promote a book to millions of viewers, all but ensuring that consumers will follow closely behind (Griswold 2008, p. 59).

Finally, it bears remembering that audiences often consume media and popular culture as collective activities savored in the presence of others, from the board games Monopoly and Risk to Wii Sports. As noted above, many readers enjoy novels and literary nonfiction as a collective pursuit by participating in book clubs (Gladwell 2002, pp. 169–75; Long 2003), and cities like Philadelphia and Chicago have organized "One Book, One City" programs that promote the shared reading of a single book (Griswold 2008, pp. 58–59). (Since 2003, the books chosen for the "One Book, One Philadelphia" project have included Lorene Cary's *The Price of a Child*, Tim O'Brien's *The Things They Carried*, Dave Eggers's *What Is the What*, and Benjamin Franklin's *Autobiography*.) Televised events such as the Super Bowl, the Academy Awards, and U.S. presidential debates draw together audiences who throw viewing parties to commemorate the occasion and share the experience with friends, as does the annual NCAA college basketball tournament, and guilty pleasures like *Smallville* and *Gossip Girl*. Peer-to-peer file-sharing software allows music listeners to exchange recordings and thus explore new sonic terrains in a collective if virtual environment, just as massively multiplayer online role-playing games (MMORGs) such as *World of Warcraft* provide opportunities for Internet video gamers to build interpersonal networks by aligning and

Gamers play World of Warcraft *at an Internet café in China. How are virtual experiences like online video games opportunities to build social networks?*

collaborating with fellow players in real time (Castronova 2005). And lest we forget: even in an age of personal iPods and digital home theaters, many American consumers still attend live theatrical and musical performances, sporting events, political rallies, and feature films in large public venues, just as they have for generations.

Producing and Consuming Popular Culture

The last few years have marked a heyday for popular culture spoofs through the emergent medium of the mash-up, in which two or more media are sampled, manipulated, and juxtaposed to ironic effect. In a four-minute clip titled *This Place Sucks,* or *TPS,* the animated heroes of DC Comic's *Super Friends*—Superman, Batman, Robin, Wonder Woman—run dialogue from the 1999 comedy *Office Space.* In *Sesame Streets,* a surreal mash-up of the Muppets of *Sesame Street* with the violent films of Martin Scorsese, Bert channels Robert DeNiro's Jake LaMotta from *Raging Bull* (1980), accusing Ernie, "You f—-ed my wife!" while Big Bird reprises DeNiro's role as Travis Bickle in *Taxi Driver* (1976), goading on Mr. Snufalupagus: "Are you talking to me? Well, I'm the only one here!" "Who the f—- do you think you're talking to?" In a much lighter parody, the Cosby Kids from Fat Albert are synched up with dialogue from the 2004 independent film *Napoleon Dynamite* to hilarious effect.

The striking thing about these mash-ups is that all evidence suggests that they are created by pop culture fans themselves—not as a function of the large-scale media production process but as a delightfully unpredictable part of the consumer experience. As much of this chapter has already illustrated, audiences often consume popular culture in highly active and creative ways. The organization of book clubs requires more than the passive absorption of a text but also its interrogation, especially as readers come together to discuss, debate, and disagree with its finer points. Digital media platforms let music fans seek out hard-to-find recordings online and develop their own playlists independent of the organized listening experience provided by the traditional album or compact disc format. In some ways, they transform culture in the very moment of its consumption. Moreover, thanks to advances in digital audio software, almost any amateur with a laptop can produce her own professional-grade music recording within a few hours, just as the rise of digital photography allows regular consumers to create, manipulate, and distribute visual images with ease and little training.

These new media technologies—as well as sixteenth-century forms of social organization, like reading groups—blur some of the distinctions between cultural consumption and production by both democratizing the tools of pop culture making, and diminishing the creator's control of how enterprising con- sumers actually make use of cultural objects in the real world. As for cultural producers themselves—filmmakers, photographers, musicians, novelists, screenwriters—our self-referential culture practically requires professional media makers to take on the pose of the consumer as part of the creative process.

Producer Danger Mouse blurred the boundaries of production and consumption of pupular culture with The Grey Album.

Quentin Tarantino's films, such as *Pulp Fiction* (1994) and *Kill Bill, Vol. I* (2003), are filled with B-movie references, as are episodes of the Fox TV series *The Simpsons.* As we discussed during the introduction, dance, pop, and hip-hop music producers regularly sample from obscure hits from the past, and disc jockeys mine the crates of their record collections for unusual contributions to the emergent stereo soundscape. In 2004 Brian Joseph Burton, better known as recording artist and producer Danger Mouse, released *The Grey Album* online—an unauthorized mash-up of the a cappella version of hip-hop impresario Jay-Z's *The Black Album* overlaid with various sampled cuts from *The Beatles,* the self-titled 1968 LP record commonly referred to as the *White Album* (for its original blank white cover). By blending Jay-Z's "99 Problems" with samples of the Beatles' "Helter Skelter," "Encore" with "Glass Onion" and "Savoy Truffle," and "What More Can I Say" with "While My Guitar Gently Weeps," Danger Mouse offered the music world a new way to think about the production *and* consumption of media and popular culture, even as he blurred the difference between the two.

Three Approaches to the Sociology of Media and Popular Culture

Now that we have explored the social and collective foundations of popular culture and its production and consumption, our next goal is to develop a comprehensive set of theoretical tools to help explain how pop cultural fads, fashions, trends, and phenomena succeed and decline over time, and what the social consequences of their popularity may be. To this end, in the following chapters, I introduce three theoretical approaches to the sociology of media and popular culture. In the next chapter, I present the *functionalist* approach, which illustrates how culture "functions" as the social glue that generates solidarity and cohesion within human groups and societies. Borrowing from research on the pro-social functions of religion and culture in the earliest primitive societies, I rely on this paradigm to explore how more contemporary collective rituals— high school football games, local parades and pep rallies, awards ceremonies—similarly serve to forge emotional bonds of recognition, identity, and trust within communities and other social groups. At the same time, I hope to demonstrate how pop culture provides the source material that allows consumers to communicate with strangers in public, just as popular television programs like *Seinfeld,*

American Idol, and *NFL Monday Night Football* provide grist for the mill around bus stations and workplace watercoolers. The functionalist approach helps to explain the popularity of professional sports, stadium rock concerts, and other large-scale media events among the members of mass audiences who might otherwise seem to have very little else in common.

In Chapter 3, I introduce the *critical* approach to media and popular culture. According to this paradigm, the ascendance of certain kinds of pop culture can be explained primarily in terms of their ability to reflect and reinforce the enormous economic and cultural power of the mass media industry. In contrast to the functionalist perspective, which suggests that pop culture is something that we as a society create for ourselves, the critical approach provides a top-down model of popular culture as a form of domination, albeit a strangely irresistible kind of domination that takes the form of sexually suggestive beer ads, professional basketball players who act like rappers (and vice versa), addictive video games, and the carnival of public spectacle ironically referred to as "reality" television. In this chapter, I apply this theoretical perspective to a number of contemporary issues in media and popular culture, particularly the ubiquity and symbolic power of brands such as McDonald's, Nike, and Starbucks.

Finally, in Chapter 4, we explore the *interaction* approach to pop culture. In contrast to the critical approach (which might explain a film's popularity on the basis of its marketing budget), the interaction approach emphasizes the power that informal processes like word of mouth and peer influence enjoy in the cultural marketplace. According to this perspective, our consumer tastes are deeply affected by the people around us, and so the success of certain kinds of popular culture depends not upon big-budget advertising, but on micro-level, small-group interactions such as those exemplified by online networking and other informal modes of cultural diffusion. In describing this theoretical approach, I address a number of related issues, including the importance of opinion leaders, early adopters, and market mavens in determining the fate of new technologies and styles of apparel, and the power of collective consumption, whether in game-playing clubs, local music scenes, or online fan fiction sites.

Fans at a football game. How do popular culture and mass media bring communities together?

friday night lights

A FUNCTIONALIST APPROACH
TO POPULAR CULTURE

Easton
Succeeds
P'burg
Not
2-day

I N THE TEXAS OIL TOWN OF ODESSA, MAGIC HAPPENS ON FRIDAY NIGHTS when the Permian Panthers high school football team takes the field. Under the bright lights of a $5.2 million stadium, the school's players, coaches, cheerleaders, and marching band perform to crowds of nearly 20,000 people who shout the home team's cheer, *"MO-JO! MO-JO!"* Odessa has survived decades of the boom-and-bust cycles of the oil industry and a long, ugly history of racial segregation, but as H. G. Bissinger (1990) observes in his best-selling book *Friday Night Lights* (later made into a critically acclaimed film and television series), the Panthers bring the citizens of this West Texas town together like nothing else. Neighbors flood the high school's pep rallies, gab about individual players' physical strengths and on-the-field statistics, wear the team's colors of black and white, and threaten the head coach whenever the Panthers lose to a longtime rival like the Rebels, a high school team from nearby Midland, Texas, the former hometown of President George W. Bush. And if perhaps this MOJO spirit seems surprising, it is only because the Permian Panthers create the kind of civic unity and excitement normally associated with beloved professional sports franchises in more populous cities, storied teams like the New York Yankees, Philadelphia Eagles, Boston Celtics, and the Chicago Cubs.

What explains the collective enthusiasm of local football, baseball, basketball, and hockey fans in the United States, or soccer fans in Brazil, or cricket fans in Australia (Foer 2004; Kaufman and Patterson 2005)? After all, such sports are forms of entertainment in which spectators watch complete strangers play competitive games with obscure rules, and in the case of professional team sports, the athletes are rarely from their "home" cities in any real sense. In fact, often the teams themselves are transplants from someplace else, like the Los Angeles Dodgers (from Brooklyn, NY), Oakland A's (from Philadelphia), Washington Nationals (from Montreal), Texas Rangers (from Washington, DC), and the Tennessee Titans (from Houston). (Teams sometimes carry over their old names to new cities, often nonsensically so, as when the New Orleans Jazz moved to Salt Lake City, Utah, but retained their identity as the Jazz even though Utah enjoys decidedly less of a regional music heritage than New Orleans, the actual birthplace of jazz.) Given the increasing mobility of professional athletes (and the obvious turnover of high school and college players, who eventually graduate), aren't sports fans really just rooting for the uniforms, as comedian Jerry Seinfeld once joked?

Actually, he wasn't all that far off—we do cheer on team uniforms, mascots, colors, and banners, at least as much as we do the players themselves—and in this chapter we rely on the tools of sociology to explain why. Specifically, this chapter describes the first of three sociological approaches used in this book: the *functionalist* approach. According to a functionalist approach to popular culture, our obsession with professional and intercollegiate athletics, celebrity magazines, and other forms of mass entertainment can be explained primarily in terms of their social uses (or literally their *function*) in generating solidarity among individuals within large and anonymous communities. Through the power of ritualistic spectator events like play-off games and rock concerts, sports and other forms of popular culture and entertainment bring strangers together in a collective spirit of camaraderie, however temporarily. Moreover, these shared moments provide opportunities for fans to express their feelings and opinions about otherwise sensitive topics of conversation, such as race relations and the ethics of work. In this chapter, I draw on the functionalist perspective to explore these social phenomena as they relate to celebrity culture, national politics, and most of all, the world of sports entertainment.

Foundations of the Functionalist Approach

In his seminal 1912 book *The Elementary Forms of Religious Life*, the French sociologist Emile Durkheim seeks to understand the social role that religion plays in the functioning of human societies. In many ways Durkheim himself was perfectly suited for this scholarly task. As a nonobservant Jew who happened to have hailed from several generations of rabbis, he was at once both intimately familiar with the myriad symbols, rituals, and beliefs of religious thought and practice yet held few personal investments in their ultimate meaning or purpose. He embarks on his intellectual journey by beginning, well, at the beginning, by describing some of the earliest religions known to humans, particularly the ancient spiritual faiths of American Indians and Aboriginal Australians. These are societies for whom religion was notably the central organizing institution of their existence: it structured their governance, work routines, and knowledge of the natural world. (This is in contrast to present-day Americans, for whom religion is only one of many forms of cultural identification and social organization, along with nationhood, ethnicity, community, and occupation, for example.)

Durkheim observed that these early religions relied very heavily on the role of signs, images, and symbols, many of which were drawn from the natural world, as in the case of totemic religions that rely on animals (e.g., kangaroos, snakes, crows) as symbols (1995, pp. 99–126). What was the purpose of these symbols? Durkheim argues that religious symbols or images represented not merely gods, or beliefs, but the religious group members themselves and what he refers to as their *collective conscience*—just as national flags may be thought to represent not only the idea of a nation, but its actual citizens. (This is one reason that some Americans view the burning of Old Glory as a deeply violent symbolic act.)

Durkheim also recognized how often these images were evoked in religious rituals and practices as a means of creating symbolic boundaries demarcating the separation of *sacred* and *profane* elements in the universe. For instance, many religions adhere to dietary codes that restrict the eating of certain foods considered dirty, filthy, dangerous, or otherwise taboo: observant Jews abstain from eating non-kosher foods such as shellfish and pork, while Islamic dietary rules forbid adherents to ingest pork as well (Douglas 1991). Likewise, the three major Western religions organize time itself into sacred occasions (Lent and Easter Sunday, the holy month of Ramadan, Yom Kippur and the Sabbath) as well as place (Jerusalem, Mecca, the Church of the Holy Sepulcher, the Western Wall, the Temple Mount). As Durkheim explains, systems of classification and boundary maintenance related to the differentiation between the sacred and the profane help societies reinforce distinctions between themselves and other groups, on the basis of insider and outsider status.

Finally, religious rituals involving large groups of people (such as the Catholic Mass) present opportunities for generating what Durkheim calls *collective effervescence,* a shared feeling of identity in which the individual members of the group (whether a tribe or a congregation) experience waves of emotion, a sense of unity and togetherness. The effervescent energy of crowds is considered so central to religious ceremonies that laws, customs, and traditions of faith all but demand that rituals be performed collectively. In Judaism, certain prayer rituals require the presence of a quorum, or *minyan,* of at least ten participants. During the annual Islamic pilgrimage to Mecca, or the hajj, three million adherents converge on the Saudi Arabian city to engage in collective worship and celebration, as Malcolm X (1964, p. 343) recollects in his *Autobiography*:

> We parked near the Great Mosque. We performed our ablutions and entered. Pilgrims seemed to be on top of each other, there were so many, lying, sitting, sleeping, praying, walking. . . . Then I saw the Ka'ba, a huge black stone house in the middle of the Great Mosque. It was being circumambulated by thousands upon thousands of praying pilgrims, both sexes, and every size, shape, color, and race in the world. . . . Faces were enraptured in their faith.

Muslim pilgrims (left) pray in Mecca, and a Sri Lankan woman (right) prays at a statue of the Buddha. According to Durkheim, religions use rituals to separate the sacred from the profane. What are the social functions of these distinctions?

To sum up, Durkheim argues that it is these basic elements of religious life— shared symbols and images, imagined boundaries separating the sacred from the profane, and rituals than help participants generate collective effervescence—that provide the social glue that binds societies together through thick and thin. Of course, Durkheim recognizes that the modern world is defined not by religiosity but secularism, a belief in science over faith in an age of unrelenting change. This worries him greatly because he fears that "there can be no society that does not experience the need at regular intervals to maintain and strengthen the collective feelings and ideas that provide its coherence and its distinct individuality" ([1912] 1995, p. 429). While religions obviously continue to flourish throughout the world, they clearly no longer have the same hold over modern individuals that they once did among Native Americans and Aborigines, if for no other reason than that our lives are organized according to the logics of a variety of competing social institutions (e.g., nation-states and their judicial systems, the global economy, science-based medicine) rather than simply religion. This is especially the case in pluralistic societies like the United States where various faiths, denominations, and sects divide entire societies into highly differentiated mosaics of religious belief. Meanwhile, in our enlightened age of invention and discovery, it appears that "the great things of the past that excited our fathers no longer arouse the same zeal among us, either because they have passed so completely into common custom that we lose awareness of them or because they no longer suit our aspirations. Meanwhile, no replacement for them has yet been created." As Durkheim poignantly remarks, "the former gods are growing old or dying, and others have not been born" (p. 429).

[handwritten margin note: summary]

[handwritten margin note: Star Trek episode]

And yet Durkheim concludes *The Elementary Forms of Religious Life* on an optimistic note: "A day will come when our societies once again will know hours of creative effervescence during which new ideals will again spring forth and new formulas emerge to guide humanity for a time. . . . There are no immortal gospels, and there is no reason to believe that humanity is incapable of conceiving new ones in the future" (pp. 429–30). What will those new gospels teach us? What kinds of symbols will emerge to reorient our identities, our social place in the world? What kinds of rituals will rejuvenate societies by generating the collective effervescence they need to thrive? What will serve as the social glue that will help bind societies together, through thick and thin?

Rituals of Solidarity and Social Cohesion in Popular Culture

A functionalist approach to popular culture emphasizes how the symbols, rituals, and practices surrounding its production and consumption can bring people together by generating a shared sense of social solidarity. The world of sports entertainment provides a powerful example. In the world of professional and intercollegiate athletics, cities and regions are represented by team franchises that employ a range of symbols engineered to foster collective attachment. Like Native American and Aboriginal tribes, sports teams are typically signified by animalistic totems, whether the Chicago Bears, Atlanta Falcons, Miami Dolphins,

How do sports teams create social solidarity?

St. Louis Rams, Cincinnati Bengals, Detroit Lions, Indianapolis Colts, Baltimore Ravens, or the Denver Broncos. (One of the reasons many civil rights groups such as the NAACP as well as scholarly organizations like the American Sociological Association have rallied against the promotion of even reverential team mascots such as the Washington Redskins or the Cleveland Indians is that they appear to dehumanize American Indians, as if they were animals.) Team nicknames, logos, and jerseys provide further means of symbolic attachment, and this is particularly emphasized during competitions that pit two teams against one another, each player's uniform emblazoned with bold colors, insignias, and other demarcating symbols used to differentiate opposing teams on the field of play, and among rival fans in the grandstands.

Just as religions create symbolic orders that distinguish among the sacred and the profane, team regalia help participants maintain the illusion of difference between opposing franchises. (I describe this difference as illusory given the manufactured nature of team identity, as emphasized by the excessive mobility of players and teams to different cities, as noted above, and the rapid creation of recent expansion teams.) Collective rituals surrounding the celebration of adversarial team differences further bolster the social integration of like-minded fans. These rituals of boundary maintenance include pep rallies, tailgate parties, celebratory parades, and the main sporting events themselves, in which athletes perform alongside support personnel such as cheerleaders, marching bands, dancers, fuzzy mascots, and the most enthusiastic of fans draped in team colors and covered with face paint. Like religious ceremonies, these rituals take place within special worlds marked off in time (March Madness, Monday Night Football, Super Bowl Sunday) and space (Chicago's Wrigley Field, Boston's Fenway Park). Such events feature incantations (cheers and fight songs) and synchronized body movements (stadium waves), and all help generate a heightened sense of collective effervescence among feverish participants.

In doing so, these rituals of solidarity allow small communities like Odessa, Texas, to feel gigantic and mythic, greater than the sum of their parts. Meanwhile, the professional sports entertainment culture of more populated cities like New York, Atlanta, Dallas, and Miami gives locals otherwise divided on the basis of national origin, socioeconomic class, race, and ethnicity a sense of commonality and even intimacy through a shared identity. This social solidarity illustrated itself during the 1990s when complete strangers embraced and high-fived one another on the streets of Chicago after the Bulls had won each of their six National Basketball Association championships, or in 2008 when Philadelphians spontaneously converged on City Hall after the Phillies won the World Series. Large cities like these often feel like anonymous, lonely worlds (Simmel [1903] 1971; Wirth 1938; Lofland 1973), and professional sports teams can bring people together in a spirit of camaraderie atypical among strangers in the urban metropolis.

Moreover, it bears remembering that while American intercollegiate and professional sports rivals attract fans of opposing teams, nearly all participants still identify with the national culture to a greater or lesser degree. (Exceptions perhaps include Canadian teams and individual athletes from abroad, such as Los Angeles Galaxy soccer star David Beckham, from the United Kingdom, and the 7'6" center for the NBA's Houston Rockets, Yao Ming, from China.) For this reason, sporting events in the United States generally emphasize American identity and national pride through a variety of rituals. Performers sing the national anthem before solemn crowds, while after the terrorist attacks of September 11, 2001, Major League Baseball home teams replaced the singing of the always light-hearted and sometimes partisan "Take Me Out to the Ball Game" with the more unifying "God Bless America." The attacks also occasioned commemorative ceremonies at professional football games and NASCAR races, replete with flag displays and a contingent of firefighters and police, the symbolic heroes of 9/11 (Collins 2004b, p. 68), just as sporting events present opportunities to honor military servicepersons and veterans during wartime. These rituals evoke the celebration of shared patriotism and national identity as a kind of civic religion and can generate an even greater sense of social solidarity and collective effervescence than the more playful, team-oriented cheering expected during game time. Of course, this sort of spirited nationalism is often generated by other public rituals as well, such as political rallies, elections, parades, and national holiday celebrations.

It is also not difficult to imagine how other kinds of popular entertainment featuring large effervescent crowds might achieve similarly social ends. Throughout rock music history, arena and stadium concerts have brought fans

Phillies fans spontaneously converged on City Hall to celebrate the team's 2008 World Series victory.

Statement by the Council of the American Sociological Association on Discontinuing the Use of Native American Nicknames, Logos and Mascots in Sport

March 6, 2007

WHEREAS the American Sociological Association comprises sociologists and kindred professionals who study, among other things, culture, religion, media, sport, race and ethnicity, racism, and other forms of inequality;

WHEREAS the American Sociological Association recognizes that racial prejudice, stereotypes, individual discrimination and institutional discrimination are socially created phenomena that are harmful to Native Americans and other people of color;

WHEREAS the American Sociological Association is resolved to undertake scholarship, education, and action that helps to eradicate racism;

WHEREAS social science scholarship has demonstrated that the continued use of Native American nicknames, logos and mascots in sport reflect and reinforce misleading stereotypes of Native Americans in both past and contemporary times;

WHEREAS the stereotypes embedded in Native American nicknames, logos and mascots in sport undermine education about the lives of Native American peoples;

WHEREAS social science scholarship has demonstrated that the continued use of Native American nicknames, logos and mascots in sport harm Native American people in psychological, educational, and social ways;

WHEREAS the continued use of Native American nicknames, logos and mascots in sport shows disrespect for Native American spiritual and cultural practices;

WHEREAS many Native American individuals across the United States have found Native American nicknames, logos and mascots in sport offensive and called for their elimination;

AND, WHEREAS the continued use of Native American nicknames, logos and mascots in sport has been condemned by numerous reputable academic, educational and civil rights organizations, and the vast majority of Native American advocacy organizations, including but not limited to: American Anthropological Association, American Psychological Association, North American Society for the Sociology of Sport, Modern Language Association, United States Commission on Civil Rights, National Association for the Advancement of Colored People, Association of American Indian Affairs, National Congress of American Indians, and National Indian Education Association;

NOW, THEREFORE, BE IT RESOLVED, that the American Sociological Association calls for discontinuing the use of Native American nicknames, logos and mascots in sport.

together in shared moments of collective solidarity and bliss, notably the live performances of superstar acts like U2 and the Rolling Stones. As a live entertainer, Bruce Springsteen has been known to give four-hour marathon concerts that energize his fans, diehards who holler along with the singer-songwriter when he performs 1970s hits like "Thunder Road" and "Born to Run." During their epic career from the late 1960s through the mid-1990s, the Grateful Dead—perhaps the most successful touring rock band of all time—regularly drew crowds of self-identified "Deadheads," dedicated fans who followed the band along their concert tour route to every show. These performances assumed the character of New Age spiritual gatherings in which audience members clad in tie-dyed and beaded clothing sang along together to surrealist tunes—"Box of Rain," "Eyes of the World," "Sugar Magnolia," "China Cat Sunflower," "Friend of the Devil," "Dark Star"—and performed free-form circle dances to improvised drum solos and guitar jams, often under the influence of psychedelic drugs such as LSD. Contemporary rock music festivals such as Lollapalooza and Bonnaroo continue to provide successive generations of music fans with shared collective experiences enjoyed in the presence of tens of thousands of amped-up fellow travelers.

In today's highly mediated cultural environment, live televised events have the potential to generate similarly effervescent experiences among what we might call an *imagined community* of viewers who, despite their lack of physical proximity to one another, still feel as if they are members of a collective audience sharing the simultaneity of a moment (Anderson 1991). Recent events include the Florida recount of the 2000 presidential election, the aftermath of the 9/11 terrorists attacks, the American-led invasion of Iraq, the devastation of New Orleans in the wake of Hurricane Katrina, and the historic election of President Barack Obama. Ironically, reproduced media images of live events can often generate as much if not *greater* feelings of solidarity among audiences, while the actual events themselves can feel chaotic, disorienting, and even boring to live spectators lost among the noisy crowds they attract. In the case of Obama's celebratory acceptance speech in Chicago's Grant Park on November 4, 2008, the occasion attracted so many people that even those who were present could only really see the candidate from afar on the jumbo video screens placed near the stage. Meanwhile, audiences watching at home not only enjoyed close-up camera shots of the president-elect and his family from the comfort of their living rooms but likely had a much better view of the effervescent crowd than the actual participants themselves.

The excitement generated by such events has led to the institution of regularly scheduled live telecasts engineered to create collective effervescence on demand. Occasions such as the annual Academy Awards ceremonies and the quadrennial Democratic and Republican presidential nominating conventions are staged affairs promoted and televised to a worldwide audience. The historian Daniel Boorstin (1961) refers to these kinds of media rituals as *pseudo-events,* happenings held simply for "the immediate purpose of being reported or reproduced" (p. 11). Competitive reality television series such as *Survivor* and *American Idol* replicate the staged features of these ritual events by filming their season finales in real time before enormous studio audiences, perhaps in the hope that the collective enthusiasm of the live spectators will rub off on home viewers.

Of course, to a large extent professional sporting events are similarly enacted for the purposes of being transformed into televised entertainment for a mass audience, which is why they are so often scheduled in prime time to conform to the needs of commercial network television. For example, because of the twelve-hour time difference between Beijing and New York, in 2008 NBC struck a deal with the International Olympic Committee to move key Summer Games events such as swimming and gymnastics to the morning so they could be shown live on prime-time American television (Carter 2008).

Popular Culture as a Resource for Public Reflection

Great literature, drama, and myth take abstract ideas and universal themes such as death, betrayal, love, envy, regret, ambition, and revenge and make them come alive by embodying them in fictional characters and their fantastic trials—Oedipus, Romeo and Juliet, Don Quixote, Dr. Frankenstein, Ebenezer Scrooge, Jay Gatsby. These myths gain their cultural power from their ability to express the otherwise ineffable sense of what it feels like to be human. In the last century, artists have taken advantage of the narrative possibilities of mass media technology to illuminate these same crucial literary themes in visually compelling ways. Obvious cinematic examples include the Orson Welles master-piece *Citizen Kane* (1941), the Francis Ford Coppola film *The Godfather* (1972) and

After President Obama's election victory, many people watching the celebration on television felt as much solidarity with the candidate and his supporters as the crowd attending the event did. Why?

its sequel *The Godfather, Part II* (1974), and the Martin Scorsese picture *Raging Bull* (1980), all which feature extraordinarily complex and self-destructive figures from Charles Foster Kane to Michael Corleone to Jake LaMotta. (Recent examples from the world of television include the HBO modern-day epics *The Sopranos* and *The Wire*, and the Emmy Award-winning AMC series *Mad Men*.) These dramas provide templates for examining the human condition, warts and all; to paraphrase the anthropologist Clifford Geertz (1973, p. 448), they are stories we tell ourselves about ourselves.

While seemingly superficial in comparison, to a certain extent the culture of celebrity and entertainment performs a similar function. In contemporary culture celebrities are treated as mythical archetypes to whom we assign all sorts of extreme attributes, whether beauty and grace, or avarice and gluttony (Gabler 2000). Regardless of how little we may care for them as individual people (Gamson 1994), we obsess over their reported comedic highs and tragic lows because their spotlighted stories provide resources for reflecting on the social world and the human experience. For example, let us take a popular staple of celebrity gossip: cheating and adultery. Tales of two-timing in Hollywood are legion and tend to be highly publicized affairs. British actor Hugh Grant got caught cheating on his longtime girlfriend, model and actress Elizabeth Hurley, when he was arrested for soliciting a prostitute in 1995. Actor Jude Law and his fiancée, actress Sienna Miller, broke off their engagement after it was revealed in 2005 that Law was sleeping with Daisy Wright, his children's nanny. Of course, the most famous case of public adultery in recent history took place not in Hollywood but in Washington, when President Bill Clinton was discovered to have carried on an illicit affair with Monica Lewinsky, a White House intern. (Their dalliances were said to have taken place in the only room in the world where the president could be guaranteed absolute privacy: the Oval Office.) He was caught during his second term, a scandal that eventually led to his impeachment by the House of Representatives in 1998 and his acquittal by the U.S. Senate in 1999.

Why were these stories so publicized, and why did readers follow them so intently? In many ways, these tales of relationships gone awry serve the same function as Aesop's fables, traditional folktales, and morality plays: they give tangible form to otherwise abstract ethical dilemmas concerning the nature of human relations and social behavior. In doing so they become readily available conversation starters, or "watercooler talk" (named for the habit of white-collar workers kibitzing by watercoolers, coffee machines, or other shared office amenities), whereas adulterous affairs and one-night stands among *actual* friends and acquaintances are generally not considered appropriate topics for public discussion, particularly in the workplace. Meanwhile, chatter surrounding the lives of famous celebrities offers ordinary people opportunities for reflection and debate on these and other sensitive issues without fear (or at least concern) of embarrassing the principal characters of such gossip. Other delicate topics regularly made available for public discourse as a result of having emanated from the world of celebrity and entertainment culture include domestic violence,

What is the social function of celebrity gossip?

drug addiction, rapid weight loss and gain, eating disorders, and the relative merits and drawbacks of elective plastic surgery. Nor do such topics end there: recall the endless speculation and deliberation sparked by the slow-speed highway chase, arrest, and court trials of former football star O. J. Simpson, accused and eventually acquitted of murdering his ex-wife and her lover in the 1990s (only to be later convicted of armed robbery and kidnapping in 2008); the late pop singer Michael Jackson, arrested and tried (and also eventually acquitted) on multiple counts of child molestation; basketball star Kobe Bryant, arrested of sexually assaulting a hotel employee (the case was eventually dropped); and multimedia juggernaut Martha Stewart, convicted and jailed for obstruction of justice and lying to federal investigators about a suspiciously timed stock sale. In each of these cases, the celebrity status of those arrested provided an excuse for the rest of us to discuss grave matters and pass moral judgment with ease.

We rely on celebrity gossip for much lighter food for thought as well. For instance, the enthusiasm surrounding celebrity pregnancies and parenthood reaches a fever pitch in entertainment tabloid magazines. In 2008 *People* paid a reported $14 million for the exclusive rights to publish photographs of Angelina Jolie and Brad Pitt's newborn twins. (The celebrity couple promised to donate the money to charity.) The babies were featured on the magazine's cover, just as Jennifer Lopez and Marc Anthony's newborn twins did earlier that year. (In comparison to Brangelina, the latter couple was reportedly paid a relatively paltry $6 million for their photo rights.) In December 2008 a single issue of *US Weekly* featured the following "news" items:

- "Nursing Confessions," on the breast-feeding regimes of actresses Jessica Alba, Marcia Cross, Salma Hayek, and Amanda Peet;
- Model and actress Rebecca Romijn, on wearing a bra during her pregnancy;
- Actress Milla Jovovich, on her one-year-old daughter's first words (apple, eyes, mama);
- Actor Jack Black, on his affection for his two sons, ages six months, and two years;
- Actor Adam Sandler, on the birth of his second daughter;
- Actor Liev Schreiber and actress Naomi Watts, on expecting their second child;

- Actress Jennifer Garner, seen shopping for produce while seven months pregnant;
- Actor Hugh Jackman, swimming with his three-year-old daughter;
- NASCAR driver Jeff Gordon, with his one-year-old daughter.

What is with this obsession over the baby children spawned by celebrities? One answer has to do with the production of entertainment news. Celebrities crave free publicity but only if it promises to reflect them in a positive light. But while celebrities encourage the publication of laudatory, puffed-up profiles and other *fluff* pieces, journalists seek to uncover *dirt*, whether professional or personal—not necessarily because it tends toward the negative and tawdry (i.e., the tales of adultery discussed above), but because it is regarded as scarce information and therefore more likely to sell to inquiring readers on the basis of its news value (Gamson 1994). In negotiations between celebrity publicists and magazine editors, baby stories are then seen as the ultimate compromise in which everyone wins: the celebrity is shown doting on her (or his) newborn children, selfless as can be, while the editors get access to the most intimate sanctuary of a famous person, the home or hospital bed, during a potentially once-in-a-lifetime event (for that particular celebrity, at least).

Of course, while this explains why magazines run such stories, it does not shed much light on why readers might care about celebrity pregnancies or births in the first place, outside of the obvious pleasure we receive from seeing cute pictures of happy babies. Here, a functionalist perspective can help provide an answer. First, bear in mind the universality of pregnancy, childbirth, and parenthood in people's lives—after all, we all came from someone's belly. Second, while childbirth obviously represents a celebrated milestone for parents, such experiences are fraught with anxieties, especially for women. Will my baby be healthy? What if she turns out to have a crippling peanut allergy? Will I ever get my body back into trim shape? Will I have to put my career on hold? Is the father around, and if so, is he up to the challenge of hands-on parenting? Widespread media coverage of childbearing and child-rearing celebrities allows for a public airing and intense discussion of these anxieties without devastating social repercussions for gossipmongers or their targets. They also permit cultural consumers to make judgments on the parenting styles of others without

The singer Gwen Stefani and her husband Gavin Rossdale pose with their son for photographers. Why do celebrities and media outlets love to feature stories about celebrity babies? Why do consumers like to read them?

necessarily appearing judgmental (and without ostracizing their friends and neighbors). This explains why Michael Jackson was so thoroughly criticized by the public in 2002 for dangling his infant child over a third-floor hotel balcony in Berlin while greeting admiring fans. Pop singer Britney Spears was similarly upbraided by the public in 2006 for driving away from paparazzi photographers with her four-month-old son Sean Preston balanced on her lap—the incident even received attention from U.S. Transportation Secretary Norman Mineta, who called her behavior "irresponsible" during an event in observance of Child Passenger Safety Week. Of course, public judgments need not be negative or abusive, as illustrated by the large numbers of fluffy news items praising the parental involvement of celebrity fathers. (A November 2008 issue of *US Weekly* quoted then President-elect Obama on its cover as confessing in a headline, "I Think I'm a Pretty Cool Dad.")

Bringing the discussion full circle, we can see how the world of professional sport also provides us with opportunities to reflect on the human condition. Certainly, as evidenced through magazines like *Sports Illustrated* and televised entertainment such as ESPN's *SportsCenter* and *NFL Monday Night Football*, media surrounding professional athletics relies on the proliferation of biographical narratives, tales of career triumph and loss, grace and virtue, heartache and victory. These stories are a staple of the sports entertainment industry, and a number of perennial narratives, or *evergreens* (Grindstaff 2002, p. 84), emerge with remarkable regularity. One set of narratives chronicles the frustrations of hard-luck franchises that success always seems to elude—Exhibit A might very well be baseball's Chicago Cubs, who have not won a World Series since 1908. Meanwhile, the Philadelphia Eagles have *never* won an NFL Super Bowl Championship, a fate that led the journalist Jere Longman to write his 2005 book *If Football's a Religion, Why Don't We Have a Prayer? Philadelphia, Its Faithful, and the Eternal Quest for Sports Salvation.* A related set of narratives feature standardized stories about long-suffering teams who break their losing streaks after years of patience, as when the Boston Red Sox broke their 86-year drought and their famed "Curse of the Bambino" by winning the 2004 World Series. (Local superstition has it that the losing streak had been caused by trading the batting legend Babe Ruth to the New York Yankees on January 5, 1920; see Borer 2008). Other narratives attach moral significance to the athletic achievements of underdogs and long shots, like the 1980 U.S. Olympic Hockey team, a collection of college and amateur players who eventually won the gold medal after beating the odds-on favorite, the Soviet Union. Athletic accomplishments based on longevity, as when Baltimore Oriole Cal Ripken, Jr., broke Lou Gehrig's record in 1995 for most consecutive baseball games played, are often framed as moral fables, as life lessons that emphasize the ethics of work and perseverance.

Another set of narratives concerns the nature of the human body and its limits. These are often stories about aging and our attempts to defy its eroding effects. In the lead-up to the 2008 Olympic Games in Beijing, China, when U.S. swimmer Dara Torres, a 41-year-old mother, made a historic career comeback by winning three silver medals, media profiles emphasized Torres's "obsessive attention to her aging body," for which she had hired "a head coach, a sprint coach, a strength coach, two stretchers, two masseuses, a chiropractor and a nanny, at the cost of at least $100,000 per year" (Weil 2008). In many ways scandals surrounding the illegal use of steroids in professional and Olympic sports similarly provide resources for reflecting on the limits of the human body and questions surrounding the blurry distinction between "natural" and "enhanced" athletic abilities, the criminality of drugs and the ethics concerning the use of biomedical technology, and ultimately, the meaning of accomplishment itself.

Finally, professional sports have long provided a dynamic context for public discussions about social inequality in America. On April 15, 1947, Jackie Robinson suited up as No. 42 and took the field for the Brooklyn Dodgers, becoming the first African American ballplayer permitted to play for a major league team since 1889. (Prior to the postwar era, black players had been segregated into a number of baseball organizations collectively called the "Negro leagues.") Robinson was arguably one of the greatest players of the game—he played in six World Series and six All-Star games, won the National League MVP, and ended his career with a .311 batting average and eventually an induction into the Major League Baseball Hall of Fame— yet at the time his invitation to join the Dodgers was so controversial that in his first months of play he braved death threats from sports fans and racial animus from some of his own teammates. But like other African American athletes whose talents and determination allowed them to break through the color barrier to achieve greatness, such as heavyweight boxing champion Jack Johnson, Robinson's courage to integrate the sport added a vital spark to a galvanizing national conversation about race and equality in America and lent support to other vocal defenders of racial justice in the years leading up to the civil rights era of the 1950s and 1960s. Indeed, over the years Jackie Robinson has become as much a symbol of the African American struggle for civil rights and racial equality as Rosa Parks and Medgar Evers, and today his legend endures for his heroism and character as much as for his athletic achievements.

Baseball great Jackie Robinson.

Rituals of Rebellion in Popular Culture

In his research on southeast Africa, the British anthropologist Max Gluckman (1963) discovered a variety of tribal rituals in which members temporarily exchange status positions related to gender roles. On a set of rites in Zululand, he reports:

> The most important of these rites among the Zulu required obscene behavior by the women and girls. The girls donned men's garments, and herded and milked the cattle, which were normally taboo to them. . . . At various stages of the ceremonies women and girls went naked, and sang lewd songs. Men and boys hid and might not go near. (p. 113)

Among the Swazi tribes of Africa, another ritual emphasizes the public denigration of the king. In this ceremony, priests assemble in the royal cattle pen, and amid the mooing cows they chant:

> You hate the child king,
> You hate the child king.
> I would depart with my Father (the king),
> I fear we would be recalled.
> They put him on the stone:
> —sleeps with his sister:
> —sleeps with Lozithupa ([the] Princess):
> You hate the child king.
>
> King, alas for your fate,
> King, they reject thee,
> King, they hate thee. (pp. 120—21)

Despite the seemingly transgressive character of both these displays, which Gluckman calls *rituals of rebellion*, their ultimate purpose is actually to restore and solidify the tribal social order. These rituals represent a kind of institutionalized protest that allows subordinate group members to momentarily let off steam without actually granting them real power for any significant period of time. (Note that among the Swazi tribes, only the king himself is permitted to organize the aforementioned ritual.) By temporarily inverting the hierarchical structure of the social order as a form of play, such rituals remind participants of the dominant status norms that organize and regulate society on a more daily basis.

Rituals of rebellion are similarly a staple of Western popular culture, and have been for centuries. In the European age of monarchs, court jesters were permitted to tease and provoke kings and queens, just as masks of former and current U.S. presidents and other political figures offer citizens the fun of ridiculing powerful people without negative consequence, albeit in a ritual that reminds us of their prestige. (After all, masquerade shops rarely sell masks resembling the faces of *ordinary* people.) These and other rituals of masquerade mark instances in which people announce their everyday identities by temporarily subverting them through the use of costumes, masks, and cross-dressing. In Philadelphia,

Members of the Trilby String Band perform during the 107th Annual Mummers Parade in Philadelphia.

the annual New Year's Day Mummers Parade brings out thousands of working-class men who march up Broad Street in sequined dresses, gowns, and face paint. During American celebrations of Halloween, children (and increasingly adults) dress in a kind of drag as well. Costumes representing criminality or evil (pirates, chain gang inmates, gunslingers, witches, vampires, devils) are popular, as are outfits resembling uniforms worn in backbreaking occupations involving often undesirable "dirty" work (French maids, nurses, cowboys).

Rituals of rebellion are similarly embedded in popular entertainment and mass culture. Satirical television shows like *Saturday Night Live* have created a cottage industry built around poking fun at politicians and other authority figures. Comedians Chevy Chase and Dan Aykroyd began this tradition on the show in the 1970s with imitative performances that emphasized the quirky foibles of presidents Gerald Ford and Jimmy Carter, just as Will Ferrell hilariously poked fun at George W. Bush's malapropisms in the run-up to the 2000 presidential election. In one sketch that aired October 7 of that year, Ferrell (as Bush) refers to his overall presidential campaign message as one of "strategery," while in the same sketch Ferrell's costar Darrell Hammond ruthlessly mocks Bush's Democratic opponent Vice President Al Gore by exaggerating his southern drawl and dismissive eye-rolling exhibited during one of the debates. In 2008 former *SNL* head writer Tina Fey regularly performed the role of the vice-presidential hopeful Governor Sarah Palin of

Alaska, skewering her rural speaking style and down-home mannerisms. Her mimicry of the candidate's sometimes convoluted syntax reached its height during a September 2008 episode in which she simply read from a transcript of a televised interview that CBS anchor Katie Couric had conducted with Palin earlier in the week.

How "rebellious" are these rituals? In many ways the ritualized character of these spoofs mitigates their potential bite—after all, if *all* famous politicians are ceremonially ridiculed in the same fashion by late-night comedians regardless of party affiliation, ideology, popularity, or competence, the barbs hurled against them lose much of their sting. In this sense, becoming a laugh line on *Saturday Night Live* or *The Tonight Show* represents little more than a flattering sign of a person's celebrity rather than a rejection of his or her governing abilities. The joking atmosphere surrounding the political swipes made by comedians in the context of mass entertainment similarly diminishes how seriously viewers will actually evaluate such criticisms.

In fact, politicians have traditionally benefitted enormously from these kinds of comedic send-ups. A stable of elected officials have personally appeared on *SNL* in order to mock their political stature on national television (and present themselves publicly as good sports): New York City mayors Edward Koch and Rudolph Giuliani, former Vice President Al Gore, and a number of 2008 presidential contenders, including Barack Obama, Hillary Rodham Clinton, and John McCain. (Gore, who lost the electoral college vote in the 2000 presidential contest despite winning the popular vote, performed a memorably funny bit of self-parody on *SNL* by begging cast members of the NBC series *The West Wing* to let him sit at a studio replica of the Oval Office desk, so he could spend a few brief minutes pretending to be the president.) Even the widely ridiculed Bush and Palin have appeared on the show, each as candidates during their respective electoral runs. Ferrell's imitation of Bush may have made him seem buffoonish but in doing so portrayed him as an "aw-shucks," all-around "regular" guy— not a bad outcome for the candidate, a highly privileged scion of a former U.S. president educated at Phillips Academy, Yale, and Harvard. As if to illustrate *SNL*'s ineffectiveness as a truly rebellious political force, after Bush became president his advisor Karl Rove dubbed his weekly meeting with senior White House aides the "Strategery Group" (Zengerle 2004).

The Darker Functions of Popular Culture

This last set of points addresses some of the darker or more insidious functions of popular culture. For much of this chapter we have explored pop culture's relatively benign and pro-social functions, including the building of social solidarity and group cohesion, the generation of collective effervescence, and the creation of resources for social reflection. But as these last examples of "rituals of rebellion" illustrate, the power of popular culture can be marshaled for a variety of purposes, and they do not benefit all members of society equally. In the case of political satire, the ritualistic nature of entertainment comedy shows like *Saturday Night Live* transforms dissent into a kind of officially sanctioned mock protest that barks but rarely bites, all while increasing the celebrity status of the targeted public figures themselves. And for what it's worth, in the last *eight* presidential elections the candidate with the best-selling Halloween mask has wound up winning the White House (Gibbs 2008).

If these collective rituals of solidarity ultimately bolster the legitimacy of those in power by artfully appropriating dissent, other celebrations of popular culture reinforce norms of social inequality in far more obvious ways. Again, the world of sports provides endless examples. High school, collegiate, and professional football teams rely on scantily clad female cheerleaders to heighten the self-esteem of male players and fans. In Olympic beach volleyball competition, rules dictate that female players must wear bathing suits, while male competitors are permitted to wear shorts and tank-top shirts. In competitive gymnastics, young girls and adolescents suffer through marathon training sessions, painful injuries, and, often, eating disorders as they struggle to please their coaches, teammates, and parents while ignoring their basic health and emotional well-being (Sey 2008).

In addition to the abuse and sexual objectification of women and girls commonly celebrated on athletic fields of play, sporting events also glorify the exploits of rich celebrity athletes who earn millions of dollars a year in salaries, bonuses, and endorsement deals. In 2008 three Major League Baseball (MLB) players collected salaries of over $20 million, each paid to play for the New York Yankees: Derek Jeter ($21.6 million), Jason Giambi ($23.4

In elite gymnastics programs, young girls and adolescents often suffer through intense training, struggle with eating disorders, and ignore injuries in the hopes of pleasing their coaches, teammates, and parents.

million), and Alex Rodriguez ($28 million). In that same year the average salary for MLB players was just over $3 million, but that may be chicken feed compared to the earnings of professional basketball players. In 2008–09 the average salary for National Basketball Association (NBA) ballplayers was $5.585 million, while eight players made over $20 million, including Tim Duncan ($20.60 million), Allen Iverson ($20.84 million), Stephon Marbury ($20.84 million), Kobe Bryant ($21.26 million), Jason Kidd ($21.37 million), and top moneymaker Kevin Garnett ($24.75 million). Meanwhile, according to *Forbes*, the most profitable sport in the world is football: the average team is worth $1 billion (the richest team is the Dallas Cowboys, valued at $1.6 billion), and six National Football League (NFL) team owners are among the 400 wealthiest Americans.

Meanwhile, the collective effervescence produced by rituals of solidarity does not always produce communal bliss but often descends into a kind of mob mentality or groupthink, sometimes with violent consequences. On Sunday night, June 14, 1992, the Chicago Bulls achieved their second consecutive championship victory in the NBA finals by beating the Portland Trail Blazers in six games. The win was immediately followed by widespread celebration on the streets of Chicago, a display of revelry that eventually erupted into destructive rioting and the looting of grocery and liquor stores in the city's South and West Side black neighborhoods. By night's end, nearly 350 stores in the city had been looted, over 1,000 people were arrested, and 90 police officers sustained injuries (Rosenfeld 1997). Riots also took place in Montreal in 1993 after the Canadiens (the city's professional National Hockey League team) won the Stanley Cup Finals, and in Vancouver, British Columbia, in 1994 after the Canucks *lost* the Stanley Cup championship to the New York Rangers. (Unsurprisingly, hockey is very popular in Canada, as is soccer in Italy, where rioting fans in Catania killed a police officer in 2007).

It is worth bearing in mind that popular culture provides not only a resource for reflection but also distraction, and again, the world of professional sports provides a number of fitting examples. (In fact, the word itself derives from the French *desporter*, which means "to divert, amuse, please, play.") Too many young men from impoverished inner-city neighborhoods risk their futures on the slim hope that they will grow up to play professional basketball, their hoop dreams pulling them from their schoolwork. (Only

The film **Hoop Dreams** *tells the story of two young men from Chicago who struggle to escape the inner city and become basketball stars.*

0.03 percent of all high school men's basketball players make it to the NBA.) Cities desperate for the glory and visibility associated with professional athletics offer sweetheart deals (such as financing new stadium construction projects) to attract and retain sports franchises while virtually ignoring their crumbling schools and public infrastructure. Finally, the collective effervescence and inspirational narratives generated by sports entertainment can be appropriated all too easily for advertising campaigns that draw on the prestige of world-class athletes such as Michael Jordan, Tiger Woods, and Maria Sharapova to sell sneakers, cameras, soft drinks, fast food, and even underwear.

Despite the value of the functionalist perspective, making sense of this darker side of sports and entertainment requires expanding our worldview to include alternative sociological understandings of how popular culture works. In the next chapter, we will explore the efficacy and relevance of our second approach to popular culture, the *critical* approach.

monsters, inc.

A CRITICAL APPROACH
TO POPULAR CULTURE

WHILE THE WORLD OF BRANDING AND ADVERTISING IS HARDLY new, today it seems as though brands have penetrated every crevice of our society. At universities, endowed professorships include the Taco Bell Distinguished Professor of Hotel and Restaurant Administration at Washington State, the Kmart Chair of Marketing at Wayne State, the Yahoo! Chair of Information-Systems Technology at Stanford, the LEGO Professor of Learning Research at MIT, and the Anheuser-Busch Professor of Management at the University of Pennsylvania (Klein 2002, p. 101). Our professional sports stadiums have been renamed for their corporate sponsors: Houston's Minute Maid Park, Washington's FedEx Field, New England's Gillette Stadium, and in Philadelphia, Citizens Bank Park and Lincoln Financial Field. Thanks to McDonald's, product placement has worked its way into morning news programs: the fast-food giant pays to have its iced coffees and other menu items featured prominently on anchors' desks in Chicago, Seattle, and Las Vegas (Clifford 2008). Around the globe, the story is the same: Taco Bell has (perhaps ironically) opened stores in Mexico City, while a Pizza Hut and Kentucky Fried Chicken stand in view of the ancient pyramids of Giza in Alexandria, Egypt. Starbucks Coffee Company maintains stores throughout the Arab world in Jordan, Kuwait, Oman, Lebanon, Saudi Arabia, Qatar, and the United Arab Emirates. As of February 2008, McDonald's had established 875 outlets across China, with plans to open an additional 125 by the end of the year (Chen 2008).

In contrast to the homegrown culture of Texas high school football discussed in Chapter 2, the proliferation of branding in contemporary culture suggests the need for a more top-down model to explain where popular culture comes from and its effect on our overall sensibilities. According to a *critical* approach to popular culture, the ascendance of certain kinds of pop culture can be explained primarily in terms of their ability to reflect and reinforce the enormous economic and cultural power of the mass media industry. In contrast to the functionalist perspective discussed in the last chapter, the critical approach emphasizes the darker aspects of popular culture—its ubiquity and dominance in our society, its consolidated ownership among a few multinational corporations, its ability to manufacture desires, perpetuate stereotypes, and mold human minds, particularly those of children. In this chapter, I apply this theoretical perspective to shed light on the organization of the media and culture industries, the increased social inequalities brought about by the ravages of global capitalism, and, of course, the power of the brand.

Image on pp. 44–45: A graphic from Adbusters *magazine criticizing corporations for encouraging consumerism.*

Foundations of the Critical Approach

In his nineteenth-century critiques of modernity, the German social theorist Karl Marx was among the first thinkers to draw attention to the problems associated with the emergence of mass culture under capitalism. For Marx, a society's culture and its symbolic imagery reflect its economic and social structure and reproduce it over time. In his great polemic, *The German Ideology,* Marx argues that the prevailing ideologies and cultural norms of any society serve to benefit its ruling classes and perpetuate their power: as an example, he observes that the emergence of codes of chivalry and valor during the Middle Ages helped to persuade untold numbers of soldiers to proudly fight to their deaths on behalf of their leaders during the Crusades. (In the context of modern capitalism, one might similarly argue that the American cult of individualism and liberty promotes entrepreneurialism, the deregulation of markets, regressive tax policies, and other social and economic programs favorable to business.) As Marx writes, "The ideas of the ruling class are in every epoch the ruling ideas: i.e., the class which is the ruling *material* force of society, is at the same time its ruling *intellectual* force. The class which has the means of material production at its disposal, has control at the same time over the means of mental production, so that thereby, generally speaking, the ideas of those who lack the means of mental production are subject to it" (Tucker 1978, pp. 172).

In later years, Marx's theories of culture and society, especially his indictment of abusive forms of ideology, would be reworked and updated by likeminded scholars throughout the twentieth century. One such thinker, Antonio Gramsci, an Italian political philosopher imprisoned during Mussolini's reign in

An image from Leni Riefenstahl's Triumph of the Will. *How is this film of Hitler's rally at Nuremberg an example of cultural hegemony at work?*

fascist Italy, recognized the ideological power of culture as an effective means of social control. In contrast to the coercive violence suggested by the deployment of police and military forces, Gramsci (1971, pp. 169—70), draws on Niccolò Machiavelli's sixteenth-century political treatise *The Prince* to explain how societies are more seamlessly controlled through the dissemination of mass media because it disarms and immobilizes its audience by engineering popular consensus through the power of persuasion. This form of dominance, often referred to as *cultural hegemony,* is most pointedly illustrated by the use of propaganda in Nazi Germany, such as Leni Riefenstahl's *Triumph of the Will,* the glorifying documentary film of Adolf Hitler's 1934 rally at Nuremberg that helped inspire millions of ordinary German citizens to submit to Nazi rule.

During Hitler's rise to power, a number of secular Jewish intellectuals from Germany fled to the United States, where many turned their attention to the power of American media and popular culture, particularly Disney, radio, jazz, and Hollywood film. Regarding commercial jazz and popular music, Theodor Adorno identifies its "factory-made" standardization as the root of its "lasting domination of the listening public and of their conditioned reflexes" (Adorno 1989, p. 202). In a 1947 essay, "The Culture Industry: Enlightenment as Mass Deception," Adorno and his frequent collaborator Max Horkheimer further assert the homogeneity and hegemonic power of commercial popular culture: "Culture now impresses the same stamp on everything. Films, radio and magazines make up a system which is uniform as a whole and in every part. . . . Under monopoly capitalism all mass culture is identical, and the lines of its artificial framework begin to show through" (Adorno and Horkheimer 1993, p. 31).

They propose a top-down theory of mass media, comparing American popular culture to political propaganda by arguing that the irresistible films and music created by culture-producing firms under monopoly capitalism—such as the Big Five movie studios of Hollywood's Golden Age (MGM, Fox, Warner Bros., RKO, and Paramount)—help their companies solidify and maintain their own economic power and social dominance. (Until the collapse of the studio system, the dominance of the Big Five was due in no small part to their earlier ownership of theater chains in addition to film studios, giving them control over the distribution of not only their own movies but those of their would-be competitors as well.) As Adorno and Horkheimer observe, "Movies and radio need no longer pretend to be art. The truth that they are just business is made into an ideology in order to justify the rubbish they deliberately produce. They call themselves industries; and when their directors' incomes are published, any doubt about the social utility of the finished products is removed. . . . The result is the circle of manipulation and retroactive need in which the unity of the system grows ever stronger" (p. 32).

To this end, Adorno and Horkheimer argue that rather than satisfy preexisting desires among audiences, the culture industries rely on advertising, popular music, and the glamour of cinema to invent new (and largely useless) desires for consumer goods, all to be fulfilled through shopping and entertainment—thus creating endless markets for the surplus products sold by department stores, fashion houses, jewelers, cosmetics firms, tobacco and liquor companies, the automobile industry, and, of course, the film studios and record companies that helped to manufacture the desires for such things in the first place.

Additionally, they argue that the formulaic amusement provided by popular culture encourages "the stunting of the mass-media consumer's powers of imagination and spontaneity," rendering working- and middle-class audiences so deluded that they overlook the source of their own exploitation as underpaid, overworked, and deprived of their autonomy and creativity as employed workers. As they write, "The sound film, far surpassing the theatre of illusion, leaves no

In 1927, Warner Bros. released The Jazz Singer, *which became the first feature-length film with dialogue, though it had only 350 words. Why did Adorno criticize "talkies" for leaving no room for imagination?*

room for imagination or reflection on the part of the audience. . . . All the other films and products of the entertainment industry which they have seen have taught them what to expect; they react automatically. The might of industrial society is lodged in men's minds" (p. 34).

In an essay on the "regression of listening," Adorno warns of the psychological impact that contemporary popular music has on its fans:

> It is contemporary listening which has regressed, arrested at the infantile stage. Not only do the listening subjects lose, along with freedom of choice and responsibility, the capacity for conscious perception of music, which was from time immemorial confined to a narrow group, but they stubbornly reject the possibility of such perception. . . . They are not childlike, as might be expected on the basis of an interpretation of the new type of listener in terms of the introduction to musical life of groups previously unacquainted with music. But they are childish; their primitivism is not that of the undeveloped, but that of the forcibly retarded. . . . There is actually a neurotic mechanism of stupidity in listening, too; the arrogantly ignorant rejection of everything unfamiliar is its sure sign. Regressive listeners behave like children. Again and again with stubborn malice, they demand the one dish they have once been served. (Adorno 1997, pp. 286, 290)

These kinds of criticisms of American popular culture would be echoed throughout the second half of the twentieth century and into our present modern age

by a vast array of scholars, public intellectuals, journalists, and artists troubled by the ever-increasing hegemony and consolidated economic power of the culture industries, the global proliferation of their products, and what some regard as an overall lowering of cultural standards. In his book *Amusing Ourselves to Death,* Neil Postman (1984) warns American readers that our collective reliance on television for our news as well as entertainment has transformed our national public discourse into "dangerous nonsense . . . shriveled and absurd" (p. 16). In a series of penetrating and incisive essays for the edgy journal the *Baffler,* cultural critic Thomas Frank pokes fun at how contemporary advertisers attempt to tap into the lucrative youth market by appropriating images of countercultural style to repackage mundane products from diet colas to sugarless chewing gum as rebellious, radical, hip, and on the bleeding edge of extreme cool, sometimes to ridiculous effect. As Frank (1997) observes, recent ad slogans include such "subversive" mantras as "Sometimes You Gotta Break the Rules" (Burger King), "The Rules Have Changed" (Dodge), and "This is different. Different is good" (Arby's). In *Fast Food Nation,* a shocking exposé and indictment of McDonald's, Burger King, and the entire corporate food service empire, journalist Eric Schlosser (2002) uncovers a gold mine of industry secrets: the subpar quality of most fast-food burger meat, the chemical additives that give McDonald's French fries their delicious flavor, the poor treatment of adolescent fast-food workers, the ad campaigns that target small children and public school districts.

Meanwhile, in the last few decades a variety of exciting social movements (many led by young people) have mobilized millions of activists against some of the culture industry's biggest offenses. They include the widespread abuse of sweatshop labor employed to produce brand-name fashion and toys in China, Vietnam, Thailand, and other Asian countries; the deplorable presentation of negative stereotypes of women and racial minorities in television, music videos, and film; and the consolidation of radio, television, and cable ownership in monopolized media markets controlled by a mere handful of companies such as Clear Channel, Comcast, and Time Warner (Klein 2002; Klinenberg 2007).

The Power of the Culture Industries

What American child cannot recognize the blue-and-white lettering of Nabisco's Oreo logo, or the smiling leprechaun who adorns every box of General Mills' Lucky Charms breakfast cereal? The global dominance of the culture industries is illustrated by the ubiquity of the world's most recognizable brands—Pepsi, Starbucks, Nike, Apple, Kellogg's, Nintendo. In 2007 Interbrand undertook a survey of the 100 Best Global Brands, as measured by financial analysts on the basis of customer demand, consumer loyalty, and forecasts of current and future revenues attributable to the brand, among other valuation strategies. Interbrand's rankings should surprise few readers: its top five brands were Coca-Cola (#1), Microsoft (#2), IBM (#3), General Electric (#4), and Nokia (#5). Other pop culture brand leaders included McDonald's (#8), Disney (#9), Mercedes Benz (#10), BMW (#13), Marlboro (#14), Louis Vuitton (#17), and Google (#20). The cultural dominance of these brands is reflected in their economic power: Interbrand estimates Coca-Cola's brand value at over $65 billion; meanwhile, the Coca-Cola Company employs over 90,000 workers, enjoys distribution in over 200 countries, markets over 450 different beverages, and sells 1.5 billion consumer servings of liquid refreshment *per day*.

The seemingly limitless variety of Coca-Cola products—Coca-Cola Classic, Diet Coke, Sprite, Dr. Pepper, A&W, Barq's, Canada Dry, Mr. Pibb, Crush, Schweppes, DASANI, Hires, Squirt, Minute Maid Splash, Fresca, Poms, Odwalla, POWERade, Oasis, Hi-C, Mello Yello—suggests a vast and sticky landscape of consumer choices at the same time that it reminds us of the dominance of Coca-Cola as an economic powerhouse. (For its own part, Coca-Cola's longtime rival Pepsi is the label behind Mountain Dew, Sierra Mist, Mug Root Beer, Lipton Iced Tea, Gatorade, Aquafina Water, SoBe Adrenaline Rush, and Starbucks Frappuccino.) Of course, as goes the concentration of the beverage industry, so goes the pop culture field as a whole. While the total output of the media, culture and entertainment industries (movies, books, television shows, compact discs, DVDs, comics, video games) seems infinite, in point of fact they represent the product of only a small handful of highly profitable multinational corporations. Most readers know that only four major broadcast networks (CBS, NBC, ABC, and FOX) control high-quality television programming on free American TV. But it may surprise some to learn that nearly all popular music sold in the United States today is released on a record label controlled by one of only four major media companies: Sony Music Entertainment, Warner Music Group, EMI Group, and the biggest, Universal Music Group. Similarly, the English-language book publishing industry is dominated by just four firms: HarperCollins, Random House, Penguin, and Simon & Schuster. The seven parent companies, discussed below, that produce and distribute most of the planet's mass-marketed music, films, books, television, and cable together are the very portrait of consolidated media and cultural power.

Sony Corporation of America. The U.S. subsidiary of the Sony Corporation employs a workforce of 180,500 people, and in fiscal year (FY) 2008 enjoyed

$88.7 billion in sales worldwide ($29 billion in the United States). Their holdings include Sony Music Entertainment, one of the four major record companies in the world; its subsidiary labels include Arista, BNA, Burgundy, Columbia, Epic, J Records, Jive, LaFace, Legacy Recordings, Provident Label Group, RCA and RCA Victor, Sony Masterworks, and Verity Records. Its motion picture arm, Sony Pictures Entertainment, includes Columbia Pictures, TriStar Pictures, MGM/United Artists, Screen Gems, Sony Pictures, and Sony Pictures Classics. Sony Pictures Television includes daytime soaps like *The Young and the Restless* and *Days of Our Lives*, and game shows like *Wheel of Fortune* and *Jeopardy!*, which air on its own Game Show Network (GSN). The company's DVDs are released through Sony Pictures Home Entertainment, and they can be enjoyed on the wide-screen televisions, DVD players, and surround-sound theater systems made, of course, by Sony Electronics.

Time Warner. The company whose Batman sequel *The Dark Knight* shattered box-office records in 2008 to become the second-highest-grossing film of all time is no joker. Time Warner employs about 86,000 people, and its Time Warner Cable is the second largest cable operator in the United States, on which viewers can enjoy their favorite programs on Cable News Network (CNN), Home Box Office (HBO), Cinemax (MAX), TNT, and truTV, all of which are also owned by Time Warner (as is The CW, a joint venture with CBS Corporation). Meanwhile, Warner Bros. Television's most successful TV series include *ER, Smallville, Without a Trace, Cold Case, Nip/Tuck, The Closer*, and *Two and Half Men.* The company releases its movies (which include the *Harry Potter* films) through Warner Bros. Pictures, New Line Cinema, Fine Line Features, and Castle Rock Pictures. Its publications include *Time, People, Entertainment Weekly, Sports Illustrated, Fortune, Money,* and the entire DC Comics empire; on the Internet, Time Warner controls the behemoth AOL (along with AOL Instant Messenger, MapQuest, and Moviefone), and at Turner Field it owns the Atlanta Braves baseball team.

Walt Disney Company. Mickey Mouse is one rich rodent. In addition to Disney's many theme parks and family resorts, Disney owns ABC Studios and the ABC Television Network (including ABC News and ABC Sports), as well as ESPN, Lifetime, and of course the Disney Channel. The company creates and distributes movies under Walt Disney Pictures and its Pixar Animation Studios, Touchstone Pictures, Hollywood Pictures, and Miramax Films; and DVDs through Walt Disney Studios Home Entertainment. They also license their global brand through Disney Toys and Disney Apparel, all sold at Disney Stores throughout North America, Europe, and Japan. Their classic films (*Snow White and the Seven Dwarfs, Pinocchio, Bambi, The Jungle Book*) are legendary, while their recent moneymakers may be even bigger: *The Lion King, Monsters, Inc., Finding Nemo*, the two *Toy Story* films and the three *Pirates of the Caribbean pictures*, the Disney Channel's *High School Musical* and its sequels, and the pop culture juggernaut that is *Hannah Montana.*

Viacom. The centerpiece of this media conglomerate is MTV Networks, which in addition to MTV itself includes some of the hippest real estate on cable television for teens—Comedy Central, VH1, Spike TV, Nickelodeon, and

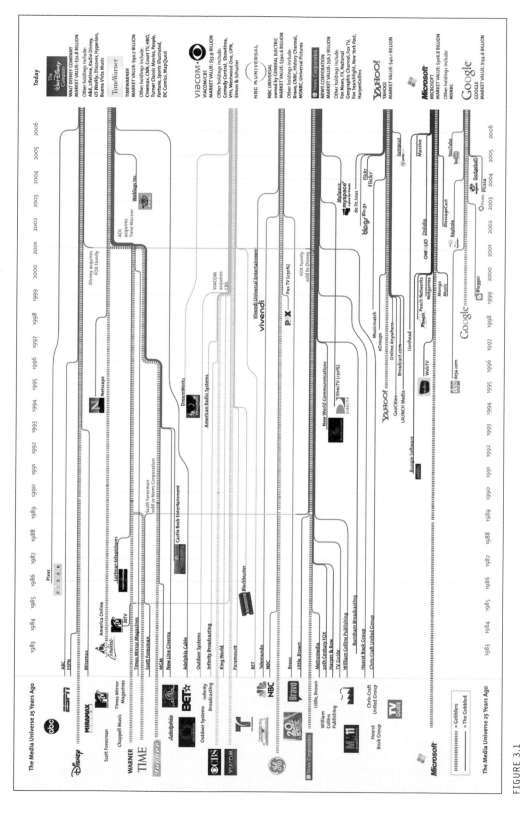

FIGURE 3.1
The Consolidation of Media Corporations

The N—as well as Rhapsody, the digital music service. To top it off, Viacom also owns Black Entertainment Television (BET) Networks, which targets African Americans and consumers of black popular culture. Viacom's motion picture arm is the Paramount Pictures Corporation, which includes Paramount Pictures, Paramount Vantage, DreamWorks Studios, MTV Films, Nickelodeon Movies, and Paramount Home Entertainment.

CBS Corporation. Formerly part of the Viacom family, the CBS Corporation owns the CBS Television Network, CBS Radio, Showtime (SHO), The Movie Channel (TMC), and The CW (owned jointly with Warner Bros.). CBS Paramount Television Network coproduces hit programs, including the entire *CSI* franchise. Meanwhile, CBS also owns Simon & Schuster, one of the four largest English-language book publishers in the world: its imprints include Scribner, Free Press, and Pocket Books.

General Electric. GE makes much more than just lightbulbs. As the owner of NBC Universal, it is the parent company of the NBC Television Network, as well as MSNBC, CNBC, USA, Bravo, Oxygen, Syfy (formerly known as the SCI FI Channel), and Telemundo, the Spanish-language television network. Its Universal Media Studios produces (or coproduces) *The Office, 30 Rock,* and all of the *Law & Order* series; and NBC Universal's movie wing includes Universal Pictures, Focus Features, Rouge Pictures, and Universal Studios Home Entertainment. The company also holds investments in A&E, the History Channel, the Biography Channel, the Sundance Channel, and TiVo.

News Corporation. Founded by media mogul Rupert Murdoch, News Corp. has its hand in a little of everything. As of March 2008, the company held $62 billion of assets and $32 billion in total annual revenues. Its motion picture arm includes 20th Century Fox and Fox Searchlight Pictures. It owns the FOX Broadcasting Company and 35 local television stations, and the cable channels FX, FOX Sports Net, and FOX News; it produces and distributes TV programming through 20th Century Fox Television and Fox Television Studios. Its publications include the *Wall Street Journal, New York Post, TV Guide*, and Great Britain's *Sun,* and the *Times* of London. The company also owns HarperCollins, another one of the four largest English-language book publishers in the world: its imprints include Avon, William Morrow, and Harper Perennial. On the Web, News Corp. owns the popular social networking site MySpace.

Alone or as a collective, these seven mega-firms wield enormous power— they control billions of dollars of assets, hundreds of thousands of jobs, and untold political influence in Washington, particularly with regard to media policy. In part as a result of their lobbying efforts, in the mid-1990s Congress passed the Telecommunications Act of 1996, which eliminated many of the caps on media ownership that formerly limited the number of newspapers and radio and television stations a single firm could control. As a result of this landmark legislation, monopolies like Citadel Broadcasting are able to own 165 FM and 58 AM radio stations. Sinclair Broadcast Group owns and operates, programs, or provides sales services to 58 television stations in 35 markets, reaching approximately 22 percent of all U.S. households. The Tribune Company owns nine newspapers (including the *Los Angeles Times, Chicago Tribune, Newsday, Baltimore Sun, Florida Sun-Sentinel, Orlando Sentinel,* and the *Hartford Courant*), 23 television stations, Chicago's WGN-AM, and the cable channel WGN America, not to mention the Chicago Cubs. But the biggest winner of the Telecommunications Act may be Clear Channel and their whopping 1,200 radio stations, or 8 percent of all the radio stations in the entire country (Klinenberg 2007).

In addition, note that for all the talk about the diversity of news and entertainment offered on the Internet, the most popular sites are owned by the globe's wealthiest media giants. According to the Project for Excellence in Journalism's 2008 report on *The State of the News Media,* the 10 most visited news sites on the Web include (in descending order) the heavily branded Yahoo! News, MSNBC (a joint venture between Microsoft and NBC Universal), Time Warner's CNN and AOL News, the *New York Times,* Gannett (the nation's largest newspaper publishing chain), Disney's ABC News, Google News, *USA Today,* and CBS News. According to the Alexa U.S. Traffic Rankings for March 2009, the 10 most

The cartoon character Bart Simpson was created for the Fox Television Network, which is owned by News Corp. Over the years, Bart has been used to market many products including candy bars, fast food, toys, and magazines.

visited Web sites overall include (again, in descending order) Google, Yahoo!, Facebook, YouTube, MySpace, Microsoft Windows Live, Microsoft Network (MSN), Wikipedia, eBay, and Craigslist. Other commercial powerhouses in the Top 20 include AOL (#11), Blogger (#12), Amazon (#13), CNN (#15), Microsoft Corporation (#16), ESPN (#19), and Comcast (#20).

When we recognize popular culture's relationship to these media giants, it tends to lose some of its glamour and aura. After all, it is hard to identify with your favorite rebel-yelling bands after you realize that their music videos are little more than commercials for one of the four major record labels, and that our rock and hip-hop heroes have been packaged and sold like soft drinks and potato chips by a multinational corporation. Suddenly, Bart Simpson doesn't seem so subversive when revealed as a marketing icon employed to boost the power of News Corp. and its stuffy *Wall Street Journal* (or its billionaire owner Rupert Murdoch).

Amid an illusionary paradise of endless cable channels, Top 40 radio stations, teen pop music groups, and beverages laden with high-fructose corn syrup, we discover that all are owned by the same minuscule number of elite parent companies beholden to shareholders concerned with profits, above all.

Perhaps it is no wonder that the cookie-cutter products of this consolidated media industry sometimes seem so boringly similar, offering the same tired sounds and identically bland tastes, even if their coatings are as deceptively differentiated as the iridescent-colored marshmallows in a bowl of frosted Lucky Charms.

Reproducing Social Inequality

The critical approach to popular culture emphasizes how the popularity of movies, cartoons, cookies, and dance music serves to increase the profits of giant corporations like Universal Music Group, Viacom, Clear Channel, Nabisco, and Coca-Cola. As our purchases of compact discs and diet soda bolster their economic power to even greater heights, they simultaneously widen the gulf between these enormous companies and their would-be competitors: independent record labels, low-power community radio stations, small-batch beverage bottlers, and locally owned newspapers. The inequality among local businesses and multinationals plays itself out on the world's stage as well, as the international dominance of American products from fast-food hamburgers to celebrity-endorsed sneakers snuffs out local traditions in faraway places like China, where the rise of global capitalism represents its own kind of cultural revolution. The social inequality existing between wealthy nations like the United States and Third World countries such as Mexico, Vietnam, Indonesia, Sri Lanka, and the Philippines is best exemplified by the conditions of export processing zones in the latter states, where millions of sweatshop factory workers stitch brand-name clothes and shoes for Nike, Reebok, Champion, Liz Claiborne, Old Navy, and The Gap for no more than a few dollars per day (Klein 2002).

While not as severe as the exploitation of Third World labor, the culture industries treat their workforce in America with a similar lack of dignity and care. McDonald's, Starbucks, and Borders Books and Music have all been accused of relying on intimidation tactics to prevent their underpaid workers from unionizing. In 1997 a Washington jury found that Taco Bell regularly forced its employees to work off the clock, simply to avoid paying them overtime (Schlosser 2002, p. 74). In 2008 the Associated Press reported that a Superior Court judge in California ordered Starbucks to pay its statewide baristas more than $100 million in back tips that the coffee chain had illegally diverted to shift supervisors. (Starbucks, a company that generated revenues of over $9 billion in 2007, immediately announced that they would appeal the decision.) Fast-food restaurants like McDonald's typically hire unskilled adolescent workers because they are thought to be docile employees willing to work for low pay without complaint (Schlosser 2002, p. 68). Meanwhile, since the 1990s, culture-producing firms from VH1 to *Men's Journal* have driven down industry wages by relying on unpaid interns as a surplus pool of free labor (Frederick 2003).

If these worker-unfriendly policies heighten the inequality between labor and capital (to use Marx's language), less-official hiring strategies employed by retailers in the culture industries exacerbate the social inequality typically experienced by women and minorities in the workplace. In 2004 the Equal

In 2008 a California judge ordered Starbucks to pay baristas in that state more than $100 million in back tips that the coffee chain had illegally diverted to shift supervisors. What are other examples of cultural industries exploiting workers?

Employment Opportunity Commission (EEOC) of the federal government, along with private plaintiffs, filed a lawsuit against the clothing chain Abercrombie & Fitch (A&F) in U.S. District Court in San Francisco, accusing the company of steering racial minorities into backroom jobs and away from the more public sales floor. (A&F settled the lawsuit out of court, at a cost of $50 million.) During the lawsuit, it became public that Abercrombie & Fitch's discriminatory hiring policies also included the staffing of young women on the basis of their sexual attractiveness. According to informants quoted in a 2000 story published in the Harvard *Crimson*, "Girls had to have shorts above a certain length. . . . A lot of the scheduling has to do with how you look. . . . They didn't put unpretty people on during peak times. The scrubby girls had to clean all the time. The greeters didn't even have to refold. . . . And it was an unspoken rule with [a manager] that girls were at or below a size six" (Marek 2000).

In addition to their often controversial hiring practices, the culture industries reproduce social inequality by reinforcing degrading stereotypes of women, minorities, and the poor in the countless images they reproduce for the mass market. Hollywood films have historically portrayed their male villains as ethnic caricatures, whether Native American (*The Searchers*), Mexican (*The Treasure of the Sierra Madre*), German (*Die Hard*), Japanese (*The Bridge on the River Kwai*), Vietnamese (*The Deer Hunter*), African American (*New Jack City*), Russian (*Air Force One*), Cuban (*Bad Boys II*), or Arab (*Syriana*). Meanwhile, female villains in film are often psychotically obsessed—Alex Forrest (played by Glenn Close) in *Fatal Attraction,* Annie Wilkes (Kathy Bates) in *Misery,* Hedy Carlson (Jennifer

According to Nancy Wang Yuen, many actors in Hollywood are pigeonholed into roles that rely on stock characterizations of ethnic stereotypes. For example, consider how Middle Eastern men are portrayed in films such as Syriana *(left). Even reality television show participants, such as Omarosa Manigault-Stallworth (right), are frequently typecast in stereotypical ways.*

Jason Lee) in *Single White Female,* Darian Forrester (Alicia Silverstone) in *The Crush*. In the movies, African American comedians from Eddie Murphy to Martin Lawrence to Tyler Perry regularly dress in drag to caricature black women as ugly and overbearing (Collins 2005, p. 125).

On the small screen, these stereotypes prevail. Hip-hop videos typically portray African American men as street thugs and black women as barely dressed objects of sexual desire. Reality TV programs often depict African American women as "no-nonsense" angry shrews: examples include Omarosa Manigault-Stallworth from the first season of NBC's *The Apprentice,* Alicia Calaway from CBS's *Survivor: Outback,* and Tiffany "New York" Pollard from VH1's *Flavor of Love* and *I Love New York*. Television talk shows such as *Jerry Springer* are likely to portray the working class as trashy and dumb (Grindstaff 2002), while family sitcoms often depict proletarian men from Archie Bunker to Homer Simpson as overweight, insensitive louts. During commercial breaks, women appear in beer advertisements for Coors Light, Miller Lite, and Bud Light as ditzy blondes, mud-wrestling vixens, and buxom party girls.

These pop cultural conventions lead to typecasting in the television and film industries, which prevent female and minority actors from finding substantial roles. According to Nancy Wang Yuen (2008), in Hollywood racial and ethnic minorities are pigeonholed into a small number of parts limited to stock characterizations and ludicrous stereotypes. Asian American performers grow frustrated when auditioning for roles that seem little more than a conflation of Asian ethnic stereotypes. According to one of her male informants, an Asian American actor in his late 50s:

> It's just that people who write these characters, most of the time they don't know very much about us. They get a very mixed image, because they don't know. They throw everything together. I mean, every Asian culture is mixed in. The name, place, culture, age, generation. It's amazing, you read, sometimes you read a character that you kind of, okay, this character's name is Vin, which is Vietnamese, right. And that he originated from Cambodia, which is another country altogether. But he's being pursued by the Tongs, which happen to be a Chinese criminal element. And that he [performs] a particular culturally specific behavior as bowing, which is Japanese. (p. 34)

Another one of Yuen's informants, a South Asian American actress, complained that casting directors consistently passed her over because her skin tone was considered too dark, or alternatively, too light (p. 41). Women of color often experience a lack of opportunity in casting sessions. According to an African American actress in her late 30s:

> It's tough when you're a woman of color. How do you explain it? Hollywood does not always consider women of color . . . for those quality roles and if there is that one role, everybody's fighting for it because it's that one good opportunity and you know normally it's gonna go to somebody that's probably a little bit more established. (p. 25)

Meanwhile, all women experience sexism in the film and television industries: even Hollywood's top-paid actresses—Reese Witherspoon, Angelina Jolie, Cameron Diaz, Nicole Kidman, Renée Zellweger, Sandra Bullock, Julia Roberts—make considerably less than their male A-list counterparts. Older actresses additionally face the indignities of ageism in the culture industries. According to another of Yuen's informants, a white actress in her 50s:

> A man's allowed to age. You see tons of gray-haired men on TV. They're the lawyers, they're the doctors, they're the policemen, they're the judges . . . but for some reason they still, in this day and age, don't populate . . . the other characters of the show with as many females as they could. . . . They've come a long way but it's still difficult. You know, if you think about it, generally there's the lead actress and she's generally young and then there's maybe a friend or an old woman, you know, and that's it. You count the number of women in a film versus the number of men, and it's amazing to me that it's still a problem, but it is. (p. 26)

Popular Culture as Social Control

When assessing the critical approach to popular culture, it is easy to see how the media and culture industries reinforce dominant stereotypes in society,

Orson Welles (center) explains to reporters that his dramatization of H. G. Wells's The War of the Worlds *was in fact just a dramatization.*

and few would deny that movie studios, television networks, and record companies are profit-making enterprises beholden to the desires of stockholders and billionaire CEOs. (In the business world of pop culture, music and movie mogul David Geffen is worth $6 billion; Nintendo's Hiroshi Yamauchi, $6.4 billion; Viacom's Sumner Redstone, $6.8 billion; Amazon's Jeffrey Bezos, $8.2 billion; News Corp.'s Rupert Murdoch, $8.3 billion; Nike's Philip Knight, $10.4 billion; and Microsoft founder Bill Gates, $58 billion.) But arguments about the hegemonic power of pop culture as a means of social control are always the most difficult to swallow. How many readers would admit that they regularly feel manipulated by television commercials, or magazine ads, or music videos? Perhaps that might have been the case generations ago, but not today, not in the twenty-first century. In October 1938 Orson Welles directed and narrated a radio adaption of the H. G. Wells's science fiction novel *The War of the Worlds,* and during the broadcast, warnings of a Martian invasion in New Jersey proved so realistic to some listeners that it caused widespread hysteria. Surely, most readers would insist, contemporary audiences would never be that gullible.

It is probably true that in these media-savvy times it would take a lot more than a radio program to generate the kind of panic experienced during the 1930s. And yet evidence suggests that we may not be as immune to pop culture's sirens as we would like to believe. It is worth noting that one of the most popular books of the 1950s was Vance Packard's classic *The Hidden Persuaders,* a biting critique of media manipulation and consumerism published in an age of anxiety surrounding the influence of mass culture. The book sold over a million copies, and yet advertising is still with us and shows no signs of dissipating anytime soon. If anything, our society is even more brand conscious today than during Packard's era.

Of course, to suggest that advertising "works" is not quite the same as arguing that male viewers of beer commercials are gullible enough to believe that all that stands between them and a rollicking threesome with a set of blonde twins is a six-pack of Coors Light. (It is just as unlikely that anyone could be *that* cuckoo for Cocoa Puffs.) Rather, cultural hegemony operates at the level of common sense; it is a soft power that quietly engineers consensus around a set of myths that we have come to take for granted, even if the Cola Wars still remain contested. What sorts of ideas? For now, let us consider just a handful.

Last season's fashions are *so* last season. Why do the makers of automobiles, designer handbags, shoes, and jeans introduce new models every year, regardless of whether their products have been substantially altered? Clearly, it is an easy way for a company to synthetically rejuvenate excitement around its brand. More important, the introduction of new products generates sales by devaluing the recently purchased styles and fashions in which consumers have already invested. Economists refer to this practice as *planned obsolescence* because it makes last season's must-have items seem obsolete and worthlessly out-of-date. Yet although based upon a completely fabricated desire, many consumers insist on replacing their perfectly fine (and sometimes hardly worn) boots and pocketbooks with newer iterations every year because they believe that the shelf lives of such goods are determined by the artificial cycles of the fashion industry rather than their durability and aesthetic beauty. (While iPods, cell phones, software, laptops, and video games are also manufactured according to a logic of planned obsolescence, rapid changes in digital technology, particularly with regard to data storage capacity, make such differences in successive models at least somewhat substantive.)

Shopping completes us. Americans have grown used to thinking of their wardrobes and other collections of consumer items and experiences as incomplete, forever requiring new purchases to fill the emptiness—even though we accumulate more today than at any time in world history. The average adult buys 48 new pieces of clothing apparel annually, while the typical child collects an average of 70 new toys per year (Schor 2005, pp. 9, 19). Even self-styled hipsters, bohemians, and other "anti-consumerists" find ways to accumulate obscure music recordings, stereo components, snarky T-shirts, and secondhand clothing (or at least duds that *look* secondhand). Each feature-film release, concert, and sporting event can easily represent what feels like a missed opportunity for fulfillment, and every purchase brings with it a kind of relief, however ephemeral.

We can all live like celebrities. Consumerism has always had a competitive edge to it in the United States, as families have tried to keep up with the Joneses living on their block. But while we have long grown accustomed to comparing our lifestyles to those of our next-door neighbors, in recent years we have

How has easy access to credit fueled consumerism over the last 20 years? What role do you think advertising and mass media play in the growth of household debt?

aimed much higher, evaluating our consumption relative to reference groups that live financially beyond our own means. As middle-class shoppers have increasingly borrowed on their credit cards to spend more and more on upper-class trappings—luxury automobiles, expensive vacations, designer apparel, stilettos, and pocketbooks—their consumer debt has skyrocketed. According to Gretchen Morgenson of the *New York Times*, in 2008 "Americans carry $2.56 trillion in consumer debt, up 22 percent since 2000 alone, according to the Federal Reserve Board. The average household's credit card debt is $8,565, up almost 15 percent from 2000." And yet this spending has not necessarily made them any happier—in fact, purchasing such accoutrements may only serve to highlight existing disparities between the middle classes and the superrich. As the economist Juliet Schor (1998, p. 5) observes in *The Overspent American: Why We Want What We Don't Need*, "Advertising and the media have played an important part in stretching our reference groups. When twenty-somethings can't afford much more than a utilitarian studio but think they should have a New York apartment to match the ones they see on *Friends*, they are setting unattainable consumption goals for themselves, with dissatisfaction as a predictable result. When the children of affluent suburban and impoverished inner-city households both want the same Tommy Hilfiger logo emblazoned on their chests and the top-of-the-line Swoosh on their feet, it's a potential disaster."

Our self-worth is determined by our looks and cultural norms of sexual attractiveness. Advertisers and fashion magazines—particularly those that rely on gorgeous actresses and models to sell products—simultaneously promote ideals of beauty and sexual desirability. Over time the proliferation of airbrushed images of perfected bodies with toned muscles, rock-hard abs, and flawless skin normalizes otherwise unattainable expectations of body definition, physical fitness, and sexual allure. Perhaps as a result, college campuses have recently witnessed an epidemic of eating disorders among women. According to a 1999 study, between 60 and 80 percent of female college students engage in regular binge eating and other unhealthy behaviors, including those associated with anorexia nervosa and bulimia. Moreover, "many college women who are at normal weights continue to express a strong desire to be thinner and to hold beliefs about food and body image that are similar to those of women who have actual eating disorders" (Hesse-Biber, Marino, and Watts-Roy 1999, pp. 385–86). These anxieties impact college men as well as women. Psychologists observe that contemporary "advertisements celebrate the young, lean, muscular male body, and men's fashions have undergone significant changes in style both to accommodate and to accentuate changes in men's physiques toward a more muscular and trim body" (Mishkind, Rodin, Silberstein, and Striegel-Moore 1986, p. 545). Correspondingly, 95 percent of college-age men report dissatisfaction with specific aspects of their bodies, particularly their chest, weight, and waist, as well as their arms, hips, stomach, shoulders, and height (p. 546).

Increased anxieties over physical appearance can be most easily observed in the recent numbers of patients receiving elective plastic surgery. According to the American Society of Plastic Surgeons, doctors performed 11.8 million cosmetic procedures in 2007, at a total cost of $12.4 billion. Of these procedures, 224,658 were performed on patients 13 to 19 years of age.

Diamonds are forever. Today we commonly think of diamonds as an eternal symbol of love and romance, marriage and commitment, and many American women expect any credible marriage proposal to be accompanied by the proffering of an engagement ring featuring a solitaire diamond. But where did such an expectation come from? In fact, it was invented by the advertising agency of N. W. Ayer, where in 1947 a copywriter coined the phrase, "A diamond is forever," for a marketing campaign for De Beers, one of the largest diamond mining and trading companies in the world (Mead 2007, p. 57). This campaign has been so influential in changing the culture of American romance that in 2000, *Advertising Age* named "A diamond is forever" the best advertising slogan of the twentieth century. (The magazine's runner-up was Nike's "Just do it.")

Brands matter. Rationally speaking, branding should not factor into our purchasing decisions, certainly not as much as pricing, quality, or convenience. Yet as we demonstrate by choosing name-brand medications over their practically identical generic or store-brand counterparts (Advil or Motrin IB over CVS's ibuprofen, Tylenol over Target's acetaminophen, Johnson & Johnson's Band-Aids over Walgreen's adhesive bandages) we respond quite favorably to branding, and associate brands with quality and reliability. Brands connote status, which is why Starbucks succeeds at selling its caffeinated beverages at expensive prices, even though according to *Consumer Reports* McDonald's coffee beats the upscale chain in its unbiased taste tests. Brands can also connote hipness and cool, which is why Ramones' punk-rock T-shirts have outsold the band's records and CDs nearly 10 to 1, and in 2004 the now-defunct New York rock club CBGB maintained a clothing line that grossed double the revenue of the actual live music venue (Walker 2008a, p. 9). Is it any wonder that Apple's celebrated iPod has outsold all other lesser known brands of portable MP3 players (over 170 million

How do corporations make their products more appealing to children?

units sold, as of 2008), even those that offer the same features for less money?

Brands are especially powerful symbols among small children. According to a 2001 Nickelodeon study, "the average ten year old has memorized 300 to 400 brands. Among eight to fourteen year olds, 92 percent of requests are brand-specific, and 89 percent of kids agree that 'when I find a brand I like, I tend to stick with it'" (Schor 2005, p. 25). Meanwhile, another study revealed "nearly two-thirds of mothers thought their children were brand aware by age three, and one-third said it happened at age two" (p. 25). No wonder that in 2005 the most popular Kellogg's breakfast cereal was Tony the Tiger's Frosted Flakes, and Quaker Oats's best-selling cereal was super-sugary Cap'n Crunch. For many years the top-selling breakfast cereal has been kid-friendly Cheerios which is owned by General Mills, the brand empire that also owns Wheaties, Trix, Lucky Charms, and Chex cereals, as well as comfort brands such as Betty Crocker, Pillsbury, Hamburger Helper, Green Giant, Old El Paso, Fruit Roll-Ups, and Häagen-Dazs.

When Popular Culture Attacks

According to the critical approach to popular culture, the primary motivation for designing and programming media and popular culture is money—not creativity, not free expression, not pleasure, and certainly not fun, but the unabashed pursuit of profit. According to such a perspective, the celebration of a film as a work of art, the cheerful adoration of a professional football team, and the joy of a cartoon as experienced by a young child each simply serve to reinforce the power and hegemony of the culture industries. This power represents the economic dominance of the corporation (through its control of capital, intellectual property, jobs) as well as a widening of the social gulf between the industrialized and developing world, multinationals and their non-unionized workers, men and women, whites and racial and ethnic minorities, and the affluent and less well-off classes in America. The hegemony of the culture industries represents a softer kind of power as well, a means of manipulating consumers through clever advertising, brand exposure, and the habituation of fashion cycles. The end result is a world that feeds on style over substance, superficiality over gravitas, and myth over reality.

Yet in recent decades the strategies of the culture industries have grown even more insidious. In their attempts to expand their market base, alcohol and tobacco companies regularly advertise to children and adolescents on Comedy Central, ESPN, and BET, and in magazines such as *Rolling Stone, Glamour, InStyle,* and *Sports Illustrated,* as exemplified by the long-standing use of kid-friendly ad mascots that have included R. J. Reynolds' Joe Camel, and Budweiser's menagerie of Clydesdales, frogs, lizards, and Spuds MacKenzie (Schor 2005, pp. 132–36). Companies advertise inside public high schools and universities through their sponsorship of athletic teams (Nike, Adidas), exclusive soft drink and fast-food vending contracts (Coca-Cola, Pepsi, Pizza Hut, Taco Bell, McDonald's, Subway, Burger King), bookstore management (Barnes and Noble), and Channel One, a video-based teaching aid that requires students to sit through commercials wedged into pseudo-educational current-events programming (Klein 2002). Meanwhile, corporations recruit young people to become *cool hunters*—that is, to research the underground trends of fashion-forward youth in order to appropriate them for mass consumption (Gladwell 1997, 2002; Klein 2002).

But while the critical approach to understanding media and pop culture provides us with a useful window into the machinations of the culture industries, it cannot answer all of the questions that interest social scientists and other scholars. For example, while the culture industries are deeply influential tastemakers, are we not equally subject to the oppositional messages delivered by competing powerful institutions of social control? (While cigarettes may be advertised to children in magazines, young people are constantly warned about the harms of smoking in their schools and by an extraordinarily well-funded medical establishment.) Moreover, given the brute dominance of the culture industries, how is it that media firms regularly fail their shareholders by losing valuable profits and market share? If they are indeed tone-deaf to the real needs and desires of consumers, where does cultural innovation and dynamic change come from? And since big-budget marketing campaigns do not always succeed in spite of the best intentions of advertisers, how do we adequately explain how less-well-promoted fads and fashions often *do* become popular over time? In spite of the critical perspective's utility, answering these questions will require an additional approach—what sociologists call an *interaction* approach, to be examined in the next chapter.

Our cultural tastes are profoundly influenced by our peers, acquaintances, and all the other people who surround us in our everyday lives.

something to talk about

AN INTERACTION APPROACH
TO POPULAR CULTURE

4

ACCORDING TO THE SOCIAL SECURITY ADMINISTRATION, THE SECOND most popular name for baby girls born in the United States in 2006 was Emma. This should not be terribly surprising: Emma is a perfectly nice name. Yet only thirty years earlier, in 1976, it was ranked only 463rd in popularity among girls. (The top five most popular female names that year were, in descending order, Jennifer, Amy, Melissa, Heather, and Angela.) How did that happen? What can explain the meteoric rise of Emma, or any name, for that matter? After all, it is not as if there are publicists out there mounting multimillion-dollar advertising campaigns urging parents to name their children Elizabeth, or Sarah, or Meredith; nor do fashion magazines push names like Madison or Abigail as this year's Sophia, or claim that Samantha is *so* 1998, when it was ranked third in the United States. (By 2006 it had dropped to tenth place.)

A Harvard sociologist, Stanley Lieberson (2000), has done extensive research on the history of naming practices in the United States, and he offers a number of creative explanations for why names change over time. He reminds us that "unlike many other cultural fashions, no commercial efforts are made to influence our naming choices" compared to "the organizational impact on tastes in such diverse areas as soft drinks, clothing, popular entertainment, automobiles, watches, rugs, lamps, vacations, food, perfumes, soaps, books, and medications" (p. xiii). He also observes that parents never name their children in a cultural vacuum but react to the choices made by other parents. Their tastes are often pulled in opposite directions: on the one hand, they want their children to have distinctive names that signal their individuality, but at the same time they rarely choose names *so* unique that they are not recognized as legitimate. (For instance, in 2004 the entertainment press mocked actress Gwyneth Paltrow and husband Chris Martin of the band Coldplay for naming their daughter Apple.) As a result, the popularity of names is always subject to constant but incremental change based on existing tastes.

Therefore, understanding the recent rise of Emma requires knowing something about the surrounding context of taste inhabited by soon-to-be parents. In 1976, Emma was not a very popular name, but *Emily* was: it was the fiftieth most popular name in the country, with a bullet. By 1982 it had jumped to No. 24, broke into the top 10 in 1991, the top five two years later, and by 1996 Emily was the most popular girl's name in America, and has remained so ever since (at least as of this writing). Over time, the popularity of Emily increased the attractiveness of Emma as a kind of spinoff, a distinctive if slight variation on a more popular theme. The frequency of parents naming their baby girls Emma trailed Emily gradually, slowly inching its way up in popularity from No. 463 in 1976 to No. 211 in 1986, No. 104 in 1992, No. 22 in 1998, No. 4 in 2002, and finally landing at No. 2 in 2003, where it remained behind Emily as the second most popular girl's name in the land for the next few years. (In 2007 it dropped to No. 3, replaced in the runner-up spot by Isabella.)

In Chapter 2 we explored the functionalist approach, which examines how societies rely on the stuff of popular culture—its symbols, stories, and collective rituals—as a kind of social adhesive that helps hold them together. In the next chapter we considered the critical approach, which characterizes pop culture as a dominating force, as the product of powerful profit-seeking media firms such as Disney, Time Warner, Sony, NBC Universal, Viacom, and Microsoft. In contrast to both perspectives, an *interaction* approach emphasizes how popular culture is created, diffused, and consumed as an outcome of social interactions experienced among small groups of individuals. While the critical approach investigates the hegemony and power of behemoth corporations, the interaction approach considers the influence of one's peers, neighbors, and informal friendship networks on the spread of pop cultural tastes in clothing styles, movies, video games, and of course, baby names. Instead of highlighting the impact of advertising and mass marketing on public opinion, the interaction approach considers micro-level, small-group processes such as interpersonal word-of-mouth communication, and social interactions within local music scenes and artistic subcultures. In this chapter, I apply this theoretical perspective to explore the diffusion of pop culture, the power of personal influence, and the importance of informal social groups on the popularity of fads and fashions in everyday life.

Foundations of the Interaction Approach

Sociologists have long emphasized the dynamics of social interaction that commonly occur within peer groups made up of individuals of relatively equal status. In *Street Corner Society,* a classic community study of Italian Americans in working-class Boston, William Foote Whyte (1943) depicts the world of "corner boys," small groups of young men who hang out on neighborhood sidewalks and street corners, barbershops, eateries, and bowling alleys, spending most of their time telling jokes, roughhousing, playing cards and dice, and defending their turf against rival gangs. In his aptly named book *The Urban Villagers,* Herbert J. Gans (1962) refers to these kinds of working-class neighborhoods as *peer group societies* in which socializing occurs several times a week not only among teenage gangs but also among close-knit groups of adult siblings, cousins, in-laws, work colleagues, church parishioners, and other neighborhood residents.

These groups obviously provide their members with camaraderie and companionship, but they also provide a space where participants develop what sociologists refer to as a *social self.* The venerated turn-of-the-century sociological theorist Charles Horton Cooley observed how individuals build their self-image from the judgments of others, or at least from what they imagine such evaluations to be ([1902] 1998, p. 164). In many ways our identity as people requires acknowledgment from society to become truly meaningful, or even to exist at all. (Even our most obviously personal identities—our first and last names—are

How does hanging out with your friends and neighbors help you develop a "social self"?

given to us by someone else, and we rely on others to use them when addressing us.) Likewise, it is only in the context of social settings and public life where people can truly express their personality and distinctiveness as individuals. In developing and recreating our social selves, we rely on our peer groups in myriad ways: we compete against our friends and acquaintances for status and prestige; internalize group-generated cultural attitudes, orientations, and tastes; and allow our comfort within the group to inform our sense of well-being.

More contemporary sociologists have drawn on Cooley's notion of the social self to explain a variety of observable small-group phenomena. Erving Goffman (1959) describes personhood as a multiplicity of roles or *presentations of self* that we strategically embody when participating in different social worlds, as illustrated by how our interpersonal demeanor shifts when we interact with our parents, high school friends, college classmates, professors, and police officers. Goffman relies on the metaphor of the theater to depict these various social roles as if they were dramatic performances enacted on a set of public stages. Meanwhile, in a seminal essay on marijuana use, Howard S. Becker (1963) observes how novice smokers must rely on more experienced users to teach them to identify the physical effects of the drug and interpret those effects as specifically pleasurable, rather than as harmful, uncomfortable, or strange. (This is analogous to how humans rely on social conditioning to recognize certain foods as delicious or even edible, such as pig's blood in Hungary, fried scorpions in China, or Spam in the United States.) Similarly, my University of Pennsylvania colleague Randall Collins (2004a) reveals how various tobacco smoking rituals performed in sacred Native American ceremonies, rowdy English taverns, sedate Turkish coffeehouses, and elegant dinner parties offer radically different emotional moods, even though each involves ingesting identical substances that otherwise provide the same physiological effect.

These observations contribute to the major argument of this chapter, that our knowledge and experience of popular culture is conditioned by the social contexts in which we interact with others. First, our consumer and cultural tastes—the music we like, the food we eat, the clothes we wear—are deeply influenced by our peers, acquaintances, and all the other people who surround us in our everyday lives. This does not mean that we slavishly adore the same rock bands praised by our classmates or that we necessarily choose our best friends based on a shared love of rap, or reggae, or Russian folk music—all it means is that the people around us *matter* in some significant way. (In fact, we often violently react *against* those closest to us, as when well-off American youth broke with the Victorian prudishness of their parents in the 1920s to embrace the red-hot blues and swing of the Jazz Age, or when the children of 1960s hippies purposefully foreswore the idealist folk-rock of the Woodstock generation for the more commercial sounds of 1980s and 1990s pop, punk, metal, and dance music.)

[handwritten margin note: foundational assumption]

Second, while the production of popular culture may be centralized among a handful of record companies, film studios, television networks, and media conglomerates, the eventual *success* of their efforts may depend just as much on micro-level processes illustrative of how chattering individuals within small groups and social scenes interact in the context of everyday life. Likewise, the viral technologies of the digital age play a significant role in reconfiguring today's production and distribution processes as well, particularly given the vast resources that Web sites like YouTube, Blogger, and MySpace offer to independent and amateur creators and new cultural authorities. In order to understand how fads and fashions succeed and fail we must examine how human groups work—how they are structured, facilitate the passage of knowledge and taste, and ultimately influence the diffusion of popular culture.

Social Networks and the Spread of Fashions and Fads

Social networks consist of individuals connected to one another through a variety of relationships, whether based on kinship, authority, friendship, romance, or work. The most primary kind of social network is a *dyad*, or a pair of individuals linked together, such as a married couple. In a dyadic relationship, individuals can be equals (as in relations among college roommates, team co-captains, or twin siblings), or have an asymmetrical or hierarchical relationship, as suggested by master-servant, king-subject, or boss-employee relations. Network ties between individuals can also be characterized according to their relative strength or weakness, which sociologists evaluate on the basis of the amount of time individuals spend together, and the emotional intensity and intimacy of their relationship (Granovetter 1973, p. 1361). For instance, marriage ties are likely to be stronger than those between coworkers or friendly acquaintances, while relations between service professionals and their clients are likely to be weaker than those among friends, even though professionals such as hairstylists, attorneys, accountants, physicians, and plastic surgeons are entrusted with access to extremely private information about their customers. In networks consisting of three individuals, or *triads*, things get complicated very quickly, since the interpersonal ties existing between some individuals may be stronger or weaker than those between others, as in the case of love triangles, or romantic dates burdened by an acquaintance who insists on tagging along as a third wheel.

When we refer to someone as "well connected," we acknowledge that they enjoy a large number of network ties—these are the people who have a thousand friends linked to their online Facebook or MySpace profile. Of course, the strength of such connections may be questionable since some people befriend as many classmates, distant relatives, and unfamiliar acquaintances as possible, all in an attempt to appear more popular than they otherwise would. Yet even though it is easy to see through such ploys, such a strategy actually can have several beneficial (if unintended) consequences because these seemingly superficial or vacuous connections, or *weak ties,* have immense practical value. When sociologist Mark Granovetter (1973) studied how people go about finding a job, he (perhaps unsurprisingly) discovered the importance of personal connections in learning about employment opportunities. But the shocking discovery he made was what *kinds* of connections matter the most in job hunting—not intimate relations and close friendships, as one might imagine, but people to whom we are *weakly* connected, even those acquaintances that one barely knows.

Why is that? The answer lies in how relationships are embedded within social networks, and the relative distance separating those networks from one another. Let's say one day I decide to quit my job as a sociology professor and writer, and given my interests in popular culture I pledge to take up a new career in advertising. Who in my social network could I turn to about possible jobs in the ad world? My closest confidant is my wife—oh, but she is a writer like myself, and knows few people in advertising. My closest friends in Philadelphia would be my next bet—but guess what? They are all sociologists, or at least professors just like me. The problem is clear: the people with whom I have the strongest personal ties in my network are very similar to me and therefore have access to the exact same kinds of information that I do—just like me, they lack firsthand knowledge of professions located outside our immediate social world. (When my undergraduate students seek out job internships they have the same problem—their best friends are all college students like themselves rather than professionals working in the occupational fields to which they are most attracted.) Our personal networks and peer groups tend to be somewhat insular and homogeneous on the basis of occupation and age (as well as socioeconomic status, educational background, religion, ethnicity, and race, among other social categories), and often at a remove from more distinctly different social worlds.

But what if I bypass my closest friends and colleagues, and instead turn to barely known acquaintances of mine with whom I have significantly *less* in common? Then things get more promising: I have a former student from years ago whose brother works at an advertising agency in Miami. I have the business cards of a few advertising copywriters and account planners who used to work at a New York agency where I once did a day's worth of consulting. One of my friends from high school is a management consultant, and I'll bet he knows people in advertising, or at least people who know people in advertising. You get the point—the further I move from my center of intimacy (reaching out to friends of friends of friends) the more likely I am to find someone at the far edges of my social circle who is more tightly embedded in a different professional network from my own. When searching for a job, *weak* social connections may ultimately prove more valuable than strong intimate ties because, although tenuous, such connections serve as a *bridge* spanning otherwise separate social worlds (Granovetter 1973).

What does any of this have to do with popular culture? Quite a lot, in fact, since the kinds of knowledge that circulate within friendship networks include cultural tastes as well, tastes for particular kinds of music, movies, novels, fashion—and birds of a feather flock together, as they say. (It is unclear whether we are simply attracted to those who share our cultural tastes or if we naturally absorb the styles of our peers; it is likely that both processes are at play.) It also means that for most people, the secret to developing new tastes in classical opera, experimental theater, underground hip-hop, postmodern art, avant-garde jazz, or other esoteric cultural styles lies in tapping persons located outside their immediate social network, just as an elderly person desiring to learn about current pop music, video games, blogging, or other kinds of contemporary consumer culture is best off seeking the guidance of grandchildren or a young neighbor. (Whenever my parents ask for assistance using new gadgets like the digital camera or iPod my wife and I recently bought them, we always tell them to go to the lobby of their high-rise apartment building and grab any twelve-year-old, who will surely know more about it than any of us.)

Moreover, social networks provide the key to understanding how everyday pop cultural trends, fads, and fashions—Crocs, trucker hats, arm warmers, over-sized aviator sunglasses—become popular. The conduits for change in fashion and taste are those persons that exist at the edges of two or more networks, subcultures, scenes, or art worlds and are therefore best positioned to bridge the wide social gaps separating them from one another.

For example, in the world of popular music, artists who sit at the intersection of multiple genres often succeed at translating specialized musical styles for more general audiences, just as the popularity of blues music among mainstream audiences owes much to the influence of American and British rock musicians steeped in the blues tradition such as Bob Dylan, Jimi Hendrix, Eric Clapton, Stevie Ray Vaughan, Led Zeppelin, and the Rolling Stones. Similarly,

Buddy Guy (left) and Eric Clapton (right) perform together at a concert in Illinois. Blues musicians such as Guy, B.B. King, and Robert Johnson influenced the style of the British rock guitarist.

Fashion designer Mark Ecko succeeded by bringing hip-hop culture to suburban consumers.

from his perch in the urban fashion industry designer Mark Ecko (born Mark Milecofsky) has succeeded in introducing the white suburban world of his New Jersey upbringing to the universe of hip-hop and graffiti culture.

Among these cultural emissaries are very special people that *New Yorker* writer Malcolm Gladwell designates in his best-selling book *The Tipping Point* (2002) as *connectors* who bridge a particularly large number of discrete and insular networks. In doing so, they efficiently spread popular cultural fads, trends, and fashions across a variety of distinctly unique groups who would otherwise never interact. According to Gladwell, connectors are the sorts of people who truly know *everyone*—yet their cultural influence lies not only in how many *total* people they know but how many *different kinds* of people they know. Gladwell suggests Paul Revere as an example. Drawing on the work of David Hackett Fischer (1994), a professor of history at Brandeis University, Gladwell attributes the American colonial hero's success in warning the local communities surrounding Boston of imminent British attack during his famous ride in April 1775 to his widespread social connections. In addition to being a silversmith, Revere served as a health officer of Boston and coroner of Suffolk County, founder of the Massachusetts Mutual Fire Insurance Company, and the president of Massachusetts Charitable Mechanic Association. He was also a noted fisherman and hunter, card player and theater lover, businessman, pub enthusiast, and Masonic Lodge member (Gladwell 2002, p. 56).

In other words, Revere's ability to spread his warning so effectively during his fateful ride stemmed not merely from the size or strength of his personal network but also from its almost abnormal diversity and openness. This also explains his special role as a linchpin of the American revolutionary movement (Fischer 1994, pp. 301–2). In the annals of American films set in suburban high schools, his postmodern fictional counterpart would be the title character from the 1986 John Hughes film *Ferris Bueller's Day Off,* or perhaps Randall "Pink" Floyd, the central figure from Richard Linklater's 1993 movie *Dazed and Confused*, as both maintain friendships among an absurdly heterogeneous assortment of football jocks and stoners, underclassmen and mean girls, cheerleaders and dropouts, nerds and prom queens, freaks and geeks. (Given the diversity of his social networks, it is no wonder that Ferris Bueller's activities during his epic day off from school feature so much cultural variety: he visits the stately Art Institute of Chicago, takes in a Cubs baseball game at Wrigley Field, lunches at a downtown gourmet restaurant, and lip-synchs Wayne Newton's "Danke Schoen" and the Beatles' "Twist and Shout" during a German American pride parade.) It is through connectors like Ferris or Pink—or rather, their real-life versions—that fads and fashions are likely to spread among social networks whose members would never otherwise interact with one another.

Cultural Diffusion and Word-of-Mouth Communication

If social networks and their connectors provide the structural machinery for the spread of popular fads and fashions, then what are the specific processes of human interaction that facilitate pop cultural diffusion through such peer groups and social circles? Market researchers emphasize the impact of *word-of-mouth* communication among consumers, especially since, unlike advertisers and public relations personnel, they have no obvious material interest in the success or failure of a particular product, brand, or lifestyle (Dichter 1966, p. 148). A recent study by the consulting firm McKinsey & Company concluded that as much as 67 percent of U.S. sales of consumer goods are based on word of mouth among friends, family, and even strangers (Taylor 2003, p. 26), while another report shows that young people rely on recommendations gleaned from word of mouth to purchase popular media such as compact discs, movies, DVDs, and games (Godes and Mayzlin 2004). Word of mouth is also thought to have been responsible for the box-office success of many "sleeper" hit films, including *The Blair Witch Project* (1999) and *My Big Fat Greek Wedding* (2002) (Liu 2006). Over time, word of mouth has also gradually turned box-office losers like *The Shawshank Redemption* (1994) and *Office Space* (1999) into popular DVD rentals and best-sellers.

While word-of-mouth processes have traditionally been conceptualized as face-to-face communication among peers and acquaintances, in the digital age consumers obviously share their opinions and customer reviews of books, films, restaurants, and retail services on Internet Web sites, message boards,

and interactive forums as well. Unlike interactions conducted in the flesh, Internet-based communications are not limited to personal network contacts nor constrained by geographic space. (They are also not temporally bound, since past consumer reviews, comments, and responses are recorded digitally and displayed online for repeated public consumption.) However, since word of mouth distributed through online Web sites is typically conducted among anonymous strangers, it more easily loses the credibility of more personal face-to-face communication among trusted friends and acquaintances.

We tend to think of word-of-mouth communication as little more than informal chitchat, but like many other cultural activities, talk can be measured and judged in a number of ways. For instance, word of mouth surrounding a new movie can be evaluated according to its *volume,* or the total number of conversations in which it is discussed; the *intensity* or enthusiasm expressed in those conversations; the *valence*, or evaluative content (whether positive or negative) of such conversations; their *dispersal* among numerous social networks or communities; and finally, their *duration* over time. Likewise, word of mouth tends to be socially patterned in consistent ways. One study suggests that conversations among consumers about retail stores are more likely to emphasize special sales events, rather than the variety or quality of available merchandise, return policies, the friendliness (or not) of employees, or everyday prices (Higie, Feick, and Price 1987). This may be due to the newsworthiness of "ONE-TIME-ONLY!" sales events that may therefore be more likely to generate talk, especially when compared to more standardized policies associated with shopping outlets.

As a general rule, while people are far more likely to talk about brands and products in a favorable manner, negative word of mouth tends to have a stronger influence and effect on consumer behavior. An early experimental study conducted at Harvard in the 1960s found that respondents were eight times as likely to receive favorable word of mouth about a certain new product; however, receivers of positive word of mouth were only 12 percent more likely to actually *buy* the product (compared to a control group), while those receiving negative word of mouth were 24 percent *less* likely to make a purchase (Arndt 1967). According to a much more recent study by two economists at the Yale School of Management (Chevalier and Mayzlin 2003), online book reviews posted on Amazon and BarnesandNoble.com tend to be overwhelmingly positive, and increases in favorable reviews lead to upticks in relative sales on their respective sites. However, extremely negative one-star reviews have a bigger impact on sales than do superlative five-star raves, which may have to do with the rarity (and thus noteworthy quality) of one-star reviews.

Meanwhile, online word of mouth surrounding new Hollywood films tends to be strongest during a movie's prerelease and opening week, with a precipitous drop in volume during the second week, followed by a continuing decline (Liu 2006). Interestingly, a film's box-office success is correlated with overall word-of-mouth volume, but not valence: in other words, movies that generate lots of word of mouth, or *buzz*, tend to do well *regardless of what the actual content of that buzz happens to be.* This suggests that word of mouth may function more effectively as a source of information rather than persuasion—at the very least, it illustrates the maxim that all publicity is good publicity (or as the saying attributed to, among others, P. T. Barnum, Mark Twain, Oscar Wilde, George M. Cohan, Will Rogers, W. C. Fields, and Mae West goes, "I don't care what they say about me, as long as they spell my name right.")

Are there people whose word of mouth matters more than others? We have already discussed the influence of connectors who bridge diverse social networks and communities, thus facilitating the diffusion of fads and fashions among otherwise isolated groups of people. While connectors owe their influence to their structural position within and among varied groups of people, others are valued for their expertise and knowledge of popular consumer culture. For example, *opinion leaders* draw on their deep familiarity and involvement with specific kinds of cultural products, categories, or genres to make informed recommendations to their peers—what kinds of ambient or drum-and-bass music to download, teen comedies to rent, or mystery novels to read. Opinion leaders tend to be experts in a particular field, often related to their occupation or full-time hobby. (For example, whenever I need a wine recommendation I turn to my friend Rod, an artist who has made documentary films in the French vineyards of Bordeaux and has written promotional copy for a Chicago wine shop; his

How would Malcolm Gladwell explain the popularity of products like Timberland boots among urban men?

fiancée is a professional oenologist, a scientist of winemaking. My wife turns to her college classmate Daryna, a former senior editor at *Wine Enthusiast*.)

Other people of influence include those who lead by example, drawing on their experience not as experts to persuade those around them but as consumers themselves. They include the *early adopters* of new products— the first person in their social network to purchase the latest eco-friendly hybrid car model, iPod iteration, or most recent computer software 2.1 upgrade (complete with bugs that they can troubleshoot, just for the fun of it). They exert *active* influence by discussing their newest purchases, demonstrating to friends and acquaintances (and anyone else who will listen to them) the exciting features of their new Amazon Kindle e-book reader, or iPhone plug-in, or Canon PowerShot digital ELPH camera, and they post their four-star customer reviews on Best Buy's and Radio Shack's Web sites. Their motives for engaging in word-of-mouth promotion may emerge out of an altruistic desire to lend their hard-earned advice to the masses or from a more self-serving need to confirm the wisdom of their purchases while showing off their status as consumer *pioneers* (Feick and Price 1987, p. 84).

At the same time, early adopters exert *passive* influence when they conspicuously consume products in public, turning onlookers and bystanders on to new fads and fashions, which is how the adoption of Hush Puppies shoes by cool kids and hip designers in New York's East Village and SoHo during the mid-1990s led to a total resuscitation of the once-moribund brand (Gladwell 2002). Similarly, the adoption of Timberland leather work boots by African American men traversing the inner city, its crumbling asphalt streets strewn with broken glass and barbed wire, helped to popularize the tough shoe among hip-hop artists and eventually the wider urban youth market, catapulting the brand into a $1.6 billion success story (Walker 2008a, pp. 82–84).

The influence of opinion leaders and early adopters tends to be product-specific, whether their expertise concerns electronic gadgets, handcrafted beers, chick-lit novels, Italian motor scooters, or salsa music recordings. In contrast, *market mavens* maintain a vast wealth of knowledge about many different kinds of products and thus perhaps even greater influence over the consumer decisions and cultural tastes of their peers. (The word "maven" comes from the Yiddish word *mayvn*, meaning expert, connoisseur, authority, or one who accumulates knowledge—often sarcastically, as in "What, you wrote one textbook and now you're supposed to be some kind of pop cultural *mayvn*?") Market mavens collect information from a seemingly limitless variety of sources. They tend to devour more consumer-based media than ordinary people and pay unusually close attention to magazines like *Consumer Reports,* lots of newspapers and television (including commercials), and even direct-mail advertising, coupon circulars, and other kinds of junk mail (Feick and Price 1987; Higie, Feick, and Price 1987). Market mavens are the kinds of people who actually read the fine print included in warranties that come with electric appliances as well as the labels of every item in their refrigerator and medicine cabinet, often in their entirety. (They are also the people who call in questions and comments to the toll-free numbers printed on packages of toothpaste, tampons, soap, and other common household goods; see Gladwell 2002, p. 276).

Yet the hallmark of mavens is not merely their obsessive quest for knowledge about brands, consumer culture, and the marketplace but their overwhelming desire to share their widely held expertise with friends, with complete strangers, with *you*. Unlike most of us, mavens do not necessarily seek out knowledge to inform their *own* purchases as much as they anticipate using such information in social interactions and encounters *with others*. According to market researchers, when surveyed, mavens tend to agree with the following statements (Feick and Price 1987):

1.   I like introducing new brands and products to my friends.
2.   I like helping people by providing them with information about many kinds of products.
3.   People ask me for information about products, places to shop, or sales.
4.   If someone asked where to get the best buy on several types of products, I could tell him or her where to shop.
5.   My friends think of me as a good source of information when it comes to new products or sales.
6.   Think about a person who has information about a variety of products and likes to share this information with others. This person knows about new products, sales, stores, and so on, but does not necessarily feel he or she is an expert on one particular product. How well would you say that this description fits you?

And so, market mavens are valued not only for their expertise about brands and consumer culture but for their desire to connect with others, sharing their meticulously collected knowledge with those with whom they interact in their everyday lives. Along with connectors, opinion leaders, and early adopters, it is their word of mouth that helps fads and fashions spread and eventually become popular.

Collective Consumption in Subcultures, Scenes, and Social Organizations

The interaction approach to popular culture emphasizes not only the relations of cultural influence among individuals within peer networks and social circles but also the dynamics of consuming pop culture collectively in socially interactive contexts: examples include *subcultures*, *scenes*, and *social organizations*. Among most sociologists, a *subculture* refers to a social world that stands apart from the larger society in some distinctively patterned way, often because its members invest in alternative identities and systems of belief and practice: examples include Amish and Mennonite communities, Black Hebrew Israelite groups, and other religious sects. But for the purposes of the present discussion, we are most interested in those subcultures in which participants appropriate the raw materials of *popular culture*—including clothes, music, dance, sports, and branding—to distinguish themselves from other consumers through the creative invention of symbolic identity and style (Hebdige 1979; Gelder and Thornton 1997).

Since World War II, American subcultures including greasers, beats, folkies, hippies, surfers, punks, skinheads, b-boys, skateboarders, riot grrls, rave kids, and indie hipsters have stood at the forefront of pop cultural reinvention, forging colorfully expressive selves through their collective consumption of both mass-produced and alternative entertainment media, advertising, and celebrity myth. During the 1960s, countercultural hippies absorbed the kaleidoscopic soundscapes of the Beatles' *Sgt. Pepper's Lonely Hearts Club Band* and the acid-rock jams of Jefferson Airplane, Love, Cream, Iron Butterfly, Big Brother and the Holding Company, and the Doors (on vinyl records, naturally), while the notorious Hells Angels motorcycle gang incorporated the Harley-Davidson brand into their outlaw image (Thompson 1967; Gitlin 1987). More recently, during the 1990s, rave kids collectively constructed a neo-hippie aesthetic identity by borrowing liberally from a range of pop cultural sources, creating a synthesis of gay urban disco music, preadolescence fashion and accessories (pajamas, stuffed animals, pacifiers, lollipops, backpacks), and Day-Glo psychedelic style. Meanwhile, the world of "wizard rock" represents one of the more unusual music subcultures to emerge in the past few years. Consisting of hundreds of bands with names like Gryffindor Common Room Rejects, the Quidditch Pitch Incident, the Dudley Dursleys, and Voldemort and the Death Eaters, musicians and their fans within this subculture perform songs based on the characters and stories surrounding the *Harry Potter* franchise at public libraries around the country. (If the idea of rock bands appropriating lyrics from fantasy literature sounds off-the-wall, it bears noting that the classic rock band Led Zeppelin recorded a number of songs that borrowed from J.R.R. Tolkien's *The Lord of the Rings* series, including "The Battle of Evermore" and "Ramble On.")

If subcultures refer to informal groups of consumers who use the stuff of pop culture to manufacture collective identity and style, then *scenes* represent the actual places where subcultural participants experience their shared identity through social interaction (Bennett and Peterson 2004). Scenes are organized according to their spatial configurations. *Local scenes* are centralized within single venues such as folk coffeehouses, honky-tonks, juke joints, and punk rock clubs, or else spread throughout urban neighborhoods or entertainment zones like Brooklyn's Williamsburg, Chicago's Wicker Park, or Philadelphia's Northern Liberties. In nightclubs as well as on sidewalks and street corners, local scenes provide a theatrical backdrop for public performances conducted among cultural consumers who show off their radical hairstyles and piercings to one another, or cutting-edge brands of designer jeans, or newly invented dance moves. These displays introduce fellow participants to the most current cultural fads and trends, and through prolonged exposure and evaluation these fashions will eventually be adopted or discarded, depending on the influence of local style makers and the vagaries of popular taste. Famous local scenes include the 1920s Harlem jazz scene, 1950s Chicago blues scene, 1980s L.A. Sunset Strip glam-metal scene, 1990s Seattle grunge rock scene, and today's country music scene in Nashville.

In an age of global media, cultural scenes can easily reproduce versions of themselves in locales across the planet. These are *translocal scenes* that circulate fashions and lifestyles in patterns of cross-national diffusion (Bennett and Peterson 2004). The international rave scene is a prime example, which during its heyday in the 1990s deployed party outposts in Ibiza, Goa, Tel Aviv, Cape Town, Tokyo, and other global cultural capitals. (Given the cosmopolitan nature of the foundations of electronic dance music, a creative hybrid of German techno and Chicago house music, the global character of these scenes should not be particularly surprising.) The worldwide dispersion of the rave scene encouraged devoted fans, or at least those among the affluent classes, to make pilgrimages to these exotic hotspots, with each trip providing opportunities for transnational encounters and the exchange of cultural currency (such as up-to-the-minute knowledge about the latest artists and DJs, dance techniques, and fashion styles) among fellow jet-setters.

Inevitably, the hyperactive mingling of local and international cultures encourages cross-fertilization and genomic mutation. At Even Furthur, an outdoor electronic music festival held annually in rural Wisconsin during the 1990s, Midwestern audiences blended together the dance music of the global underground with death metal to produce an interbred "darkside" scene. The hybrid nature of this heavy metal-rave crossover revealed itself among dancers head-banging to techno music peppered with Black Sabbath covers, mixing Ecstasy with other synthetic drugs, and merging the rave-based symbolism of PLUR (Peace, Love, Unity, Respect) with the skull-and-bones aesthetics of the occult (Champion 1997; Reynolds 1999; Grazian 2004). Other globally circulating music scenes have produced similarly innovative cultural permutations, including Britain-based Bhangra-pop fusion, and Japanese jazz music (Atkins 2000; Bennett 2000, 2001).

Of course, in the digital age, global encounters surrounding the consumption of popular culture need not take place in face-to-face settings. In the last several years online Internet-based scenes—or *virtual scenes*—have brought

Aaron Yonda (left) and Matt Sloan, creators and filmmakers of Chad Vader, prepare before taping an episode. Yonda plays the part of Chad, Darth's younger brother, in a Star Wars parody. The short videos have been viewed 9.5 million times on the video-sharing sites YouTube and MySpace.

together fans from all over the world (Bennett and Peterson 2004). Virtual music scenes covering genres from Afro-Cuban jazz to alternative country to New Jersey-based rock rely on Internet sites with downloadable recordings and videos, concert listings, blogs, forums, and Listservs to generate interactive discussion and debate among consumers and creators alike (Lee and Peterson 2004). The Web site TelevisionWithoutPity.com features viewer-driven online forums organized by TV program, with discussion threads further categorized by season, episode, character, and a seemingly limitless array of discussion topics. (Threads related to the CBS competitive-reality show *Survivor* include "Gender and Class Issues in *Survivor*," "Challenge Chatter," "If You Were Chosen . . .", and "You Know You're Obsessed with *Survivor* When . . ." Meanwhile, the thread "Welcome to Tribal Council: The Meet Market," attracts fans of the show who want to communicate with other viewers to discuss personal topics completely *unrelated* to the show itself.)

In addition to providing opportunities for online conversation, virtual scenes also provide distribution nodes for fan-produced content and drama, and opportunities for role-playing. Fan fiction sites invite participants to contribute their own stories based on the characters, settings, and themes from the *Harry Potter* series as well as *The Lord of the Rings, Pirates of the Caribbean, Smallville, The West Wing,* and practically any other pop cultural touchstone one can imagine. On Atom.com, fans post homemade digital films that spoof everything from soap operas to *Star Wars*—fan films parodying the latter include *The Eyes of Darth Tater, Clone Trooper Down, Jedi Gym,* and *Quentin Tarantino's Star Wars* (Jenkins 2006). Meanwhile, the online synthetic world *Second Life* allows television fans to direct their avatars to the virtual Upper East Side world of *Gossip Girl* where they can receive text messages, shop for designer outfits, and mingle at Manhattan rooftop parties, just like the snarky characters from the CW series.

As the proliferation of fan Web sites suggests, subcultures and scenes are often formalized into *social organizations* that provide more-or-less stable arenas for human interaction surrounding the collective consumption of popular culture. On the more administratively casual end of the spectrum, the number of American college-educated women participating in local book clubs has escalated since the 1980s (Long 2003, p. 19). Book clubs typically select works of literature or nonfiction to be discussed in depth at meetings held once a month in members' homes or in libraries, bookstores, or cafés. By personally reflecting on these books in one another's presence, group participants develop new and enriched ways of understanding not only literature but society itself and their place within it, a sensibility that the sociologist Elizabeth Long refers to as "a potentially transformative way of being in the world" (pp. 110–13). As for the books themselves, the buzz generated by two-hour book-club discussions often carries over into the conversations and reading recommendations that participants make outside the context of the group; this word of mouth can dramatically impact the sales and overall popularity of book-club favorites (Gladwell 2002, pp. 173–74).

Like book reading, informal game playing also tends to revolve around semi-organized social groups. The Harvard political scientist Robert D. Putnam (2000, p. 103) has written on the enormous popularity of group-based card playing in the United States during the twentieth century. In 1940, 87 percent of U.S. households owned a deck of playing cards, more than owned radios or telephones. In 1958 the U.S. boasted 35 *million* bridge players, or almost one-third of all American adults. In 1961, 20 percent of adults belonged to a regular card-playing club, and in the mid-1970s nearly 40 percent of all adults played cards at least once a month, or *four times* the number of moviegoers (pp. 103–4). Today, American adults still play about 500 million card games a year, and while contract bridge is mostly played by senior citizens, poker playing among young people—particularly betting games such as No-Limit Texas Hold 'Em—has grown tremendously in recent years, especially among high school and university students. (However, on college campuses, poker-playing parties have faced serious competition from the more socially isolating world of online casinos; see Schwartz 2006.)

In contrast to small-bore, informal organizations such as book-reading and card-playing clubs, gaming communities commonly rely on the efforts of more institutionalized social entities such as locally controlled sporting associations such as Little League baseball, youth soccer, and bowling leagues. Larger and more formal social organizations coordinate national and international competitive gaming events that corral thousands of fanatic cultural consumers into hotels and convention halls for concentrated interaction lasting days on end. The United States Chess Federation claims 80,000 members and 1,200 affiliated chess clubs and organizations; it runs tournaments year-round, including

Players at the Phoenix Scrabble Tournament in Arizona. More than 150 competitors from across the United States and Canada participated in the four-day tournament to win $8,800 in prize money.

the U.S. Chess Championship, which dates back to 1845. The World Series of Poker, owned and operated by Harrah's Entertainment, hosts events around the country, including Atlantic City, Lake Tahoe, New Orleans, and an annual tournament in Las Vegas that in 2007 attracted over 54,000 entrants from 87 different countries, and awarded nearly $160 million in prize money. Las Vegas also hosts the annual Classic Gaming Expo, where fans break records playing 1980s arcade games from Ms. Pac-Man and Donkey Kong to Burger Time and Centipede. As writer Joshua Bearman (2008, p. 65) observes, the Expo represents "an important moment of social interaction for a crowd that, by all available visual evidence, spends a considerable amount of time alone."

Meanwhile, the National Scrabble Association, an independent organization funded by Hasbro, the world's biggest toy company and maker of the classic board game, oversees 2,300 active tournament players, 200 local clubs, and 150 tournaments a year, including a national and world championship. According to Stefan Fatsis's book *Word Freak* (2001), Scrabble clubs and tournaments are intense meeting grounds where die-hards who share an obsession with the game discuss strategy, gossip about their fellow competitors, and pore over notebooks full of arcane vocabulary lists. Some enthusiasts literally wear their gaming obsessions on their sleeves, showing off T-shirts that read "SCRABBLE PLAYERS DO IT ON THE TILES" and "DOES ANAL RETENTIVE HAVE A HYPHEN?"

Hasbro sponsors Scrabble competitions because such events help promote their product to the masses while increasing the identification that the most active players have with the brand. According to the former marketing vice president for Selchow & Righter, the company that manufactured Scrabble (along with Parcheesi and Trivial Pursuit) and funded its competitive players association until they were bought out in the 1980s, "We are in the games-making business. We are not in the altruism business. . . . We conduct these tournaments and we invest money in these tournaments so that the world at large will know about Scrabble, will go out and buy Scrabble games" (pp. 176–77). Yet the game's devoted community of competitive players is homegrown, having developed organically among fans participating in local game-playing clubs years before company sponsorship was forthcoming—just as other kinds of fan clubs, tournaments, and events surrounding media and pop culture consumption often emerge out of the interpersonal networks of eager consumers. Perhaps the most infamous of these events are the *Star Trek* conventions first organized in 1972—three years *after* the science-fiction TV show went off the air (Walker 2008b, p. 14). At these gatherings, thousands of "Trekkies" or "Trekkers" (as fans

A few of the 125,000 comic book fans attending Comic-Con International at the San Diego Convention Center. Originally showcasing comic books and science fiction, the convention has expanded over the years to include a wider range of pop culture, such as anime, manga, animation, toys, collectible card games, video games and Webcomics.

of the show are known) walk the convention floor dressed in Vulcan regalia and kibitz over esoteric trivia about otherwise obscure plot twists.

Today these fan-oriented sci-fi events have been dwarfed by comic book conventions such as Comic-Con International, which takes places annually in San Diego, and Wizard World, a traveling convention held in Philadelphia, Chicago, Los Angeles, and Arlington, Texas. These conventions are hugely popular: in 2008 Comic-Con counted nearly 125,000 attendees. These events attract thousands of autograph-seeking fans of comic books, graphic novels, movies, and video games as well as players of fantasy card games such as Magic: The Gathering, who compete at tables spread throughout the convention floor. In addition, these events feature participants who don homemade costumes or expensive, professional-quality superhero outfits. At Wizard World, such participants include *Star Wars* fans who voluntarily provide make-believe security for convention organizers while dressed as Imperial Storm Troopers. Some of these fans are members of the Fighting 501st Legion, a group of costume enthusiasts who dress as *Star Wars* villains for charity events held by organizations such as the

American Cancer Society, March of Dimes, Make-a-Wish Foundation, and the Special Olympics. (Members of their sister fan-driven organization, the Rebel Legion, dress as *Star Wars* heroes like Luke Skywalker, Han Solo, Princess Leia, and Queen Amidala.)

The Blurry Boundary between Marketing and Reality

Given the efficacy of cultural diffusion strategies best understood within the interaction approach to popular culture, it is no wonder that the advertising and public relations industries have incorporated them into their standard business practices. For example, publicists actively seek out connectors, opinion leaders, early adopters, and other fashion-forward people of influence as special guests for their promotional events when hyping new urban nightclubs, restaurants, cafés, or cocktail lounges. According to Danny Lake, a nightlife public relations consultant from Philadelphia:

> I was branding [a local bar and restaurant], and they wanted to be hip and cool. . . . So we created a tribute series. First, we paid tribute to the guys at La Colombe [a downtown espresso cafe that attracts a European clientele] because they make the best coffee in the city. We told them we were going to do this: we were going to have a party in their honor on a Wednesday night in June. And what did we want from them? We wanted them to invite all their friends, colleagues, allies, customers, everybody that's hip and cool like them. And we threw that party, and it was a great success and we exposed all of their people to our brand. . . .
>
> We identified twenty hip and cool movers-and-shakers, people that could expose our brand to people that they were connected to. (You know the word *connectors*?) . . . It was a huge success and it really expanded their visibility through the right audience. . . . When the guests came in, we asked them for their e-mail address. So we said, "Welcome to the party, it is complementary admission, but we'd really like one thing: your e-mail address." Attract a better element; make it look better; create this perception that the place is *a place to be* because the right people are there. (Grazian 2008b, pp. 81–82)

Public relations agents recognize that connectors not only make desirable yet discrete customers themselves but also have access to informal friendship networks of glamorous partygoers and big spenders like themselves. In fact, in recent years Gladwell's book *The Tipping Point* has served as gospel throughout the public relations universe. In particular, marketing and advertising executives have grown attached to his discussion of the role that the well-connected play in generating contagious word of mouth and buzz necessary for the viral marketing of various cultural fads and fashions.

In addition to the promotion of nightlife and entertainment venues, the marketing of pop culture from independent cinema to brand-name beverages relies ever more heavily on the value of social networks, subcultures, and word of mouth. Although the 2002 romantic comedy *My Big Fat Greek Wedding* was filmed on a shoestring budget for a reported $5 million, the picture went on to gross over $240 million at the U.S. box office, in part because, according to the marketing magazine *Brandweek*, "Greek charities, organizations, and churches were recruited to spread word of mouth about the movie" while "free screenings, attended by the film's cast members, were promoted by Greek Orthodox priests" (Taylor 2003, p. 26). The recent revival of the Pabst Blue Ribbon beer brand owes its success to the clandestine or *stealth marketing* of the Pabst Brewery Company, which quietly underwrites indie events thrown by bike messengers, skateboarders, art galleries, independent publishers, and other bohemian outposts of the urban underground. Similarly, the Austrian company responsible for the energy drink Red Bull stages and promotes extreme sporting events—including a 2001 kiteboarding race from Miami to Cuba—as publicity stunts designed to tap into the hip networks of subcultural youth and other cool kids (Walker 2008a).

Finally, such stealthy promotional strategies meet their match when compared to the efforts of *reality marketing* firms such as BzzAgent, which sends its volunteer army of ordinary people out into the world to promote such brands as Ralph Lauren Blue perfume, Lee jeans, and Al Fresco chicken sausage in their everyday lives, simply by casually chatting up the friends and acquaintances in their social networks (pp. 165–88; on reality marketing, see Grazian 2008b, pp. 86–90). Of course, this strategy works because the kinds of people who sign on with BzzAgent take pleasure in talking about brands and popular culture, just as market mavens do. But the genius (or tragedy, depending on your point of view) of reality marketing is that it has taken the advertising industry's appropriation of word-of-mouth communication to its logical conclusion, effectively confusing the difference between marketing and reality, buying in and selling out. As the next chapter illustrates, the boundary separating the two has perhaps never been more blurred than it is today.

Run-D.M.C., one of the most influential hip-hop groups of the 1980s, were major innovators in the New York City music scene. Why are urban centers such as New York incubators for creative culture?

bright lights, big city

CREATING POPULAR CULTURE

FOR THE LAST ONE HUNDRED YEARS OR SO, NEW YORK CITY HAS BEEN an incubator for some of the nation's greatest achievements in home-grown art and music. The Harlem Renaissance of the 1920s spawned a generation of African American writers, poets, artists, composers, and musicians from Langston Hughes to Duke Ellington. During the 1940s and 1950s the Abstract Expressionist movement, as represented by painters like Jackson Pollock, Robert Rauschenberg, Jasper Johns, and Willem de Kooning, turned New York City into the experimental capital of the world. In the 1960s, singer-songwriter Bob Dylan rose to prominence in the streets and cafés of Greenwich Village. Farther uptown Andy Warhol created his famous Pop Art lithographs and silkscreen paintings at his famous studio, the Factory, where he also made experimental films and managed the art-rock band the Velvet Underground. In the 1970s and 1980s, the downtown scene featured the punk and art-rock music of the Ramones, Television, Blondie, and Talking Heads, and the spirited painting of Jean-Michel Basquiat. Meanwhile, in black neighborhoods in Queens and the South Bronx, 1980s rap artists from Run-D.M.C. to Grandmaster Flash and the Furious Five helped to popularize the hip-hop sounds of the city.

So what is so special about New York City? According to the most basic tenets of American sociology, cities are unique social worlds because of their *urbanism,* as measured by their number of residents, population density (or residents per square mile), and degree of human diversity (Wirth 1938). These three characteristics make cities vital engines for the production of art, music, and other forms of entertainment and popular culture, in part because they encourage the formation of urban subcultures. As we discussed in the last chapter, *subcultures* are collective social worlds that stand apart from the larger society in some distinctively patterned way, often by investing in alternative symbolic identities and styles of living. According to Claude Fischer (1975), a sociology professor at UC Berkeley, the massive and anonymous crowds of residents, commuters, and visitors that flood city centers give urban dwellers the incentive to pull together into a *multiplicity* of social groups that serve as protective pockets of intimacy and camaraderie. The diversity of cities ensures *variety* among subcultures, while the human density of heterogeneous residents tightly sequestered in local neighborhoods bolsters the *intensity* of such groups. The large populations of cities also supply subcultures with a critical mass of participants necessary for their *vitality* and *longevity* over time.

So again, what is so special about New York City? According to the U.S. Census Bureau, it boasts a population of 8.3 million residents, making it the largest city in the United States. It is also among the most racially and ethnically diverse: its population is 27 percent Latino, 26.6 percent black, 9.8 percent Asian, and 4.9 percent multiracial. The New York metropolitan area also has the fourth-highest population density in the country. This makes New York an ideal location for the germination of subcultural life, as illustrated by the growth of so many NYC art worlds and popular music scenes (as well as other kinds of subcultures, such as immigrant enclaves and minority religious sects) throughout the twentieth century.

Other American cities fulfill a similar promise of cultural vitality by drawing on their size, racial and ethnic diversity, and other qualities of urbanism such as mixed-income neighborhoods, concentrations of commercialized entertainment, and institutions of higher education and fine arts. Philadelphia, the sixth-largest city in the country, has a significant African American population (43.2 percent), and perhaps for this reason it has given birth to three distinct traditions in black popular music: the hard bop jazz of the 1950s and 1960s (locals included John Coltrane, Hank Mobley, Jimmy Smith, and Clifford Brown); the 1970s soul music known as the "Philadelphia Sound" (exemplified by songs like Joe Simon's "Drowning in the Sea of Love," the O'Jays' "Backstabbers" and "For the Love of Money," and the theme song from the TV show *Soul Train*); and the 1990s neo-soul movement, an alternative hip-hop/rhythm-and-blues (R&B) hybrid genre that includes the Roots, Jill Scott, and others. (Meanwhile, the white teen pop music of the 1950s was popularized by Dick Clark on *American Bandstand*, which was taped in a TV studio at 46th and Market streets in West Philadelphia, and many of its signature performers—Bobby Rydell, Fabian, Frankie Avalon—grew up in the same working-class Italian American neighborhoods of South Philadelphia; see Hodos and Grazian 2005). Today, visual artists and rock musicians migrate to Philadelphia to take advantage of inexpensive rents; available studio space in defunct industrial buildings, warehouses, and lofts; the city's abundance of gallery spaces and small music venues; and its universities, art colleges, and conservatories, whose young, enthusiastic students make up a large proportion of the city's current audience for local artistic and popular culture, and perhaps some of its future creators as well (Pressler 2005, 2006; Grazian 2008b).

In this chapter we explore how the creation of popular culture is shaped by its immediate social context, urban or otherwise. While in Chapter 3 we looked at the role that large mass media films play in the production of pop culture (a topic we will revisit in Chapter 6), now we focus our attention on the actual artists and support personnel who create and disseminate the stuff of popular culture, including disk jockeys (DJs), special-effects animators, television writers and actors, novelists, and musicians of all genres, from classical to blues, jazz, rock, and rap. Of course, the specific context in which cultural creators work does not always determine what they will produce—after all, who could explain how a second-generation Jewish immigrant from the Bronx named Ralph Lifshitz wound up as the fashion designer Ralph Lauren, whose Polo brand brought elite country-club style to the masses—but it almost always makes a difference. In this chapter we will use the tools of sociology to examine exactly *how* context matters by taking into account not only the actual places and moments in which creators make popular culture but the significance of less obvious realities as well, including occupational and organizational norms, aesthetic and social conventions, technological change, and the law.

A Reflection Theory of Culture

It has become commonplace to suggest that popular culture serves as a mirror that, as a society, we hold up to see our own reflection as illuminated in our songs and soap operas, our movies and myths. We imagine that the heroic characters of great American novels—Huck and Jim from Mark Twain's *The Adventures of Huckleberry Finn*, Captain Ahab from Herman Melville's *Moby-Dick*, Dean Moriarty from Jack Kerouac's *On the Road*—reflect our frontier individualism and rugged fearlessness. We see our iconoclasm and revolutionary spirit in classic films such as *Rebel Without a Cause* (1955) and *One Flew Over the Cuckoo's Nest* (1975), and also in sci-fi epics like *Star Wars* (1977). This same national rebelliousness and pride can be read into the poetry of Walt Whitman, the folksongs of Woody Guthrie and Pete Seeger, and the rock 'n roll of Chuck Berry, Elvis Presley, and Bob Dylan. As Americans we know and accept these truths, just as we embrace baseball, Cracker Jack, hot dogs, roasted turkey, and apple pie as quintessential to our very being, our national soul.

Or do we? Upon a second look, the synchronicity between our popular culture and social order seems to slip. After all, pop culture is a complicated organism, more than simply a sponge that easily absorbs the multiple realities that make up a national way of life. (If only it were so easy—then *every* American novel would be as revelatory as those penned by Twain or Melville, just as every pop song would be as important as Bob Dylan's "Blowin' in the Wind" or "Like a Rolling Stone.") As we have discussed in earlier chapters, popular culture is the product of collective work coordinated among innumerable creators and support personnel, often under the auspices of a profit-seeking multinational company. If our novels and music are reflections of the cultural zeitgeist, they are also reflections of other sociological realities. Let us briefly discuss three such realities: the *technological constraints* under which popular culture is manufactured and performed; the *organizational apparatus* that structures how it is promoted and sold; and the *legal system* that regulates the entire process. In doing so, we can see not only how popular culture reflects society and the social order but how it reflects *the cultural production process itself.*

Let's work backward: first, how exactly does popular culture reflect its surrounding legal context? To take just one example, changes in copyright law have an enormous impact on the content of popular culture. In fact, Wendy Griswold (1981), a sociology professor at Northwestern University, argues that the distinctiveness of the so-called "American" frontier character that emerged in nineteenth-century novels like *The Adventures of Huckleberry Finn* and *Moby-Dick* can be attributed in large part to the specific quirks of American copyright law. For most of the nineteenth century, U.S. publishers recognized the copyright of American authors yet refused to pay royalties to British and European writers. Since these publishers passed the savings along to consumers, novels by foreign authors were considerably less expensive than books penned by American writers.

(For example, between 1876 and 1884 the average prices for imported and domestic books were $0.64 and $1.04, respectively.) To compete successfully in what had become an unfair market, American authors were therefore forced to create characters and plots that differed substantially from those found in British and European novels by writers like Charles Dickens and Gustave Flaubert—thus giving birth to distinctive "American" title characters from Melville's *The Confidence-Man* to Twain's *A Connecticut Yankee in King Arthur's Court*.

How do we know that these differences were a response to copyright law and not born out of some essential American ideology or way of life? Because in 1891 Congress passed the Platt-Simmonds Act that finally extended copyright protections to foreign authors for the first time, and after this, the differences between British and American novels radically declined? While some characterizations and themes unique to American literature obviously persist, notably those concerning race, the convergence of national book cultures brought about by the transformation of U.S copyright law is otherwise nearly undisputable. As Griswold observes, "The American authors had greater incentive to deviate from the norm, to write on nontraditional themes that European authors had not effectively monopolized. After 1891, there was no longer the same incentive for deviation, the novelistic imperatives took over, and the American authors swung into line with everyone else" (p. 760).

What role did American copyright law play in the creation of cultural icons such as Huck Finn?

A more recent example of how changes in copyright law impact the content of popular culture can be found in two very special rap albums: *Paul's Boutique,* recorded in 1989 by the rock-rap fusion group the Beastie Boys, and the 1990 Public Enemy album *Fear of a Black Planet*. Both of these records enjoy enormous critical acclaim: *Time* included *Paul's Boutique* on its list of the 100 greatest albums of all time, while *Spin* rated *Fear of a Black Planet* the second-best album of the 1990s. Both albums offer a sonic soundscape practically unmatched in the history of pop music, in part because of the sheer number of music and film samples packed within each of their tracks. *Fear of a Black Planet* alone samples at least

Public Enemy performing in the late 1980s. Why do most albums have far fewer samples than Public Enemy's classic Fear of a Black Planet?

90 classic recordings, including those by James Brown, George Clinton, the Temptations, Eric Clapton, Grandmaster Flash, and Sly & the Family Stone. Meanwhile, *Paul's Boutique* features over *one hundred* samples from the Beatles, Jimi Hendrix, Curtis Mayfield, Isaac Hayes, Pink Floyd, Led Zeppelin, the Ramones, the Sugarhill Gang, and, interestingly enough, Public Enemy.

Of course, plenty of contemporary hip-hop CDs rely on sophisticated sampling techniques, but still, it is rare for an artist or producer to employ nearly as many samples as these two albums do; most usually include no more than one or two per song. Why? The answer lies in a highly influential judicial court case: *Grand Upright Music, Limited v. Warner Bros. Records Inc.*, in which the U.S. District Court for the Southern District of New York granted an injunction against Warner Bros., finding that the label had illegally released a recording by rapper Biz Markie that sampled the 1972 Gilbert O'Sullivan song "Alone Again (Naturally)" without first acquiring permission from the copyright owners. This ruling ultimately transformed hip-hop forever by discouraging music producers from oversampling copyrighted recordings, because while permissions were never guaranteed and were often prohibitively expensive, the threat of exposure to potential lawsuits from injured parties had now reached new heights. And guess when this court case was decided? That's right— in 1991, shortly after the release of *Paul's Boutique* and *Fear of a Black Planet*. Those two albums were among the last albums recorded by major labels (Capitol and Def Jam/Columbia, respectively) before *Grand Upright Music* changed the music industry irrevocably, perhaps forever. Today such adventures in sampling require digging into the public domain for available recordings or else releasing CDs and digital files featuring mash-ups and remixes as illegal bootlegs available online, as artists like Danger Mouse and Girl Talk have done. (The *New York Times Magazine* columnist Rob Walker [2008c] calls Girl Talk's copyright-flouting music "a lawsuit waiting to happen.")

These examples illustrate how popular culture reflects the specific legal system that regulates its production. Let us now move on to our next concern: how does popular culture reflect the organizational apparatus that structures the way music, film, books, and television programs are promoted and sold? For instance, of the thousands of music recordings released every year, only a

industry issues

very small fraction of them ever receive any radio or television airplay, and the songs chosen (or rejected) for promotion through these public venues reflect the organizational arrangements that shape the selection and distribution process. Again, 1980s popular music provides a nice example—in this case early '80s British new wave music as represented by synthesizer-pop glam bands like Duran Duran, Culture Club, the Human League, and the Eurythmics. What explains the dominance of this music genre in the United States in the early 1980s? In fact, in many ways it seems downright *unreflective* of American society at large, or at least the musical styles performed by the most popular American artists at that time, particularly the R&B-influenced pop music of Michael Jackson and Prince, and the hard rock of Journey and Van Halen.

However, the success of British new wave music in the early 1980s almost perfectly reflects the organizational apparatus of the music industry as exemplified by the emergence of MTV, the 24-hour cable music channel. Since its debut in 1981, MTV has relied on promotional music videos produced by major record labels for a large proportion of its on-air content. (This has changed in recent years as MTV has increasingly emphasized reality television programs like *The Real World, Making the Band, The Hills,* and *The City* among its offerings.) But as sociologist Paul Lopes (1992, p. 68) points out, in the early 1980s "no significant video production of pop music existed in the United States," whereas music videos had long been a source of television programming in—you guessed it- Great Britain. As a result, MTV was forced to rely almost entirely on imported videos promoting new British artists for its programming in the channel's first years of existence, thus inadvertently jump-starting the popularity of new wave music here in the United States. Sure enough, the success of the genre reached its peak shortly thereafter, in 1983, when new wave performers made up 43 percent of all new artists on *Billboard* magazine's annual albums chart, and 50 percent of new artists on the singles chart (p. 66).

Even before songs make it into MTV's rotation, they first must be selected for release by a profit-seeking record company. In recent years, the music industry has relied on market testing pop singles to potential consumers by playing them small bursts and snippets of songs, sometimes over the phone (Gladwell 2005, p. 166). Of course, this evaluative strategy privileges particular types of pop songs—short, fast tunes with studio effects and catchy hooks that are immediately gratifying but may not withstand repeat listening on overzealous Top 40 radio stations. It also effectively filters out certain kinds of recordings from the production process altogether, including songs that emphasize lyrical and/or sonic complexity that may demand more listener attentiveness than that required during market testing, and innovative forms of music that listeners may not immediately assimilate because they sit uncomfortably between traditional genres. In this manner, contemporary popular music directly reflects the organizational strategies employed during the production and selection process.

Of course, one may simply argue that today's pop music is more a reflection of *audience preference* than the production process, just as long as test marketing represents an accurate indicator of what people want. But the task of uncovering audience preferences is hardly a scientific endeavor, especially since listeners cannot "prefer" new music with which they are unfamiliar. It bears remembering that some of pop music's most successful artists began their careers with very small fan bases and only over time gained the kind of traction and consumer approval that test marketing presupposes should be instantaneous and effortless. In 1973 Columbia Records took a chance by releasing two albums by a relatively unknown male singer-songwriter who had developed a following along the New Jersey shore, and although the recordings received critical acclaim they sold poorly. In today's era of test marketing and immediate profit-seeking, he surely would have been dropped by the record label. Fortunately, Columbia released his third album in 1975, and although it garnered no hit singles, a handful of its songs found a home on album-oriented rock (AOR) radio stations, including "Thunder Road," "Tenth-Avenue Freeze Out," "Jungleland," and the album's title track, "Born to Run." Since then, that singer-songwriter, Bruce Springsteen, has sold over 65 million albums in the United States and 120 million worldwide, including his 1984 album *Born in the U.S.A.,* which at 30 million copies sold worldwide makes it one of the best-selling albums of all time. (He has also won 18 Grammy Awards, and in 1999 he was inducted into the Rock and Roll Hall of Fame.) My point here is not to lionize Springsteen but to illustrate how his music and career reflect an older (and now outdated) organizational apparatus that structured product selection in the music industry during the 1970s—an industry that in recent years has embraced more formal test-marketing strategies that (for better or worse) have transformed what popular music looks and sounds like in today's global cultural marketplace.

technology issues

Finally, how does popular culture reflect the technological constraints that shape its production and distribution to the public? On one level the answer is as obvious as the shift in music from acoustic jazz to electric R&B to synthesized pop to digital techno beats, or the transformation in film from silent black-and-white cinema to "talkies" to Technicolor to CGI animation. Of course, the reality is more complicated, particularly since technologies of the past have a strange way of influencing the present. For example, why are most pop songs about three or four minutes long? The technological context of music production in the earliest years of the recording industry provides an answer. From the 1910s until the end of the 1940s, popular music was typically recorded on "seventy-eights": double-sided, 10-inch shellac discs that spun at 78 rpm (or revolutions per minute). These discs could hold only about three minutes of sound per side, so naturally the hit songs of the 1920s, 1930s, and 1940s were produced as three-minute recordings. (The less standard 12-inch disc could hold a whopping three-*and-a-half* minutes per side.) This probably does not seem like a big deal, except that until the age of recorded music, composers and performers had never really been constrained in this particular way—consider the expansive length of most classical symphonies or operas. Early American blues and folk music were even less inhibited because they were based on oral traditions in which songs were passed along from musician to musician without a written score and often included improvisational passages that the player would invent anew with every performance. In such a context, songs had *no* determined length: they simply ended when the performer stopped playing. Therefore, the technology of the early recording era not only determined what a song sounded like—it determined what a song, in fact, *was*.

Still, none of this explains why most pop songs *today* should be only three or four minutes long. After all, long-playing (or LP) records were invented in 1948, while digital recording technologies and data storage capacities allow us to record songs of virtually *any* length, from three minutes to three hours, or days or months. But of course, few contemporary listeners would sit through a three-hour song (I can barely get my students to sit through a one-hour lecture), because over time we have become conditioned as a society to define down the duration of our songs. In this manner, the three-minute pop song is what sociologists call a *survival* from the past: once born out of technological neces-

How did the technological limitations of early records shape the form of popular music?

sity but now destined to remain an aesthetic and cultural constraint all its own, today's three-minute pop song is a reflection of the technological context in which popular music was recorded between 1910 and 1948.

Of course, the technologies of the digital age—namely the conversion of music to MP3 data files that can be purchased online, shared among users, inserted into homemade playlists and mix CDs, played on personal iPods in any sequence, and turned into ringtones—have transformed the way we habitually experience music in many other ways. One in particular stands out: we are more likely to think about songs as cultural and aesthetic entities unto themselves than as component parts of albums or CDs. After the invention of the LP record in 1948, artists increasing began releasing music in album format, which soon gave rise to the *concept album* as a cohesive musical work intended to be heard in its entirety in one sitting, its songs woven together by common stylistic virtues and lyrical themes. The first concept albums were jazz recordings such as Duke Ellington's *Black, Brown and Beige* (1958) and John Coltrane's *A Love Supreme* (1965). During the 1960s and 1970s critics began to take popular music more seriously with the release of a series of experimental rock concept albums, notably the Beatles' *Sgt. Pepper's Lonely Hearts Club Band* (1967), the Kinks' *The Kinks Are the Village Green Preservation Society* (1968), and the Who's *Tommy* (1969). (Later concept albums include Marvin Gaye's *What's Going On* [1971], David Bowie's *The Rise and Fall of Ziggy Stardust and the Spiders from*

Mars [1972], Pink Floyd's *The Wall* [1979], the Flaming Lips' *Yoshimi Battles the Pink Robots* [2002], and Green Day's *American Idiot* [2004]).

Yet as enduring as the concept album might once have seemed, it may be destined to remain a relic of the past, if only because digital technology makes it so much easier to purchase (or otherwise duplicate) and consume individual songs rather than entire albums. In fact, in 2008 total album sales (CDs and full-album downloads) dropped to 428 million, a whopping 45 percent decrease since 2000; meanwhile, over a *billion* songs were downloaded that same year, a 27 percent rise from 2007 (Sisario 2009). What makes this market shift extra-fascinating is that for all practical purposes, it revives the emphasis on recorded three-minute singles that dominated the popular music industry from the 1910s through the 1950s, albeit as a response to a set of technological conditions not likely dreamed of by the pop stars of yesteryear.

Cultural Conventions

This last section illustrates how, although technological changes may have theoretically liberated the creators of popular culture, surviving artifacts from the past (like the three-minute song) persist because habits can be stubbornly difficult to break. The dominance of the three-minute song exemplifies the power of *cultural conventions*, the taken-for-granted rules and agreed-upon assumptions that make social activity possible (Becker 1982). In worlds of popular culture creation, common conventions include the stable use of well-defined language and terminology; standardized materials, tools, and technology; systems of musical theory and notation (keys, scales, chords, time signatures); codified genre types and aesthetic styles; and rituals of participation, including the spatial and temporal boundaries that lend shape to performances.

dfn

Conventions make pop cultural production enormously more efficient than it would otherwise be. Picture a trio of rock musicians preparing to play "Smells Like Teen Spirit," the lead single from Nirvana's 1991 album *Nevermind*. Even if the players have never heard the song, standard conventions of musical structure, genre, and style can be mobilized to describe its fundamentals to the musicians, including its key (F minor), the four power chords that make up the song's dominant guitar riff (F5-B♭5-A♭5-D♭5), and instrumentation (guitar, bass guitar, vocals, drums). Like many rock songs, "Smells Like Teen Spirit" is organized in a conventional manner around a set of verses, a repeating first and second chorus, and a 16-bar guitar solo that echoes the vocal melody. (In fact, the simple formal structure of the song has been compared to other hit songs from the classic rock era, including "Louie Louie" by the Kingsmen and "More Than a Feeling" by Boston.) Armed with a familiarity of modern rock conventions, virtually any competent musician could perform a halfway-decent rendition of the Nirvana song with little practice—perhaps not as brilliant as the original, but passable nonetheless.

To further illustrate how conventions simplify and improve coordinated efforts among cultural creators, imagine how time-consuming it would be if every new group of musicians had to invent an entirely new system of scales, chords, tones, and notation for themselves. Conventions are also reflected in the standardized tools and materials used to produce popular culture (i.e., digital video recorders, guitar effects pedals, oil and acrylic primers), and the physical infrastructure needed for its distribution and exhibition (i.e., fiber-optic cable networks, concert venues, multiplex cinemas, museum gallery spaces). Given the widespread adherence to cultural conventions, novelists need not program their own word-processing software, just as jazz musicians do not need to build their own brass instruments, nor do movie directors need to design their own screen projectors on which to show their films.

Of course, the stability of conventions eases the production of popular culture but ultimately limits its creative possibilities—that is, cultural *conventions* make culture *conventional*. Pop music artists sometimes record double albums of brand-new material but rarely triple albums, which caused critics to call the 1999 release of the Magnetic Fields' three-CD set *69 Love Songs* "as much an eccentric New York art project as a pop album." American feature films are rarely longer than four hours, which is why Quentin Tarantino's 247-minute epic *Kill Bill* had to be released to theaters as two separate films in 2003 and 2004.

Meanwhile, some constraints are embedded in the culture-making tools or exhibition spaces themselves. Alto saxophones have a more limited octave range relative to other instruments like the piano, just as calligraphers who rely on mass-produced inks may be hamstrung by the retail availability of certain colors, hues, or textures. Artists who create impossibly large murals or sculptures may have difficulty finding gallery or museum spaces in which to exhibit their work or buyers who make purchases for private collections displayed in their homes. (Such works are usually erected in outdoor public spaces.) The physical characteristics of most local rock music venues (notably building size and age) prevent the use of pyrotechnics and stage effects common to plus-sized arena and stadium concerts. The heavy metal band Great White learned this the hard way in 2003 when they headlined a show at the Station nightclub in West Warwick, Rhode Island. The spray of sparks set off at the beginning of their set accidentally ignited the flammable soundproofing material surrounding the stage, and the resulting fire claimed the lives of one hundred people, including the band's guitarist.

Not all dismissals of convention leave behind this sort of tragic destruction: in fact, many conventions are relatively easy to break, although in doing so one risks confusing audiences and critics alike. For example, my word-processing software, Microsoft Office Word, gives me hundreds of fonts to employ in my writing, but convention discourages me from **using** multiple fonts *in* the same *sentence* or paragraph. The use of unconventional tools or materials in popular culture can easily generate either approval or outrage. Fans reacted with delightful surprise when the Beatles featured an Indian sitar on their 1966 rock 'n roll album *Revolver* (as heard on at least two tracks, "Love You To" and "Tomorrow Never Knows"), and the indie rock band the Decemberists opened their 2005 album *Picaresque* with a blast from a Jewish *shofar*, a ceremonial ram's horn traditionally blown during the holidays of Rosh Hashanah and Yom Kippur.

The Beatles in New Delhi, India, in 1966. Guitarist George Harrison learns to play the sitar from a Sikh teacher as the other members of the Beatles look on.

On the other hand, British painter Chris Ofili generated controversy by incorporating elephant feces into his work, most famously in 1999 when New York mayor Rudolph Giuliani threaten to pull the Brooklyn Museum of Art's municipal funds when it ran an art exhibit that included Ofili's dung-adorned *The Holy Virgin Mary.* The exhibit in question, fittingly called *Sensation,* also included Damien Hirst's *A Thousand Years,* a piece composed of flies, maggots, and a cow's head, and Marc Quinn's *Self,* a sculptural rendering of the artist's head made from nine pints of his own frozen blood. Of course, in keeping with the overall theme of the chapter, we must bear in mind the context-specific nature of these cultural unconventionalities and taboos—after all, the sitar is hardly an unconventional instrument in *Indian* popular music, and it is not uncommon for dried animal dung to be used on occasion in African arts and crafts from pottery to baskets and even paper.

Cultural Creativity as Collaborative Activity

In *The Sociology of Philosophies,* University of Pennsylvania sociologist Randall Collins (1998) observes that the great philosophical ideas of the ages from ancient Chinese Confucianism to German Idealism and French Existentialism emerged not from the minds of individual geniuses as much as from their interactions within small communities of teachers and mentors, pupils and disciples, colleagues and rivals. Their meetings, discussions, debates, and arguments provided a fertile context for the development of refined thought, just as artists working and kibitzing together inevitably share techniques and styles, evaluate each other's work, and push each other to excel. These collective worlds of creativity formed among friends, which sociologist Michael P. Farrell (2001) calls *collaborative circles,* provide a kind of dynamism that propels innovation and rebelliousness in the arts. This observation explains how an intimate group of friends who studied and socialized together in Paris helped give birth to the most important art movement of the nineteenth century. Today, many of their names—Edouard Manet, Pierre-Auguste Renoir, Claude Monet, Camille Pissarro, Paul Cézanne, Edgar Degas—are as famous as their paintings of landscapes, water lilies, fruit bowls, and ballet dancers, and in many ways their French Impressionist style was invented not only in their art studios but at Café Guerbois on the rue des Batignolles in Paris, where these painters began gathering in the late 1860s for weekly Thursday night meetings filled with noisy conversation and impassioned argument. Moreover, despite the romantic stereotype of the solitary artist alone at his easel, the Impressionists frequently traveled together to sites of natural beauty where they could paint in each other's company. According to Farrell's description of their experiments painting in the Forest of Fontainebleau just outside Paris, "while working side by side, the young painters shared ideas about what art should be and began to develop their own vision. The group was like an amoeba that sends out a pod in one direction, pulls it back, then sends another one out in a new direction as it feels its way toward nourishment" (p. 34).

Collaborative circles like the French Impressionists are common fixtures in the history of literature and the arts. During the 1920s a group of expatriate writers living in—where else?—Paris, most notably Ernest Hemingway, Gertrude Stein, James Joyce, Ezra Pound, and F. Scott Fitzgerald, constantly shared ideas about writing while drinking carafes of wine in cafés, hotels, brasseries, and studio apartments. In his posthumously published memoir *A Moveable Feast*, Hemingway describes Paris as "the town best organized for a writer to write in that there is," in part because of its availability of book vendors, libraries, and quiet cafés convenient for writing, but also for the richly sociable spaces of the city where intellectual worlds flourish (1965, p. 180). Back in the United States, the poets, novelists, and storytellers of the 1940s and 1950s Beat Generation, including Allen Ginsberg, Jack Kerouac, William S. Burroughs, Herbert Huncke, and John Clellon Holmes gathered at Columbia University, Times Square, and other New York City outposts, and their experiments with marijuana and heroin, Eastern mysticism, jazz music, and homosexuality found their way into their stunningly adventurous writing, particularly in works like Ginsberg's *Howl*, Burroughs's *Naked Lunch* and *Junky*, and Kerouac's *On the Road*.

Like literature and art, the production of popular culture also relies on the collective activity and social interaction generated within vibrant collaborative circles of creativity. In American jazz and blues music, the ritual of the jam session provides a fitting example. The jam session dates back to the 1920s

Several Beat writers and artists at a diner in New York City in the late 1950s. Clockwise around the table, they are poet Gregory Corso (back of head to camera), painter and musician Larry Rivers, writer Jack Kerouac, musician David Amram, and poet Allen Ginsberg.

when musicians would congregate in after-hours clubs in Chicago, New York, and other U.S. cities to practice their craft by improvising with fellow artists in noncommercial settings as an alternative to the concerts, dances, and other public appearances where they typically performed for paying audiences. Held in the backrooms and basements of intimate nightclubs and secret speakeasies, these jam sessions were gathering places for musicians where they played and experimented with new ideas, networked and talked shop with fellow performers, and competed for in-group status among their peers (DeVeaux 1997; Grazian 2008a). Its socializing function among artists led African American writer Ralph Ellison to celebrate the jam session in a 1959 essay for *Esquire* as the "jazzman's true academy." As he explains:

> It is here that he learns tradition, group techniques and style. For although since the twenties many jazzmen have had conservatory training and were well grounded in formal theory and instrumental technique, when we approach jazz we are entering quite a different sphere of training. Here it is more meaningful to speak, not of courses of study, of grades and degrees, but of apprenticeship, ordeals, initiation ceremonies, of rebirth. . . . His instructors are his fellow musicians, especially the acknowledged masters, and his recognition of manhood depends on their acceptance of his ability. . . . [The jam session is] a retreat, a homogeneous community where a

collectivity of common experience could find continuity and meaningful expression. (reprinted in [1964] 1995, pp. 208–9)

Elsewhere in his essay Ellison pays tribute to the jazz greats of the 1940s who soloed and accompanied one another in the famous jam sessions at Minton's Playhouse on 118th Street in Harlem: Dizzy Gillespie, Charlie Parker, Thelonious Monk, Coleman Hawkins, Ben Webster, Roy Eldridge, Charlie Christian, and Lester Young. At New York jazz joints like Minton's, these legends collectively created the bebop sound over 60 years ago; yet even today, jazz and blues jam sessions provide opportunities for musicians to converge and perform together in an inviting environment that encourages risk-taking and experimentation. This is especially the case in contemporary blues clubs in Chicago, where jam sessions continue to provide a collaborative context for musical creation among strangers. In many ways, it is the cultural conventions of the blues genre itself—a reliance on traditional blues scales, chord progressions, time signatures, stanza lengths, norms of improvisation, and a repertoire of standards—that reduce the potential for confusion that might otherwise arise among musicians playing together for the first time (Grazian 2008a, p. 53).

Ensemble work in television production provides another key illustration of how collaborative worlds lend themselves to the creation of innovative popular culture. Take the creative team behind the children's educational TV program *Sesame Street*, a motley bunch of puppeteers, writers, actors, stagehands, educators, composers, and animators, to say nothing of Jim Henson's hyperactive Muppets. According to Michael Davis's book *Street Gang* (2008), the show's cast and crew had always indulged in practical jokes, competition among songwriters, and the myriad small-group interactions common among creative collaborators. According to Frank Oz, the puppeteer who lends his voice to beloved characters such as Bert, Grover, and Cookie Monster, "Fucking around [in the studio] was the key to *Sesame Street*. It allowed for that affectionate anarchy that Jim [Henson] reveled in" (p. 221).

The collective creativity generated by ensemble acting and tag-team writing has similarly made *Saturday Night Live* (*SNL*) one of the most successful sketch-comedy shows in TV history. Since its debut in 1975, the NBC late-night program has relied not only on the onscreen antics of its stars but the "affectionate anarchy" celebrated by its actors and writers off-camera as well. According to Tom Shales and James Andrew Miller's oral history *Live from New York* (2002), in its early years the show's studios at New York's Rockefeller Center resembled a 1970s coed college dormitory, with sketch writers and cast members pulling all-nighters, sharing drugs, sleeping with one another, and of course, experimenting with all manner of jokes and outrageous performance. In this creative environment the Not Ready for Prime Time Players—Dan Aykroyd, John Belushi, Chevy Chase, Jane Curtin, Garrett Morris, Bill Murray, Laraine Newman, and Gilda Radner—reinvented television comedy, and future *SNL* stars like Eddie Murphy, Billy Crystal, Mike Myers, Chris Farley, Adam Sandler, Chris Rock, and Will Ferrell, among others, followed in their footsteps. (Famous *SNL* writers

Two cast members from the early years of Saturday Night Live, *Jane Curtin and Bill Murray, perform the "Weekend Update" newscast sketch.*

from past seasons include comedian and U.S. senator Al Franken, *Seinfeld* and *Curb Your Enthusiasm* co-creator Larry David, late-night talk-show host Conan O'Brien, and actress Tina Fey, the creator and star of the NBC comedy *30 Rock*, which is based on her experience as an *SNL* head writer.)

Finally, it should be noted that just as the cafés of Paris provided an arena for provocative debate among the Impressionist painters and later for expatriate American writers like Hemingway and Fitzgerald, today's urban nighttime hotspots similarly serve as a meeting ground for cultural creators who live and work in cities. In *The Warhol Economy*, urban planning professor Elizabeth Currid (2007) illustrates how New York City artists, musicians, fashion designers, and other makers of pop culture interact with one another in Chelsea art galleries, Williamsburg rock clubs, and East Village cocktail lounges. Crowded DJ nights, art openings, and fashion show after-parties provide a dynamic backdrop where creative people discuss their work, share innovative ideas, and build trusting collaborative relationships. As Currid reveals in a chapter fittingly titled "The Economics of a Dance Floor," urban nightlife scenes are also ideal contexts for developing contacts with cultural creators across social networks, particularly within industries that reward artistic workers who can successfully bridge otherwise divergent commercial fields, whether music composition, photography, acting, digital animation, new media production, book publishing, graphic arts, or film editing. Of course, these nightlife zones of creativity are not particular to New York but thrive in other urban centers of art and pop culture production as well, including Los Angeles, Chicago, Miami, Philadelphia, and San Francisco.

Arts and Crafts

In his book *Art Worlds*, sociologist Howard S. Becker (1982) observes that we often distinguish between two kinds of cultural creativity closely identified with one another: arts and crafts. According to Becker, when making *art* one relies on aesthetic skill and judgment to produce a genuine articulation of one's individuality, creativity, and unique vision. In this sense the creator produces art for purely expressive or otherwise nonutilitarian reasons—"art for art's sake," as they say. Examples might include abstract painting, avant-garde poetry, or performance art. In contrast, *crafts* refer to similarly creative endeavors performed for the purposes of making a useful object or providing a specific service, usually for a paying client or consumer. Like art, craft production relies on aesthetic skill and judgment as well, as illustrated by the talents of commercial artists, TV cameramen, shipbuilders, photojournalists, and pastry chefs.

Yet as dissimilar as these categories may seem, in many cases arts and crafts refer to the *exact same types* of activities made different only because they are infused with alternative meanings as shaped by their cultural context; and when circumstances shift, their social designations as art or craft may change as well. For instance, the production of motorcycles is typically thought of as a craft: while they can possess a certain aesthetic beauty in their design, motorcycles are generally appreciated as vehicles purchased by consumers to be driven at high speeds on highways and roads rather than shown in an art museum—that is, until 1998, when the Solomon R. Guggenheim Museum in New York hosted an exhibit titled "The Art of the Motorcycle," which showcased 114 motorcycles of all vintages and models. This is an example of *craft becoming art*, as utilitarian commodities are consecrated as art objects by legitimizing institutions like museums (Becker 1982, pp. 273–88). Perhaps oddly, home and office furnishings provide another example: desks and armchairs designed by the architect Frank Lloyd Wright appear on permanent display at the Art Institute of Chicago, and office furniture is regularly exhibited at the Smithsonian's Cooper-Hewitt National Design Museum in New York. While wedding planners commonly hire disc jockeys to play preselected music for party guests, since the late-1970s disco, dub, house, and hip-hop DJs have become pop artists in their own right by spinning, sampling, scratching, and remixing records (Brewster and Broughton 2000). By employing twin turntables as expressive musical instruments, DJs transform craft into art.

How common is this transformation from craft to art? In many ways the consecration of early Renaissance art itself represents such a categorical shift. In an examination of fifteenth-century Italian painting, Michael Baxandall (1972) observes that frescoes and portraits during that time were funded not by benevolent patrons but by wealthy clients who commissioned "great works" by negotiating complex contractual arrangements with artists for hire. These contracts obligated the artist to conform to the aesthetic wishes of the buyer in excruciating detail, from the use of certain paints and colors (especially gold, silver, and ultramarine, given their high cost) to the specificity of the artwork's subject matter. In 1485, the Florentine painter Domenico

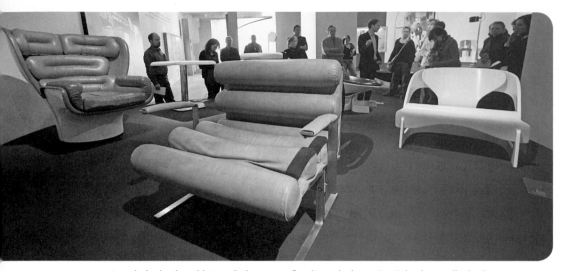

Armchairs by the mid-twentieth-century furniture designer Joe Colombo, on display in an art museum.

Ghirlandaio contractually agreed to incorporate "figures, buildings, castles, cities, mountains, hills, plains, rocks, costumes, animals, birds, and beasts of every kind" into a set of frescoes for the choir of the Basilica of Santa Maria Novella in Florence (pp. 17—18). When his 1488 masterpiece *Adoration of the Magi* was commissioned, Ghirlandaio was contracted to "color and paint the said panel all with his own hand in a manner shown in a drawing on paper . . . in every particular according to what *I, Fra Bernardo [the client] think best* . . . with powdered gold on such ornaments as demand it . . . and the blue must be ultramarine of the value about four florins the ounce" (p. 6; emphasis added). Of course, today we honor Ghirlandaio and his most accomplished apprentice, Michelangelo, as inspired and expressive artistic geniuses rather than commercial craftspeople, yet in many ways that is exactly what they were. (This observation does not take anything away from their talents but simply asks us to reevaluate the context of social relations in which they produced their work.)

Just as social circumstances can transform craft into art, examples of *art becoming craft* abound as well (Becker 1982, pp. 288—96). Struggling theatrical actors sometimes take on roles in industrial training videos, while American movie stars frequently earn big paychecks acting in TV commercials shown abroad: examples include Samuel L. Jackson shilling for Barclays Bank in Great Britain, and Sylvester Stallone selling ham in Japan. Orchestral violinists, cellists, clarinetists, and other instrumentalists often make ends meet by working as commercial studio musicians in the Hollywood film and television industry, as do classical music composers and conductors (Faulkner 1971). Rock musicians age into this professional craft as well. After the British rock band the Police broke up in the 1980s, their drummer, Stewart Copeland, began a new career composing soundtracks for film, television, and video games: his movie credits include Francis Ford Coppola's *Rumble Fish* (1983), John Hughes's *She's Having a Baby* (1988), and Oliver Stone's *Wall Street* (1987) and *Talk Radio* (1988).

For artistic creators, performing the work expected of craftspeople—that is, producing culture in a commercialized context for a paying clientele or audience—often requires that they compromise their expressive or aesthetic vision in the interests of satisfying the mainstream tastes of consumers. As Gary Alan Fine (1992), a professor of sociology at Northwestern University, observes in his research on restaurant cooking, chefs must balance their own culinary judgment against the expectations and desires of average customers who, as a group, tend to prefer their meat and fish entrees overcooked and add too much salt and pepper to otherwise optimally seasoned dishes. In chain restaurants like Applebee's, Bennigan's, Chili's, and T.G.I. Friday's, chefs are also bound to corporate promises and customer expectations that the same dishes—Loaded Potato Skins, "Oh, Baby" Back Ribs, Death by Chocolate—will taste exactly the same in any restaurant location, from Carlisle, Pennsylvania, to Cartersville, Georgia, to Carlsbad, New Mexico. (Chili's has outlets in each location.) And since restaurant diners will wait only so long for their orders to be prepared, behind kitchen walls chefs regularly cut corners to an unsettling degree; this is why, according to Fine, "when food falls on a dirty counter or floor after being cooked, cooks will wipe or rinse it, and then serve it, with the customer none the wiser" (p. 1281).

Buying In and Selling Out

The myth of the romantic artist is an enduring one: it is easy to imagine the lonely painter or poet isolated in his garret studio, tortured by his inner demons as he creates his imaginative masterpieces. Unconcerned with money, his art alone—the unique expression of his human vision and inspired genius—keeps him alive. This myth easily lends itself to the world of rock music: exemplars of the beatified rock artist include John Lennon in his post-Beatles career; Jim Morrison, the lead singer of the 1960s rock band the Doors; Kurt Cobain, vocalist and lead guitarist of the 1990s Seattle grunge band Nirvana; and the 1990s indie rock singer-songwriter Elliot Smith. Not coincidentally, all four died tragically, solidifying their mythical status as pop cultural martyrs.

But sociology punches a number of holes in this timeless myth of the solitary artist. As this chapter illustrates, cultural producers tend to work collectively in collaborative circles and other social groups (just as Cobain performed closely with Nirvana's bassist Krist Novoselic and drummer Dave Grohl), and their creations are modeled in accordance with prevailing cultural conventions and social expectations. While popular culture may express something of the artist's personality or identity, his or her output also reflects its social context, particularly the production process in which it is embedded. These contextual realities include the technological constraints that shape the manufacture and performance of pop culture, the organizational apparatus that structures its promotion and distribution, and the legal system that governs the overall process. At the same time, institutions of cultural consecration and legitimacy such as the Guggenheim Museum, the Art Institute of Chicago, and the Rock and Roll Hall of Fame help to mold and shift public perceptions of cultural value and propriety.

As for the obvious suggestion that authentic artists are far more concerned with expressing themselves creatively than with making money, it bears remembering how many try to excel at both. Certainly, almost all pop culture creators strive for aesthetic expressiveness and artistic excellence on even their most commercially oriented projects. Recent Hollywood blockbusters have managed to combine commercial demands with artistic vision: as the *New York Times* critic Manohla Dargis (2008) wrote of the Batman film *The Dark Knight*, "pitched at the divide between art and industry, poetry and entertainment, it goes darker and deeper than any Hollywood movie of its comic-book kind." According to Stephen Oakes, a director of animation and special effects who produces television advertisements and promotional spots, commercial artists use client-based projects as outlets for their own creative vision: "In the production companies, in the creative teams at the ad agencies, I would say that we don't spend much time worrying about the home viewer. It is mostly ourselves as peers. We are trying to entertain ourselves and our friends—we are trying to get away with as much fun as possible while doing the job that the brand manager has set forth for us" (Ohmann 1996, p. 79). In fact, Oakes and his colleagues rely on TV advertising and music videos as testing grounds for developing experimental concepts and techniques. Regarding his work creating promotional ads for MTV during the 1980s, he recalls:

> It was a wonderful opportunity, because they said, "Here is the budget; do whatever you want; just make sure it ends up with the MTV configuration, the logo." Well, that was my dream job. And we did come up with some pretty wild stuff that came from the artist's interest. We did one that was based on a woman's personal watercolors, and she was the director of it. We did some sculptural model things. We did an MTV logo made out of time lapse of frozen chemicals that did funny things during its melting. We ran it in reverse so all this glop sort of swirled together and made the MTV logo. Each one of those was like a little visual experiment. Some were more successful than others, but the stakes weren't that high. It was a kind of novelty workshop. (pp. 78—79)

At the same time, pop cultural creators in most fields of production, particularly in fashion, television, filmmaking, and popular music, typically seek out professional and commercial success at least as much as any artistic ideal. In rap music, artistic success is *specifically* defined in monetary terms, as baldly proclaimed by the title of the rapper 50 Cent's 2003 multiplatinum album *Get Rich or Die Tryin'*. In a context of commercialized culture, money connotes artistic status; or, in the words of the late blues singer Barkin' Bill Smith, "It's not about havin' fun. It's about *makin' money*—now *that's* what it's all about! . . . Hell, then you can go out and *buy* your own fun!" (Grazian 2003, p. 151).

Meanwhile, among rock musicians, licensing songs for use in television commercials, soundtracks, and video games, along with other branding efforts that for years musicians, critics, and fans have lambasted as "selling out" (Klein 2009), are today considered business as usual, even among bands with serious punk ethics or indie credibility, simply because there are so few alternative ways of earning a livable wage as a recording artist. In his memoir *Black Postcards* Dean Wareham (2008), the lead vocalist for the indie rock bands Galaxie 500 and Luna, explains that most touring bands on independent labels must forgo musicians' salaries and typically only make money on the road from T-shirt sales and other merchandising schemes (p. 181). As for performers on major labels, album royalties are often only paid out to blockbuster acts like Madonna and U2, whose records earn enough to recoup their original production, marketing, and touring costs. According to Wareham, "All the money that gets spent on making and promoting your record means that sometimes you are only digging

The rapper 50 Cent performing a track from his album Get Rich or Die Tryin'. *How does commercial success connote status in hip-hop culture?*

yourself a hole, a deep pit of record company debt. You may get a 14 percent royalty rate, but with all those expenses being charged to your account you are never going to see royalties anyway" (p. 111). In contrast, licensing fees for TV commercials and other ancillary markets are guaranteed and generally paid up front. As the *New York Times* pop music critic Jon Pareles (2008) observes, "Musicians have to eat and want to be heard, and if that means accompanying someone else's sales pitch or video game, well, it's a living." Another *Times* writer, John Leland (2001), puts this in recent historical perspective: "Fourteen years after Nike outraged Beatles fans, and the surviving Beatles, by using "Revolution" in a sneaker ad—Michael Jackson controlled the publishing rights to the song—the revolution is over, and the advertisers have largely won." If this is "selling out," writes Leland, then many bands today are more than willing to "buy in."

The agent Ari Gold, played by Jeremy Piven on the television show *Entourage*, is an example of one of the many types of decision makers who participate in the media industry.

risky
business

HOW THE MEDIA AND
CULTURE INDUSTRIES WORK

I T COULDN'T MISS. HISTORICAL WAR EPICS HAD BEEN ALL THE RAGE since Ridley Scott's 2000 hit *Gladiator* earned five Academy Awards, including Best Picture, and a domestic box-office prize of $188 million. And so in 2004, Academy Award-winning director Oliver Stone made *Alexander*, a film based on the life of the mighty conqueror Alexander the Great, for $155 million. The film featured two previous Oscar winners—Anthony Hopkins and Angelina Jolie—along with a long list of stars that included Colin Farrell, Val Kilmer, Christopher Plummer, and Rosario Dawson. And yet in spite of its great promise, the film was roundly panned by critics, a $34.3 million box-office bomb.

That same year, Mel Gibson directed a morbidly violent film depicting the arrest, trial, and crucifixion of Jesus Christ in gruesome and graphic detail. Filmed on a relatively modest budget of $25 million, the movie had no stars in any of the major roles, and all of the dialogue was spoken in Aramaic, Latin, and Hebrew, with English subtitles. Upon its release, *The Passion of the Christ* was castigated by a wide range of dissenters, including *New York Times* film critic A. O. Scott, who wrote, "*The Passion of the Christ* is so relentlessly focused on the savagery of Jesus' final hours that this film seems to arise less from love than from wrath, and to succeed more in assaulting the spirit than in uplifting it. Mr. Gibson has constructed an unnerving and painful spectacle that is also, in the end, a depressing one. It is disheartening to see a film made with evident and abundant religious conviction that is at the same time so utterly lacking in grace." *The Passion of the Christ* went on to gross $370 million in domestic box-office receipts, making it the twelfth-top-grossing film of all time.

One of the most firmly held truths in the media industry is that "all hits are flukes," or as the Academy Award-winning screenwriter William Goldman has suggested of the uncertainties surrounding success in Hollywood, "Nobody knows anything" (Faulkner and Anderson 1987; Bielby and Bielby 1994).

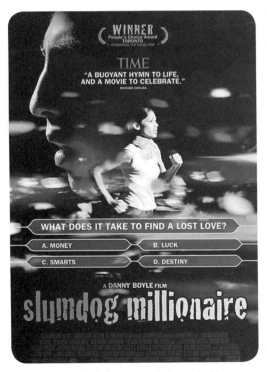

The conventional wisdom among industry insiders was that Slumdog Millionaire—a movie about Who Wants to be a Millionaire? that was set in India and had half its dialogue in Hindi—had little commercial appeal. But they were wrong: The film grossed over $360 million worlwide in the year following its August 2008 release, and it won the Academy Award for Best Picture.

And yet media and pop culture-producing firms exert a great deal of effort seeking out talent, trying however futilely to predict box-office winners, ratings champions, best-selling authors, and multiplatinum artists. This raises an interesting question: given the strong uncertainty of success in today's mass media market, how do cultural producers go about choosing which films, books, television programs, and music projects on which to take their chances?

Conventional wisdom would suggest that in such cases, quality would be most paramount. But what *is* quality? How does one recognize it, and according to whose standards? Instead, I would argue that decision making in the media industries is primarily driven by the *minimization of risk*. In the absence of a crystal ball that can predict commercial success, decisions are usually made rationally in a context of risk aversion and caution. Of course, this contradicts the wild image of corporate media instigators in the popular imagination—MTV, Death Row Records, Jerry Bruckheimer Films. And yet behind their façade of racy content portrayed in spring break specials, reality TV dating shows, hip-hop videos, and shoot-'em-up blockbusters, these and other media outlets operate no differently than insurance companies that employ great bureaucratic mechanisms to effectively manage risk.

The Organization of the Media Industries

To understand how this process works, one must remember that the stuff of popular culture—movies, compact discs, DVDs, television shows, video games, novels, comic books, magazines—are products sold by multinational corporations in the interest of making billions of dollars in annual profit under market capitalism. In emphasizing this, I do not intend to belittle or disparage pop culture, particularly given that this capitalist system has generated many of the most innovative artistic works of the last century. Nevertheless, aesthetic and cultural brilliance should not prevent the sociologically minded from observing how our favorite cultural products are just that—products for sale that are selected for production, manufactured, marketed, and distributed within a highly regimented organizational system.

Sociologist Paul Hirsch (1972) illustrates how this system operates as if it were a giant processing machine. The production process begins with a surplus pool of creative talent made up of starving artists, guitar heroes, table-serving actors, cutting-edge filmmakers, and would-be great American novelists. To eventually succeed as cultural producers, these creative workers must meet the immediate needs of profit-seeking firms, whether music companies such as Reprise Records, film studios like Focus Features, or book publishing behemoths like Random House. In organizational jargon, we might say that this labor pool of willing artists, musicians, and actors push up against the edge of what Hirsch would call a protective *input boundary*. This input boundary operates as a filter used by record labels, movie production houses, and other firms to hand select a small group of creative talent from the enormous pool of media hopefuls for eventual mass cultural diffusion and possible stardom.

Anna Wintour, editor-in-chief of Vogue, *is one of the most powerful cultural gatekeepers in the United States. She was also the inspiration for Meryl Streep's character in the film* The Devil Wears Prada.

Facilitating in this winnowing process are *boundary spanners*, personnel responsible for making connections between individual artists and corporate media firms. Some of these boundary spanners are managers, agents, or other emissaries representing creative personnel, while others serve as talent seekers for media companies, such as A&R (artists and repertoire) scouts in the music industry, casting directors in film and television, and acquisitions editors in book publishing. Through countless auditions and evaluations, social networking at multiple meetings, and other assorted trust-building exercises, a select number of creative artists who manage to break through the aforementioned input boundary are eventually hand-picked for temporary contract work (more on this below) with a media company, whether it be to write and submit a novel for publication, costar in a motion picture, or record a hip-hop CD.

Upon manufacturing a variety of cultural products, mass media firms must successfully market these wares to a set of media and communication outlets that will promote them on glossy magazine covers, newspaper features pages, entertainment television news programs, and popular Web sites. To do this, a second group of boundary spanners—in-house support personnel that include publicists, press coordinators, radio promoters, and sales representatives—selectively champion their firm's most promising films, CDs, or other offerings with every available means at their disposal across a second filter, a fittingly named *output boundary* that must be successfully traversed if these products are to gain the attention of the entertainment press, and eventually the public.

The boundary-spanning personnel situated at the receiving end of this deluge of corporate solicitation serve as *gatekeepers* responsible for selecting and disseminating an even smaller set of cultural products to the public. Working as magazine editors, television news producers, entertainment journalists, movie reviewers, book critics, and high-profile bloggers, gatekeepers are theoretically entrusted with the responsibility of making thoughtful recommendations to pop music fans, fiction readers, film buffs, and the like. In this manner, the primary audience for movies, books, and recordings are not everyday consumers but those professional evaluators entrusted to offer reliable suggestions to the public. Given their importance to the overall output of the media and culture industries, Hirsch refers to these gatekeepers as *surrogate consumers,* since they are expected to make choices on behalf of their readers and viewers, ordinary paying customers like you and me.

As one can see, at the input and output boundaries within this organizational system, industry professionals are required to make multiple decisions in a context of uncertainty, in which success is virtually impossible to predict with any reliability. At the input boundary, decision makers at media firms ask themselves: should we sign this singer-songwriter? How do we know her music will still sound fresh by the time we release her CD a year from now? Are movie audiences ready for a sci-fi thriller about the destruction of New York City, given the real-life horrors of the September 11 terrorist attacks? Although historical books about the American founding fathers and the U.S. Civil War usually sell better than most other nonfiction subgenres, aren't the bookstores already saturated with these tomes?

Meanwhile, the output boundary presents further opportunities for second-guessing among media firms in reaction to the fickleness of audiences and cultural consumers, and the vagaries of the marketplace. Should we promote our new pop music boy wonder, or our more seasoned hit maker? Given the space constraints of the *New York Times Book Review,* should we push Tom Wolfe's new novel (which will garner plenty of press attention regardless of what we do), an academic treatise on an important but completely obscure topic, or a first book written by the son or daughter of a celebrity author? Since our test marketing demonstrates that audiences have a hard time relating to the title character of our upcoming studio feature (given his three heads), should we send this film straight to video, let it quietly die in the theaters, or put our dear careers on the line for it, since its quirky director has a proven track record? Of course, media outlets have to take similar gambles regarding which celebrities to feature on their covers or profile in their Arts and Entertainment sections—after all, magazines and newspapers are beholden to their paying customers and subscribers just as much as any other media producer. In an unpredictable and inherently volatile environment in which "all hits are flukes," corporate media firms seem to have little choice but to allow their decisions to be driven by their aversion to risk.

Going with What You Know

So how do the media and popular culture industries actually go about making decisions designed to minimize risk? One common strategy is to adhere to traditional genre categories and other types of cultural conventions. As discussed in previous chapters, the use of established genres represents an attempt to classify similar kinds of music recordings, novels, films, and other media or cultural products according to recognizable stylistic criteria, audience expectations, and market efficiencies. For example, TV soap operas (*Days of Our Lives, The Young and the Restless*) are identified by their melodramatic scripts, overly theatrical acting, consistent themes of love, lust, betrayal, and revenge, and their largely female audiences. Exemplars of film noir (*The Maltese Falcon, The Third Man*) take place in cities haunted by shadows and feature casts of morally complicated characters that include lonely heroes, femme fatales, and confidence men, while teen comedies (*American Pie, Superbad*) almost exclusively take place in middle-class suburbs and emphasize the social politics of high school and the anxieties of adolescent dating and sexual identity.

Within the culture industries, these genres serve as organizational devices useful for making the production process more efficient, particularly given that production teams often work on genre-specific projects. Creative departments in the recording industry are organized by music genre, and boundary spanners in a number of media-related fields (A&R personnel in the music industry, acquisitions editors in book publishing) work in dedicated genre areas as well. At the distributional end of the media industry, promotional outlets like radio stations are studiously classified by genre, and the sales floors of bookstores, record shops, and video rental stores are similarly organized into conventional categories: true crime and romance and women's studies, classical music and R&B, science-fiction and horror. Meanwhile, online retailers like Amazon allow for genre categorization at an even more specified level. (As an example of this specificity, while Barnes and Noble shelves books under the category "sociology," Amazon further differentiates among suburban sociology, research and measurement, social situations, and the sociology of death.)

As a result, it is exceedingly uncommon for the media industries to promote cultural products that do not cleave to common types of genre conventions or stylistic boundaries, particularly in a context of unpredictability. Music artists who defy industry-defined genres are far less likely than others to be signed to a recording label, attract radio airplay, be sold in retail venues that measure and evaluate sales for industry publications like *Billboard,* matched with similar performers for live touring opportunities, succeed abroad in the international market, or have their songs covered by other artists. According to author Malcolm Gladwell (2005), such unconventional artists also tend to test market poorly, since mainstream audiences may initially regard their music with suspicion or confusion. For this reason, as an emergent music genre, rap music took years to gain acceptance in the recording business during the 1980s despite its proven popularity and commercial success (Lopes 1992; Negus 1998).

American television has demonstrated similar biases throughout its history. Traditionally, TV programming schedules have been insistently dotted with highly formulaic types of offerings, including medical dramas, police mysteries, family situation comedies, and tabloid talk shows. This conventionality excludes quite a lot of viable and innovative programming options. In fact, according to Marc Cherry, the creator of the ABC drama *Desperate Housewives*, he originally pitched his show as an hour-long comedy but received little enthusiasm from studio/network executives: after all, who among them had ever heard of an hour-long comedy? It was not until he changed his sales pitch—not the premise of the show, mind you, but just its packaging—*by reframing the program as a primetime soap opera.* In other words, selling the show as a suburban *Melrose Place* proved easier than revising the conventional half-hour sitcom.

Of course, after the runaway success of *Desperate Housewives* in 2004, ABC capitalized on their good fortune by adding even more hybrid soap opera comedies to their primetime schedule, including *Grey's Anatomy* in 2005, and *Private Practice* and *Dirty Sexy Money* in 2007. But this copycat strategy alone was hardly deemed a silver bullet by the network. To further minimize risk, the casting directors for these shows all turned to actors with proven track records. *Grey's Anatomy* starred Ellen Pompeo, who played the romantic female lead in

Shonda Rhimes, creator of the series Grey's Anatomy and Private Practice, and actress Kate Walsh, who appears on both shows.

the 2003 film *Old School,* and 1980s heartthrob Patrick Dempsey. *Private Practice* featured TV stars Amy Brenneman (*NYPD Blue, Judging Amy*) and Tim Daly (*Wings, The Sopranos*), while *Dirty Sexy Money* starred Peter Krause from the critically acclaimed HBO series *Six Feet Under,* and veteran actor Donald Sutherland (*M*A*S*H*, National Lampoon's Animal House, Six Degrees of Separation*).

Yet according to research by sociologists William Bielby and Denise Bielby (1994), network executives are even more likely to hire prominent *writer-producers* with successful projects under their belts than potentially bankable actors or celebrities. And notably, the writers and producers of these aforementioned series all had well-known reputations for working on previous hit shows. TV creator Shonda Rhimes developed *Private Practice* only after her earlier project, *Grey's Anatomy,* became a Nielsen-rated Top 10 smash hit. *Dirty Sexy Money's* creator Craig Wright was a writer on *Six Feet Under* and the blockbuster science-fiction drama *Lost,* which in turn was created by J. J. Abrams, the executive producer of earlier TV hits like *Felicity* and *Alias* who later went on to direct action films like *Mission: Impossible III* and *Star Trek.* In fact, in an article aptly titled "All Hits Are Flukes," Bielby and Bielby (1994) illustrate that in a context of demand uncertainty, creators, writers, and/or producers with successful track records are selected over famous celebrities by network programmers by a factor of two to one. In recent years, these television hit makers have included David E. Kelley (*L. A. Law, Picket Fences, Chicago Hope, Ally McBeal, Boston Public, The Practice,*

Boston Legal), Darren Starr (*Beverly Hills 90210, Melrose Place, Sex and the City*), and Mark Burnett (*Survivor, The Apprentice, Rock Star, Are You Smarter than a 5th Grader?*). And yet the résumés of even these seasoned pros are far from untarnished and include such failed series as *Models Inc., Snoops, Miss Match, Kitchen Confidential,* and *The Apprentice: Martha Stewart.* After all, in the end all hits are flukes, and nobody knows anything.

The Secondary Market

In recent years the growth of 24-hour cable networks, the DVD industry, TiVo, DVR, video on demand, and the Internet has permanently altered our temporal experience of television and cinema. Thirsty for available quality programming, cable channels regularly air reruns of contemporary popular shows, while inexpensive and convenient digital technology allows consumers to build their own extensive video libraries, whether on DVD or their laptop hard drives. In fact, the *secondary market* for popular culture, which represents all alternative opportunities to generate profit from a cultural product beyond its domestic sale in its original format, has increasingly dominated its more glamorous primary market counterpart as a more reliable and less risky revenue stream for television and film studios, book publishers, and music recording companies.

Secondary markets are associated with a number of strategies for minimizing risk because they create a host of profit-making opportunities without incurring additional development or production costs. For example, as suggested in Chapter 5, licensing the rights to a music recording for use in another media format can provide a new source of untapped revenue as well as increase public exposure for the artist. As media and communication scholar Bethany Klein (2009) observes, in an era of decreasing album sales, song licensing for commercial use in television advertising or movie soundtracks has become a lucrative way for musicians and their record companies to generate compensatory income and added promotional buzz. According to Klein, the results have altered the calculus of how pop music today is marketed and sold. Starting in 1999, the electronic dance music artist Moby successfully licensed all 18 tracks of his album *Play* for use in motion pictures, television shows, or commercials. The late singer-songwriter Nick Drake's 1972 title track recording from the album *Pink Moon* was licensed for a Volkswagen commercial in 2000, an appearance that revived interest in Drake's largely forgotten catalogue. According to journalist Naomi Klein (2002), the late-1990s reissue of Louis Prima's big band hit "Jump, Jive An' Wail" for use in a Gap commercial practically jump-started the neo-Swing revival of that decade. Of course, the secondary market often transforms dormant product into big sales by disengaging it from its original context, sometimes to strange effect—witness the placement of Iggy Pop's 1977 recording of "Lust for Life," a driving, energetic song about the punk singer's heroin addiction, in a commercial for Royal Caribbean Cruise Lines (Klein 2009, pp. 101–4). (The ad conveniently edits out all references to drugs, liquor, torture films, and stripteases.)

Other efforts at tapping into the secondary market can be similarly advantageous as strategies of leveraging ready-made cultural product for risk-free gain. A domestic movie can easily be repackaged for the global marketplace, where it may make more than double its original box-office take. The 2006 film *The Da Vinci Code* grossed nearly $220 million in the United States, only to then grab up a whopping $540 million abroad. That same year, the James Bond thriller *Casino Royale* took in $167 million domestically and an additional $420 million in the non-U.S. market. The global market can even save a film that bombed its first time around. Directed by Luc Besson in 1997, the over-the-top science-fiction comedy *The Fifth Element* starred Bruce Willis and cost $90 million to produce, only to gross $64 million in the United States. Film critic Janet Maslin of the *New York Times* panned the picture, arguing that "Mr. Besson pitches this gaudy epic at a teenage audience

A poster promoting The Da Vinci Code *in Beijing, China.*

that values hot design over plot coherence, hollow excitement over reason. The story describes a mission to save humanity, but as far as the film itself is concerned, it's already gone." No matter—this quirky film earned over $200 million abroad, which accounted for 76 percent of its total box-office take. (As I argue below, it is increasingly common today for films to be produced specifically for the international market by relying on nonstop action and special effects over witty dialogue, which may partially explain why Sylvester Stallone and Jean-Claude Van Damme still have movie careers.)

Just as the global box office remains a potentially greater source of profit than domestically released cinema, the home entertainment market has increasingly become more lucrative than feature films. In 2004, movies sold to retail stores generated 63 percent of all Hollywood studio motion picture revenues in the United States, while theatrical box-office sales represented a lackluster 21 percent. As John Gertner (2004) reported in the *New York Times Magazine,* "The major studios—now owned by publicly traded multinational corporations—are increasingly aware of the fact that even as their theatrical divisions produce the glamour and buzz, their home-video divisions generate an increasing portion of the cash. (At one studio, they call DVDs 'the corporate A.T.M. machine.')"

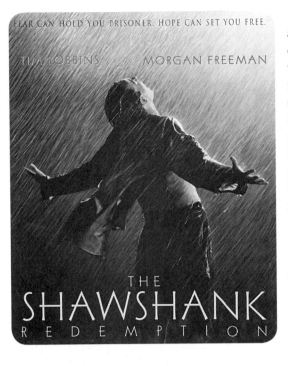

With DVD sales exceeding $15 billion annually (Gertner 2004), even films that could not capture an audience during their theatrical release can achieve financial redemption on video, including movies *about* redemption. When *The Shawshank Redemption* debuted in 1994, it was a commercial failure, grossing a paltry $18 million, and no wonder: it was a 142-minute prison film with an incomprehensible title and no obvious audience. Even after receiving seven Academy Award nominations, including Best Picture, it went on to earn only an additional $10 million at the box office. And then, after years of late-night watching and word-of-mouth whispers from mesmerized viewers, it finally broke free from its darkened cell. According to *Chicago Sun-Times* film critic Roger Ebert, "In one of the most remarkable stories in home video history, it found its real mass audience on tapes and discs, and through TV screenings. Within five years, *Shawshank* was a phenomenon, a video best seller and renter that its admirers feel they've discovered for themselves. When the *Wall Street Journal* ran an article about the *Shawshank* groundswell in April 1999, it was occupying first place in the Internet Movie Database worldwide vote of the 250 best films; it's usually in the top five." (Actually, as of April 2009 it was once again in first place, tied with the perennial favorite *The Godfather*.)

In television's secondary market, the most profitable risk-minimizing strategy is literally in reruns, as primetime shows that have already demonstrated their durability as hits find repeat success in syndication. However, syndication is lucrative in another way as well. While the licensing fees networks pay to studios for first-run primetime programs do not typically cover even the costs of production, the earnings to be gained from syndicated programming are exceedingly more remunerative, and this is where studios recoup their investments. This secondary market is so profitable that during the last several years, television producers have begun creating programs *specifically designed* to perform well in syndication, particularly the two branded series *Law & Order* and *CSI: Crime Scene Investigation*, along with their many spinoffs.

How? Most obviously, both series feature last-minute plot twists that encourage (or at least do not *discourage*) multiple viewings among fans who may remember the basic outlines of a rerun show without quite recalling how it ends. Moreover, both the *Law & Order* (NBC) and *CSI* (CBS) series are procedural dramas featuring plot-driven narratives in which teams of criminalists made up of police detectives, prosecutors, medical examiners, forensic scientists, and lab technicians—all characters whose interior lives rarely seem to change—work on cases assured to be solved within the temporal confines of each episode. By avoiding the serialization common to other kinds of dramas like soap operas, the producers of *Law & Order* and *CSI* make it easier for audiences to view episodes out of sequence, a clear advantage for syndicated programming. (Similarly designed procedural dramas include CBS's *Criminal Minds, Without a Trace, Numbers,* and *The Mentalist.*) It is therefore no wonder that these series are among the most aired of any syndicated dramas currently on cable television.

Overproduction and the Need for Blockbusters

Success is extremely difficult to predict in the pop culture industries, particularly given the high probability that any single product will bomb. In some ways, media firms inflate this high failure rate by introducing an avalanche of surplus

Why are dramas such as CSI: Miami *so popular in syndication*

offerings each season. In the United States, record companies release close to 30,000 new CDs a year. In 2006, book publishing houses released 291,920 new titles and editions, while an all-time high of 607 Hollywood films were released domestically during that same year. Of course, most of those discs, books, and movies never made a dime, but no matter. Media conglomerates rely on an established strategy of *overproduction,* a crude market logic that assumes that among their nearly infinite offerings, a few big-budget blockbusters—along with a smattering of surprise "sleeper" hits—will generate enough profit for their studios, distributors, publishers, and record labels to cover the losses incurred by everything else.

For example, in 2007 the top-grossing film was *Spider-Man 3*. Released by Columbia Pictures, the film brought in a whopping $337 million at the U.S. box office and nearly $550 million abroad, making it one of the highest-grossing motion pictures of all time. Fortunately for its parent company, Sony, the film's tremendous success allowed Columbia to subsequently take a loss on *Walk Hard: The Dewey Cox Story,* a musical comedy released in December of that same year. (Co-written by Judd Apatow [*The 40-Year-Old Virgin, Knocked Up*], the film parodies the Oscar-winning biopics *Walk the Line* and *Ray.*) With a box-office take of only $18 million, the movie cost nearly double what it grossed, and after only 24 days it dropped out of theaters. But no matter—just one *Spider-*

Man 3 can pay for itself along with more than twenty commercial bombs as underachieving as *Walk Hard.*

Of course, such a business model can only work if media firms are assured that blockbusters as triumphant as *Spider-Man 3* can rise out of their offerings—no easy feat, given that "blockbusters are nearly impossible to predict" (Faulkner and Anderson 1987, p. 891). In the motion picture industry, the considerable rewards to be gained by investing in potential blockbusters drive the recurrent demand for highly visible directors, producers, and cinematographers, but only those who have enjoyed recent box-office success (hence the oft-quoted Hollywood truism, "You're only as good as your last credit"). To increase their chances of creating a smash hit, this very select pool of elite filmmakers controls multimillion-dollar budgets that have grown exponentially since the 1970s. Of course, the drastic overspending on such film projects only increases the need among studios to produce windfall profits in order to simply break even, which generates even *greater* demand for blockbusters. Taken to its logical conclusion, this cycle of bet-raising resembles an endless round of no-limit gambling, "an enormously high-rolling crap game" (p. 885).

Within this crazed financial context, the need for blockbusters encourages a variety of emergent strategies that media firms hope will minimize risk, at least on the margins. Movie studios gravitate toward films with a built-in audience and promotional engine, particularly sequels, prequels, remakes, and spinoffs. In fact, to a certain extent this strategy has demonstrated success in the past, especially if we look at the Top 20 all-time box-office hits in the United States (see Table 6.1). Of these motion pictures, 10 are sequels or prequels of previously successful films, representing the *Batman, Star Wars, Shrek, Pirates of the Caribbean, Spider-Man,* and *Lord of the Rings* franchises. (Meanwhile, only two of the original films released in these series—*Star Wars* and *Spider-Man*—make this prestigious list.) Also, half of the films in the Top 20 are spinoffs or adaptations from best-selling novels (*Forrest Gump, Jurassic Park, The Lord of the Rings*), comic books and graphic novels (*Spider-Man, Batman*), action figures (*Transformers*), and even a Disney World theme-park ride (*Pirates of the Caribbean*). Meanwhile, for all intents and purposes Mel Gibson's *The Passion of the Christ* was adapted from a longtime best-seller, while *Titanic* could be interpreted as a loose remake of the award-winning films *Titanic* (1953) and *A Night to Remember* (1958).

TABLE 6.1

Top 20 All-Time USA Box Office (as of April 2009)

1.	*Titanic* (1997)
2.	*The Dark Knight* (2008)
3.	*Star Wars* (1977)
4.	*Shrek 2* (2004)
5.	*E.T. The Extra-Terrestrial* (1982)
6.	*Star Wars: Episode I: The Phantom Menace* (1999)
7.	*Pirates of the Caribbean: Dead Man's Chest* (2006)
8.	*Spider-Man* (2002)
9.	*Star Wars: Episode III: Revenge of the Sith* (2005)
10.	*The Lord of the Rings: The Return of the King* (2003)
11.	*Spider-Man 2* (2004)
12.	*The Passion of the Christ* (2004)
13.	*Jurassic Park* (1993)
14.	*The Lord of the Rings: The Two Towers* (2002)
15.	*Finding Nemo* (2003)
16.	*Spider-Man 3* (2007)
17.	*Forrest Gump* (1994)
18.	*The Lion King* (1994)
19.	*Shrek the Third* (2007)
20.	*Transformers* (2007)

The production of these films also represents a risk-averse way to satisfy the international cinema market. By drawing on the recognition of global brands while emphasizing endless action sequences and slick effects over dialogue and character development, these movies effortlessly translate to non-English-speaking audiences. The all-time box-office blockbusters worldwide (see Table 6.2) include four *Harry Potter* pictures, the three *Lord of the Rings* films, three *Star Wars* movies, two films each from the *Spider-Man* and *Pirates of the Caribbean* franchises, and one film apiece from the reliable *Batman, Jurassic Park,* and *Shrek* series. Meanwhile, the remaining three motion pictures in the Top 20 all rely on either computer-generated imagery (or CGI), artful animation, or fireballs galore: *Titanic, Finding Nemo,* and *Independence Day.*

Furthermore, these kinds of films easily lend themselves to branding and merchandising opportunities, as best exemplified by the *Star Wars* juggernaut. Hasbro maintains an exclusive license to manufacture and sell all manner of *Star Wars* toys, collectible dolls, action figures, games, puzzles, and candies

TABLE 6.2
Top 20 All-Time Worldwide Box Office (as of April 2009)

1. *Titanic* (1997)
2. *The Lord of the Rings: The Return of the King* (2003)
3. *Pirates of the Caribbean: Dead Man's Chest* (2006)
4. *The Dark Knight* (2008)
5. *Harry Potter and the Sorcerer's Stone* (2001)
6. *Pirates of the Caribbean: At World's End* (2007)
7. *Harry Potter and the Order of the Phoenix* (2007)
8. *Star Wars: Episode I: The Phantom Menace* (1999)
9. *The Lord of the Rings: The Two Towers* (2002)
10. *Jurassic Park* (1993)
11. *Harry Potter and the Goblet of Fire* (2005)
12. *Spider-Man 3* (2007)
13. *Shrek 2* (2004)
14. *Harry Potter and the Chamber of Secrets* (2002)
15. *Finding Nemo* (2003)
16. *The Lord of the Rings: The Fellowship of the Ring* (2001)
17. *Star Wars: Episode III: Revenge of the Sith* (2005)
18. *Independence Day* (1996)
19. *Spider-Man* (2002)
20. *Star Wars* (1977)

until 2018. They include a "Darth Tater" Mr. Potato Head, *Star Wars* 3-D Monopoly game, and a Destroyer Droid Yo-Yo. Meanwhile, shorter-term promotional deals have associated the films' heroes, villains, and Wookies with Taco Bell, KFC, Pizza Hut, Pepsi, Frito-Lay, Colgate, and Fruit of the Loom.

These kinds of licensing deals help movie studios minimize risk by providing an additional source of company revenue upfront during the often expensive film-making process. In fact, on some occasions such enterprises actually finance the production of the film itself. For example, in 1999 Hasbro paid Lucasfilm nearly $590 million for exclusive toy licensing rights to the *Star Wars* franchise, a figure that approximated the budgets for all three prequels (*The Phantom Menace, Attack of the Clones,* and *Revenge of the Sith*). In addition to providing needed financial support, licensing and merchandising schemes like these help movie studios promote their action pictures directly to their target markets—generally young and impressionable consumers already addicted to cola, fast-food burgers, and video games. Finally, the promotional synergy surrounding a film's marketing campaign can elevate its national release to the status of a cultural event, as illustrated by the midnight crowds that now regularly accompany opening night theatrical premieres. In this manner, motion picture studios gamble that the promotional machinery behind their films can inflate super-hyped expectations of their commercial success into self-fulfilling prophesies.

The celebrated triumphs enjoyed by these types of films may suggest a predictable formula for engineering a blockbuster smash: brand recognition and popularity, expensive computer-generated graphics, dumbed-down dialogue, explosive pyrotechnics, youth appeal, and plenty of merchandising potential. But in the end, all hits are still flukes, as illustrated by the movies that followed this formula and proved dreadfully disappointing at the box office in recent years. In 2006 Wolfgang Peterson, the director of the wildly successful hit *The Perfect Storm* (2000), took the creative reins of *Poseidon,* a $160 million remake of a 1970s cult-classic feature about yet another sinking ship. Although the film shared the same disaster plot as *Titanic,* the all-time box-office champion, it was the film itself that eventually sank, grossing only $60.7 million. In 2004, *Catwoman* featured the beloved actress Halle Berry as a slinky superhero in skintight leather, yet this $100 million movie grossed only $40.2 million. In spite of the eventual success of the *Pirates of the Caribbean* franchise, the 1995 stinker *Cutthroat Island,* budgeted at $98 million, collected a paltry $10 million at the box office, driving its production company Carolco Pictures into bankruptcy.

Need more evidence? In 1995 Oscar-winner Kevin Costner directed and starred in the futuristic sci-fi epic *Waterworld.* The film was made at a whopping cost of $175 million, only to gross $88.2 million at the box office. Then there is the sad case of the 2002 flop *The Adventures of Pluto Nash,* a $100 million film starring

Mr. Potato Head as "Darth Tater."

comedian Eddie Murphy that managed to gross only a measly $4.4 million. Many other so-called "can't-miss" films starring celebrity actors Tom Hanks (*The Bonfire of the Vanities*), Arnold Schwarzenegger (*The 6th Day*), Sandra Bullock (*Speed 2: Cruise Control*), John Travolta (*Battlefield Earth*), Brad Pitt (*Meet Joe Black*), Bruce Willis (*Hudson Hawk*), and Jennifer Lopez (*Gigli*) have met similar box-office fates.

As for the toy companies that help finance the production of Hollywood blockbusters, even the most successful franchises can hang their merchandisers (and financiers) out to dry. Although the first five *Harry Potter* films had grossed well over $4 billion worldwide, the toy manufacturer Mattel endured dragging sales with each new release, and in 2006 chose not to renew their licensing contract with Warner Bros., blaming the wizard franchise for the company's overall sales slump. As a result, the studio granted its "master toy license" to National Entertainment Collectibles Association, a company that planned on marketing its wares to a wealthier and perhaps even more spendthrift set of consumers than the preteen readers of the J. K. Rowling series—her adult fans.

Gaming the Gatekeepers

The conventional view of popular culture suggests that in a market system, mass media firms target everyday people and their desires, and it is the fickleness of those desires that makes success so unpredictable. However, this is not entirely the case, given that the primary audiences for movies, books, and recordings are not everyday consumers but the gatekeepers responsible for distributing and marketing culture directly to the public. As explained above, professional evaluators of mass culture can be thought of as *surrogate consumers*; therefore, for media firms to get their products out to the public requires that they promote their wares to *Entertainment Weekly* and *People* editors, *Washington Post* book reviewers, *Chicago Tribune* film critics, and radio programmers for Clear Channel and local independent stations. These editors, critics, and journalists choose a minute percentage of the thousands of CDs, movies, and books released each year to incorporate into their publications' editorial content, whether as short reviews, lengthy profiles, or even as a magazine cover. These surrogate consumers also include book and music buyers for retail outlets like Borders Books, Barnes and Noble, and increasingly, Wal-Mart and Target.

How do surrogate consumers make decisions regarding which cultural products to promote? The history of popular culture is filled with sordid tales of bribery and other criminal activities designed to manipulate the cultural dissemination process. During the early days of rock 'n roll, it was discovered that radio disc jockeys had been accepting side payments from record companies to play specific singles on the air. This abusive practice, known as *payola* (a mash-up of "pay" and "Victrola," an early record player model manufactured by the Victor Talking Machine Company), eventually attracted attention from the U.S. Congress and became illegal in 1960. From the 1980s to the 2000s, record companies attempted to get around this inconvenience by hiring *independent record promoters* to serve as middlemen who could indirectly pass money along to radio stations and thereby evade payola laws. But in 2005 and 2006 the New York State attorney general (and later governor) Eliot Spitzer prosecuted and eventually received settlements from the four major labels (Warner, Sony BMG, Universal, and EMI) for exploiting this loophole, with the Federal Communications Commission (FCC) ruling this practice illegal as well.

Of course, similar kinds of strategies are still legal (if ethically problematic) and widely practiced. Book publishers pay bookstore chains to prominently place their titles on their front tables, aisle endcaps, and in other high-visibility areas (Miller 2007). Film critics enjoy lavish, all-expenses-paid press junkets in return for previewing and hyping upcoming movies. And as business writer Daniel Gross (2005) points out, "The Web is one gigantic payola machine, from Amazon.com to the exploding realm of paid search."

But the contemporary age of giant multinational media conglomerates offers an even simpler model of gatekeeper cooptation. Making side payments to disc jockeys requires conspiratorial cooperation, but parent companies have a much easier time simply marketing their products across their own promotional platforms. In this manner, the *synergy* existing among the acquired subsidiaries or merged parts of a large media corporation represents a more contemporary strategy of minimizing risk within the culture industries. For example, Time Warner owns both Home Box Office (HBO) and the magazine *Entertainment Weekly,* and therefore was able to run an "exclusive" behind-the-scenes cover story on the filming of the final season of the HBO drama *The Sopranos* in an April 2007 issue, as well as multiple puff pieces about the cable channel's hit show *Entourage*. (Time Warner also owns Time Inc., which publishes more than 145 magazines worldwide, including *Time, People, Sports Illustrated, Fortune, InStyle,* and *Essence.*) Similarly, Rupert Murdoch's News Corporation owns the FOX television network, which has aired a number of hit programs over the last several years, including *American Idol, The Simpsons, The X-Files* and *24.* What else do these four shows have in common? They have all been featured on the cover of *TV Guide,* which News Corp. also owns.

In addition to magazine coverage, shared corporate ownership across multiple television properties provides similar opportunities for monopolistic abuse. From 1998 to 2000, ABC aired the critically acclaimed Aaron Sorkin comedy *Sports Night,* a parody of ESPN's news program *Sports Center*—an all-too-convenient programming decision given that the Disney Corporation owns both ABC *and* ESPN television networks. (In one telling episode of *Sports Night* the female lead played by Felicity Huffman oozes with excitement after seeing the Broadway production of *The Lion King,* yet another Disney product.) Sony Pictures Television owns the popular game shows *Jeopardy!* and *Wheel of Fortune,* both of which it promotes by showing reruns on its Game Show Network (GSN). A recent merger between NBC and Universal formed the NBC Universal Television Group, which not only owns the NBC network but the entire *Law & Order* franchise that began airing on NBC in 1990. The inclusion of the monstrously successful franchise was said to have clinched the deal for NBC, presumably because of the opportunities for cross-promotion to audiences of both its primetime and syndicated episodes.

Flexible Production and the Economics of Reality TV

Once we get used to thinking about decision making in the culture industries in terms of minimizing risk, certain recent cultural trends suddenly begin to make more sense. Take reality television. Many critics explain the proliferation of reality TV by pointing out the blurring of news and entertainment and the democratization of celebrity in American popular culture, yet a candid look at the economics of reality TV provides an even better explanation. First, reality TV programs are relatively inexpensive to produce, especially when compared to star-studded comedies and dramas. In its final season, all six members of the regular cast of the NBC hit show *Friends* were paid $1 million each *per episode,* while even anonymous character actors are typically paid competitive union wages as members of the Screen Actors Guild. Meanwhile, reality TV participants are often paid little more than small stipends to cover their expenses, and many dip into their savings to finance their hiatus from their day jobs. Since reality television shows do not rely on traditional scripts, producers also avoid the expensive costs of hiring writers and paying out their royalties. It bears observing that it was during the 1988 Writers Guild of America strike that networks introduced the first generation of reality-based television programs, notably the bare-knuckled law enforcement shows *Cops* and *America's Most Wanted.* The union-resistant nature of this type of programming was reaffirmed during the 2007 Writers Guild strike two decades later when reality shows were left virtually unaffected even as TV production work in more mainstream sectors came to an abrupt halt.

Another way that reality TV programming contributes to an overall strategy of minimizing risk concerns the flexible norms of production permitted by the genre. Conventional television comedies and dramas are produced over the course of a season in which major networks and studios often plan for a 22-episode run. (Cable networks have increasingly experimented with 10- or 12-episode runs per season.) But the flexibility of reality television allows for much smaller, low-commitment runs of five or six episodes per season, while even the most successful exemplars of the genre from *Dancing with the Stars* to *Survivor* feature slim seasons of only 8 to 15 episodes each. The shortened lengths of these seasons allow producers to take chances on cutting-edge programming with minimal risk, and unlike with narrative comedies and dramas, producers can tinker with the most basic premises of their reality shows during hiatuses. This is best illustrated by programs like *Survivor* and *MTV The Real World,* both of which switch locales as well as casts each season.

Finally, the proliferation of reality programming represents an industry shift toward genres that most easily lend themselves to product-placement advertising campaigns. In recent years the rise of technological advances that allow for commercial-free television viewing, including DVDs, TiVo, DVR, video on demand, and various online outlets have increased anxieties among networks, which have looked to product placement as a means of recouping lost

How do sociologists explain the popularity of reality television hits such as Dancing with the Stars *(left) and* Survivor *(right)?*

ad revenue. Regardless of their merit or entertainment value, reality TV shows are perfect platforms for incorporating the brands of corporate sponsors. Like traditional game shows such as *The Price is Right,* competitive reality programs can easily feature branded products as prizes: on *Survivor,* starving contestants often win name-brand sodas, beer, chips, and candy bars during reward challenges, and savor them on camera. The producers of home improvement shows like *Trading Spaces* regularly strike product-placement deals with toolmakers and big-box retailers. Meanwhile, narrative reality shows can get away with introducing brands of cola and designer fashion as simply part of the organic fabric of everyday life. In extreme cases such as the MTV reality soap opera *The Hills,* in which the central heroine Lauren "L. C." Conrad happily interns at *Teen Vogue* while assisting high-end fashion designers like Marc Jacobs, it is unclear who exactly is promoting whom.

Shifting the Burden of Risk

The low-to-nonexistent wages paid to reality TV stars suggest a final set of strategies employed by the media industries to minimize risk under volatile market conditions. Sociologists Gina Neff, Elizabeth Wissinger, and Sharon Zukin (2005) observe that in a variety of creative occupations from computer software design to fashion modeling, workers increasingly take on risks and expenses formerly shouldered by their employers. Neff and her coauthors appropriately depict these jobs as *entrepreneurial labor* since these workers invest their own capital and sweat equity in their careers for the improbable opportunity to gain potentially lucrative rewards in return. In the culture industries, creative workers often contract out their labor on a short-term basis to work on specific earmarked projects: a photo shoot in Acapulco, a Web page for an advertising agency, a seasonal run of a television series, the index for a nonfiction book, the final editing of a feature film. These short-term contracts prevent companies from having to absorb the expenses associated with hiring creative workers on a full-time basis (including their training costs, health insurance, retirement benefits, and vacation time) as well as the financial liabilities involved in maintaining a highly paid workforce during unpredictable economic downturns.

Instead, these risks and costs are borne by the creative workers themselves. Serving as independent contractors, a variety of entrepreneurial workers—graphic designers, television actors, photojournalists, digital animators, commercial studio musicians, mystery novelists, video game designers—often pay continually out of pocket for training courses (or in the case of fashion models, gym memberships, personal trainer sessions, and dance or "movement" classes), expensive equipment, and self-promotional portfolio materials ranging from personal Web sites and demo CDs to expensively produced short films and video compilations. Given that résumé-boosting prestige projects (e.g., modeling work for high fashion magazines) frequently pay less than more mundane yet consistent media and cultural work (e.g., chain store catalog work), building an impressive portfolio often requires workers to accept high-profile but low-paying assignments over more lucrative opportunities. Additionally, these freelance workers endure the risks associated with job instability in an already mercurial marketplace and the pressure to constantly market themselves to potential clients and employers at professional networking events.

By shifting the burden of risk to the worker, the corporate strategy of hiring entrepreneurial labor allows media and culture-producing firms to minimize fixed overhead costs such as employee training and benefits. Another strategy for transferring risk involves the royalty system commonly used to organize payment in a variety of creative fields, particularly music recording and book publishing. According to this system, musicians, songwriters, and novelists are contracted to work for a small percentage of the earnings generated by their product. By distributing this royalty payment after the product has eventually been released to the public (provided it is released at all), media companies insure themselves against the unpredictability of the marketplace since they are only obligated to pay their creative artists *after* they have proven their financial viability.

These kinds of royalty-based deals also require the cultural worker to shoulder market risk in an additional way. Rather than invest in their creative artists' initial production and promotional expenses, media companies bill such costs to the artists themselves, as a charge against their future royalties. Musicians of all genres unfortunate enough to sign a run-of-the-mill record deal may receive an advance on their royalties to be disbursed for recording studio time, music video production, and a national road tour, only to find themselves eventually in debt to their own music label, even if their album is a moderate hit.

A final strategy of the media industries simply does away with workers' wages altogether. Since the early 1990s, the so-called glamour industries represented by popular name-brand record companies, fashion houses, hip-hop magazines, film studios, advertising firms, and television networks have increasingly relied on the free labor provided by unpaid internships. These are typically jobs in which college students perform menial tasks—photocopying, delivering faxes, answering phones, cold calling, filing, proofreading, fact checking, ordering lunch, fetching coffee—without being paid anything other than the opportunity to gain the "professional experience" thought necessary for eventual longer-term employment in the creative sector. As Jim Frederick (2003) observes, these lousy jobs sell themselves on false promises and inflated credentials while seducing impressionable youth eager to subject themselves to certain drudgery and untold humiliations for the cachet signaled by the coolness quotient of celebrity companies like MTV and BET, *Cosmopolitan* and *Rolling Stone*—especially if the perks include free concert tickets, record release party invitations, promotional CDs, and the slim opportunity for a chance encounter with a supermodel or rock star. In violation of the 1938 Fair Labor Standards Act, most of these internships fail to provide young employees with useful professional skills while even the *symbolic* value of internship "experi-ence" declines as these demeaning, unpaid jobs grow ever more popular among collegiate and postgraduate workers. Meanwhile, the surplus of giddy pop culture fanatics clamoring to work for free drives down wages and salaries for all *other* creative workers throughout the mass media industries at all levels of the job hierarchy. In doing so, the intern economy represents yet another attempt by culture-producing firms to minimize risk and decrease expenses under conditions of unpredictability and volatility, albeit on the young backs of their biggest fans.

How do films such as *Titanic* portray different types of culture and use them to represent characters' class affiliations?

the rules of the game

CULTURAL CONSUMPTION
AND SOCIAL CLASS IN AMERICA

THE 1997 BLOCKBUSTER FILM *TITANIC* IS AS MUCH A STORY ABOUT social stratification on the high seas as it is about the 1912 disaster itself. The top-grossing motion picture of all time, James Cameron's *Titanic* presents, in its first half, a world divided economically and culturally on the basis of social class, where the wealthy live on the upper decks and enjoy first-class accommodations—private cabins, formal dining, fine cigars—while third-class passengers enjoy raucous parties full of music and dancing, albeit while cooped up in steerage. Just as in other films about social class and cultural mores (Jean Renoir's *The Rules of the Game*, Whit Stillman's *Metropolitan*, Robert Altman's *Gosford Park*), in *Titanic* the lines dividing the culture and tastes of the affluent classes from the poor could hardly be drawn in a more stark manner.

Rightly or wrongly, we commonly distinguish between different kinds of culture by relying on labels such as "highbrow" and "lowbrow," and associate them with their respective class affiliations. (The terms are an unfortunate survival from the nineteenth-century pseudoscience of phrenology in which intelligence was measured by the size of one's forehead, or literally the height of his or her brow.) In the most stereotypical sense, *highbrow* culture (or simply *high* culture) refers to the fine arts consumed by the affluent classes—classical music and opera, ballet and modern dance, abstract painting and sculpture, poetry and literary fiction. We might also include less traditional forms of high culture enjoyed by contemporary cosmopolitan audiences: National Public Radio programs like *This American Life* and *All Things Considered*, PBS television news shows such as *The News Hour* and *Frontline*, and world music recordings from Sufi chanting to Tuvan throat singing. In many ways high culture is merely synonymous with the traditionally humanist conception of culture itself, as the most intellectual and civilizing of leisurely pursuits. (When we say someone is *cultured*, we usually mean that he or she is familiar with *high* culture, just as we might go to an art museum or the symphony to "get some culture" [Grisword 2004, p. 4].)

Meanwhile, *lowbrow* or *low* culture typically refers to the kinds of mass culture stereotypically associated with working-class (or so-called *lower*-class) audiences, including rap, blues, heavy metal, and country music; professional wrestling, stock car racing, rodeos, and monster truck rallies; and gory horror films, gross-out comedies, and pornography. This pejorative label—*low* culture— suggests a set of activities and amusements lacking in virtue and associated with sexuality and the *lower* half of the body, certainly relative to its highbrow counterparts. Outrageous moral panics surrounding the imagined sexual and moral degradations of lower-class American culture seem to be a routine occurrence in our national discourse. In a 1985 *Newsweek* article about heavy metal entitled "Stop Pornographic Rock," the writer complains:

My 15-year-old daughter unwittingly alerted me to the increasingly explicit nature of rock music. "You've got to hear this, Mom!" she insisted one afternoon . . . , "but don't listen to the words," she added, an instant tip-off to pay attention. The beat was hard and pulsating, the music burlesque in feeling. . . . Unabashedly sexual lyrics like these, augmented by orgasmic moans and howls, compose the musical diet millions of children are now being fed at concerts, on albums, on radio and MTV. (quoted in Binder 1993, p. 761)

These kinds of anxieties about lower-class culture in the United States have historically emphasized the liveliness and ribaldry of African American popular culture, often in hysterical overtones. In 1921, *Ladies' Home Journal* published a piece that asked, in all seriousness, "Does Jazz Put the Sin in Syncopation?"

Jazz disorganizes all regular laws and order; it stimulates to extreme deeds, to a breaking away from all rules and conventions; it is harmful and dangerous, and its influence is wholly bad. . . . The effect of jazz on the normal brain produces an atrophied condition on the brain cells of conception, until very frequently those under the demoralizing influence of the persistent use of syncopation, combined with inharmonic partial tones, are actually incapable of distinguishing between good and evil, right and wrong. (quoted in Appelrouth 2005, p. 1503)

Today it is admittedly difficult to imagine that the brilliant (not to mention thoroughly inoffensive) music performed by 1920s jazz greats like Duke Elllington and Louis Armstrong could have ever generated such fearful hysteria. Another article that same year exclaimed "Unspeakable Jazz Must Go!"

Those moaning saxophones and the rest of the instruments with their broken, jerky rhythm make a purely sensual appeal. They call out the low and rowdy instinct. All of us dancing teachers know this to be a fact. We have seen the effect of jazz music on our young pupils. It makes them act in a restless and rowdy manner. . . . They can be calmed down and restored to normal conduct only by playing good, legitimate music. (p. 1505)

Considered lowbrow at the time, jazz in the 1920s was even attacked for ruining the culture of elites, especially classical music. In 1929 the *New York Times* ran a piece entitled "Composer Sees Jazz as Feverish Noise," in which Sir Hamilton Harty, the conductor of Great Britain's Halle Orchestra, warns readers, "When future historians look upon the present epoch they will call it a machine age of music. They will see that in an age that considers itself musically enlightened we permit gangs of jazz barbarians to debase and mutilate our history of classical music and listen with patience to impudent demands to justify its filthy desecration" (quoted in Appelrouth 2003, p. 125).

Aretha Franklin singing at the inauguration of President Barack Obama.

Do these kinds of cultural class divisions still hold in contemporary American life? In terms of a high/low distinction, our national culture sometimes seems schizophrenic. At the 2009 inauguration of President Barack Obama, classical musicians Itzhak Perlman and Yo-Yo Ma performed on the same grandstand as soul and gospel singer Aretha Franklin. Past honorees of the John F. Kennedy Center for the Performing Arts in Washington, D.C., include orchestral conductor Zubin Mehta and rock legends Pete Townshend and Roger Daltrey of the Who; ballet dancer Mikhail Baryshnikov and country music singer Willie Nelson; opera singer Luciano Pavarotti and R&B performer James Brown. Blues music, an expressive cultural form that grew out of the life experiences of impoverished descendants of African American slaves, is regularly performed at Carnegie Hall, Lincoln Center, and the White House (as is the jazz music once defamed by the *Ladies' Home Journal* and in the *New York Times*), while classical music is now performed at chic downtown nightclubs in New York City (McCormick 2009). Affluent white teenagers adore hip-hop music, while underprivileged African American youth appropriate Tommy Hilfiger's yacht-club clothes and other preppy brands (Polo, Nautica, Munsingwear) as inner-city fashion (Klein 2002, pp. 75–76). Meanwhile, much of our mass culture—notably professional men's football, baseball, and basketball—is celebrated by audiences from *all* social classes and walks of life.

Of course, cultural differences among social classes do abound: wealthy urban professionals are far more likely than the poor to listen to classical music and opera, decorate their homes with abstract art, and read books for pleasure (Peterson 1992; Halle 1993; Griswold 2008). But as illustrated by the preceding examples, the social organization of *taste*—one's preference for particular styles of fashion, music, cinema, or other kinds of culture—is dizzyingly complex. While the last two chapters emphasized the social and institutional worlds in which popular culture is created, we now turn toward an exploration of not only taste, but *consumption*—the reception, interpretation, and experience of culture. Are cultural tastes patterned in some sociological way? How might different consumers read and interpret the same cultural objects in different ways? How are these meanings shaped by larger social or contextual forces?

In this chapter we will attempt to tease out the complex relationship between cultural consumption and social class in America by examining the fluid nature of taste and class cultures, and how easily they change over time. We will try to under-stand how the persistence of certain cultural differences among audiences helps to maintain socioeconomic inequality among social classes. Finally, we will try to explain why the class boundaries surrounding the consumption of American popular culture seem so blurry and confusing, and have been for the last 150 years or so.

The Invention of Class Cultures in America

Like all cultural conventions, distinctions between highbrow and lowbrow culture and taste are socially fabricated and prone to drastic change over time. How do we know this? A brief cultural snapshot of nineteenth-century American society may be instructive. Today, we think of the plays of William Shakespeare as decidedly highbrow, largely considered the height of artistic and literary accomplishment. Students study *King Lear* and *Hamlet* in university courses, and write Ph.D. dissertations on the allegorical design of *Othello*. Audiences sit in silent awe during live performances of Shakespeare's tragedies, particularly those staged by the most prestigious thespian troupes in the world: Britain's Royal Shakespeare Company, the Shakespeare Theater Company in Washington, D.C., and the Public Theater in New York.

Yet during the nineteenth century, Shakespeare's plays were considered *popular culture*—and not only in England but in the United States. Working-class Americans as well as elites shared a deep familiarity and fondness for his plays. In his 1840 publication of *Democracy in America*, Alexis de Tocqueville reports, "There is hardly a pioneer's hut which does not contain a few odd volumes of Shakespeare. I remember reading the feudal drama of *Henry V* for the first time in a log cabin" (1988, p. 471). According-ing to historian Lawrence W. Levine (1991), Shakespeare's plays were regularly performed on steamboats and makeshift stages in min-ing camps and breweries as well as in more metropolitan theaters in Philadelphia and San Francisco. As Levine observes, "Shakespeare was performed not merely alongside popular entertainment as an elite supplement to it; Shakespeare was performed as an integral part of it. Shakespeare *was* popular enter-tainment in nineteenth-century America" (p. 163).

In many ways, Shakespeare's wide-spread popularity among Americans in the mid-nineteenth century should not be par-ticularly surprising. His plays matched the

When did Shakespeare become highbrow? An 1849 portrait of Charlotte and Susan Cushman as Romeo and Juliet in act 3, scene 5. Charlotte (left) was considered the most powerful actress on the nineteenth-century stage and was the first American actress to attain critical theatrical acclaim.

mass tastes of the period: they are laden with dry humor and wit, as are the novels of Mark Twain, and his scenes are melodramatic and full of ghosts, just like the poems and short stories of Edgar Allan Poe. His most famous soliloquies, such as *Hamlet*'s "To be or not to be . . . " speech, offer the kind of oratory familiar to a nation whose public life required studied attentiveness to lengthy preachers' sermons, and political speeches and debates. Unlike contemporary readers, nineteenth-century Americans would have had little trouble deciphering Shakespeare's Elizabethan English, since the most popular book of the era was the King James Bible, first published by the Church of England in 1611—the same year that Shakespeare introduced his comedies *The Winter's Tale* and *The Tempest*. Moreover, American audiences would have sympathized with Shakespeare's worldview that placed the individual human being at the center of the universe, a creature of free will with ultimate responsibility for his or her own destiny: indeed, this is how Americans viewed themselves.

But perhaps the biggest reason that Shakespeare's plays were considered popular culture has to do with the social organization of American entertainment in the nineteenth century. Unlike the highbrow/lowbrow distinctions of today, 150 years ago Americans enjoyed a national popular culture consumed and experienced collectively by the masses, by people from *all* social classes. Live entertainment performances were attended by a microcosm of society, arranged according to socioeconomic status—aristocratic gentlemen and ladies luxuriated in the boxes, the merchant and professional middle classes sat in the orchestra, and working-class audiences crowded the gallery, or balcony. (As an illustration of the intense racial segregation of the period, African American attendees of all classes were relegated to the balcony as well.) During performances of Shakespeare, those in the cheap seats would express their derision of an inept actor by pelting him with eggs, apples, potatoes, carrots, lemons, cabbages, pumpkins, and in at least one reported instance, a dead goose (Levine 1991, p. 168).

Likewise, American entertainment blended diverse genres and styles in ways that would be thought blasphemous by today's standards. Theaters presented Shakespearean plays alongside acts by magicians, dancers, acrobats, and comics (p. 164). According to Princeton sociologist Paul DiMaggio's (1982) research on nineteenth-century Boston, concerts featured the mingling of classical music compositions, Italian opera, devotional and religious songs, and popular tunes (p. 34). As for other entertainment spaces,

> Museums were modeled on Barnum's: fine art was interspersed among such curiosities as bearded women and mutant animals, and popular entertainments were offered for the price of admission to a clientele that included working people as well as the upper middle class. Founded as a commercial venture in 1841, Moses Kemball's Boston Museum exhibited works by such painters as Sully and Peale alongside Chinese curiosities, stuffed animals, mermaids and dwarves. For the entrance fee visitors could also attend

the Boston Museum Theatre, which presented works by Dickens and Shakespeare as well as performances by gymnasts and contortionists, and brought to Boston the leading players of the American and British stage. The promiscuous combination of genres that later would be considered incompatible was not uncommon. As late as the 1880s, American circuses employed Shakespearean clowns who recited the bard's lines in full clown make-up (p. 34).

Today, the idea of *King Lear* being performed at the circus stretches and boggles the mind, as does the image of rowdy working-class audiences hurling rotten vegetables down from the balconies of the Metropolitan Opera House. So what happened? Well, the Industrial Revolution happened, creating a new upper-class American elite of successful entrepreneurs, bankers, and businesspeople. (The richest men in American history—John D. Rockefeller, Cornelius Vanderbilt, John Jacob Astor, Stephen Girard, Andrew Carnegie—first amassed their great fortunes in the nineteenth century during this time.) This *nouveau riche* (literally "new rich") class enjoyed untold wealth, but few of the refinements that grow from an aristocratic upbringing—in fact, many came from rather humble backgrounds. These increasingly status-conscious industrialists therefore drew on the trappings of European nobility—family crests, indulgences in French cuisine, classical art and music—in crafting newfound cultural tastes and symbols of distinction for themselves (Beisel 1993). To this end, in the late-nineteenth century this new bourgeoisie began erecting class boundaries concretized in elite arts and cultural organizations, including the Boston Symphony Orchestra and the Museum of Fine Arts, the Art Institute of Chicago, New York's Metropolitan Museum of Art, and the Philadelphia Academy of Music (Zolberg 1981; DiMaggio 1982).

With these elite institutions, the upper classes of the Gilded Age successfully *invented* the highbrow/lowbrow class-based cultural distinctions that today we take for granted. This invention of class cultures required conscious efforts at boundary maintenance and social exclusion, most obviously through the development of special entertainment venues, so-called legitimate theaters and museums in which to consecrate and present classical music, opera, drama and art as "serious" culture for upper-class audiences. By making ticket prices and subscriptions prohibitively expensive and strictly enforcing dress codes and rules of social etiquette (no throwing cabbages allowed, I presume), the elite effectively excluded members of the working classes from participating in these new worlds of cultural esteem. By the turn of the twentieth century, the American upper classes had eventually succeeded in bifurcating the nation's once diverse mélange of popular culture—Shakespearean tragedy, circus clowns, acrobats, contortionists, mermaids, dwarves—into separate stylistic offerings of "serious" and "popular" culture, each redefined on the basis of class and prestige. Given the wholly manufactured nature of this prestige, it is perhaps fitting that the word *prestige* itself was originally used to describe the illusions, tricks, and fakery of magicians and jugglers.

Class Status and Conspicuous Consumption

For the American upper classes, attendance at classical symphonic music and Shakespearean theater performances represented part of a larger set of rituals and customs designed to exhibit status and distinction in public. In his classic work *The Theory of the Leisure Class*, Thorstein Veblen ([1899] 1994) coined the term *conspicuous consumption* to describe these status displays since they represent attempts to show off one's wealth through the flagrant consumption of expensive and luxurious goods and services, particularly those considered wasteful or otherwise lacking in obvious utility, like diamond bangles or high-heeled shoes. Even today, upper-class tastes tend to emphasize *form over function* as well as *quality over quantity*, which is why expensive restaurants often serve tiny portions of elaborately presented foods, such as salmon sashimi or Spanish tapas. Of course, the very wealthy not only enjoy an excess of money but also free time, as displayed in pursuits that Veblen called *conspicuous leisure*. They include playing sports that emphasize specialized technical skill and elaborate training, such as golf, polo, fencing, or equestrian riding, and studying dead languages like ancient Greek.

The conspicuous consumption of luxury SUVs, summer homes, ski vacations, and spa treatments has a noteworthy counterpart—the purposeful *avoidance* of popular culture associated (rightly or wrongly) with working-class tastes. Health crazes among the affluent typically revolve around the denigration of foods preferred by poor people, chiefly inexpensive yet efficient sources of protein, fat, and carbohydrates: fried chicken, cheeseburgers, tacos, pizza, and so forth. According to sociologist Bethany Bryson (1996), when asked about their music preferences and dislikes American respondents are most likely to express disapproval for those genres associated with less educated audiences: heavy metal, country, gospel, and rap. Pejorative class-based characterizations like "ghetto," "trailer-park," and "white-trash" are commonly affixed to low-status behaviors and styles as a strategy of dismissal.

If affluent Americans studiously avoid symbolic or cultural associations with the working class, the opposite is almost certainly not true, since the members of all social classes often try to emulate the conspicuous consumption of the superrich, at least in superficial ways. While poor African American youth embrace Tommy Hilfiger and Polo country-club fashion, young inner-city mothers adorn their babies in expensive brand-name clothes like Reebok and Nike (Anderson 1990, p. 125). Another example

Yachts at the dock in Nantucket Harbor. Over the past decade the island has come to be dominated by the conspicuously superrich.

might be the widespread popularity of designer knockoff handbags, wallets, earrings, and sunglasses, replicas of high-priced brands from Prada to Chanel to Louis Vuitton. (Perhaps as a means of competing with the imitation jewelry industry, Tiffany and Co. sells a small heart-shaped charm for $80, which caters to a significant market of consumers who desire the celebrity luster of the Tiffany brand but cannot afford their $7,100 diamond bracelet.) More audacious emulators of the rich and famous hire personal paparazzi firms like Celeb 4 a Day to follow them around with cameras while nightclubbing. Meanwhile, the success of the $161 billion American wedding industry depends on the strength of the fantasy that everyday people deserve the trappings of wealth—limousines, glamorous clothing, catered cocktail parties, ice sculptures, endless glasses of champagne—if only for one special evening (Mead 2007).

Cultural Capital and Class Reproduction

One might reasonably ask what is at stake here. If cultural consumption is all about image making, why do the images matter so much? After all, the billionaire who drives a beat-up pickup truck and wears discount-store clothes (as Wal-Mart's founder Sam Walton did) still has his overflowing bank accounts. Yet in fact, quite a lot might be at stake, if we bear in mind that cultural tastes and consumer habits have social consequences that extend far beyond one's wardrobe or iPod playlists. Rather, cultural tastes have value and can be transferred to others, converted into financial wealth, and ultimately help to reproduce the class structure of our society.

This is admittedly a big claim, so let us start with the basics. In his venerable book *Distinction*, French sociologist Pierre Bourdieu (1984) discusses his concept of *cultural capital*—one's store of knowledge and proficiency with artistic and cultural styles that are valued by society, and confer prestige and honor upon those associated with them. Cultural capital refers to one's ability to appreciate and discuss intelligently not only the fine arts but elite forms of popular culture as well, such as art-house cinema and foreign films, critically acclaimed novels, television and NPR radio programs, and sophisticated magazines like *Harper's* and *The New Yorker*. It also includes one's experience with cosmopolitan culture, particularly one's fluency in foreign languages, and the cultivation of taste for global, international, or fusion cuisine. Cultural capital also refers to one's familiarity and competence with the rules of dress and etiquette appropriate for upper-class social situations, such as knowing how to tie a necktie in a Windsor knot, when to applaud during symphonic concerts, and how to eat sushi with chopsticks in an expensive Japanese restaurant.

Why call this kind of knowledge cultural *capital*? Bordieu uses the term *cultural capital* because it shares many of the same properties as economic capital or wealth. Like wealth, cultural capital is unevenly divided among the social classes, largely because it tends to be *inherited*, passed among generations within families. One's taste and appreciation for the fine arts is never derived naturally but taught through constant exposure and positive reinforcement, often at a young age. The homes of upper-class families are brimming with collections of novels and nonfiction books, paintings and drawings, atlases and maps, and all kinds of music. Wealthy families introduce their children to the arts by taking them to museums, plays, and concerts, and by sending them to private piano, violin, and ballet lessons. They take them to exotic ethnic restaurants, bring them on European vacations to world capitals like Paris and Rome, and send them to college preparatory boarding schools. In doing so, parents try to cultivate in their children the same sense of respect and esteem (if not actual affection) for the fine arts and cosmopolitan culture that they themselves have come to appreciate, or at least value.

Of course, the transfer of cultural capital from upper-class parents to their children can be a pricey proposition—think of the expense of all those years of ballet and music lessons, foreign travel, and private school. In this sense, economic capital itself can be *converted* into cultural capital as an investment. In fact, the returns on such an investment can be substantial given that once accumulated, cultural capital can be converted back into economic capital. High-paying law firms and consulting agencies screen their applicants not only on the basis of their intellect and academic achievement but on their cultural skills and habits as well. During interviews, recruiters evaluate candidates on their business attire and hygienic appearance, and their articulateness in English and fluency in other languages. Once hired, new employees may be expected to socialize with their bosses or associates while skiing or playing golf (both expensive recreational pursuits requiring years of training), or else they may be asked to entertain clients at dinner parties at fancy restaurants—they will need to know how to order wine from a sommelier, correctly distinguish between their salad and entrée forks (the salad fork is always on the outside), and know how to properly break and butter their dinner roll (in small pieces). In much of the business world, the rules of the game privilege those with impressive levels of cultural capital, and access to high-income occupations (or otherwise prestigious jobs in higher education, publishing, or the performing arts) may require it. During the application process and on the job itself, recruits who make the most of their cultural capital are able to convert it back into economic wealth, as represented by the financial rewards of the high-paying job itself.

If cultural capital is therefore transferable (from parents to kin), and convertible (to economic rewards), then it is hardly a stretch to hypothesize that over time the organization of cultural tastes and consumer habits might work to reproduce the class structure of our society. Upper-class adults use their cultural capital to secure lucrative jobs and invest their incomes in cultivating the same tastes and cultural skills in their children, who eventually generate enough cultural capital of their own that they can effectively continue the cycle. In doing so, the upper classes reproduce themselves over and over again, in perpetuity if they wish, leaving behind those who lack basic competence in elite cultural consumption themselves and the resources to train their children to do all that much better.

Of course, when accessing how cultural capital operates in the United States, we must remember that our industries and social institutions not only discriminate on the basis of socioeconomic class, but race, ethnicity, and gender as well. As University of Pennsylvania anthropologist Philippe Bourgois (2002) discovered during his research among young Puerto Rican men in New York City, the tough style of interpersonal communication they developed while on the streets of East Harlem was completely incompatible with the white-collar culture of the corporate world, a sad fact that consistently resulted in job termination for these otherwise hardworking employees. Research also suggests that within the business world, familiarity with professional sports probably matters much more than knowledge of the fine arts (Erickson 1996); this could give males a powerful advantage over equally qualified women when competing for jobs and promotions. (Obviously, since the 1970s the female audience for American sports has grown tremendously, particularly among active women who participated in high school or intercollegiate athletics at earlier ages, and so to a certain degree this is changing.)

We should also bear in mind that different professions may reward different kinds of knowledge. For example, in today's global postindustrial economy, *technical* expertise likely matters more than cultural capital, especially in professions such as financial services, investment banking, real estate development, insurance, engineering, and software development. These fields employ many smart workers admired more for their mathematical prowess than their aesthetic sensibilities and who often work in hidden backstage settings rather than face-to-face with clients. In fact, during the Internet boom of the 1990s, startup firms regularly hired computer programmers whose dress ranged from casual to slovenly, and who pulled all-nighters by gorging on leftover pizza and cola between games of ping-pong and foosball. (My guess is that the salad/entrée fork distinction was somewhat irrelevant in this environment.) Alternatively, many jobs in the media industries—advertising, publishing, Web site design, music and film editing—obviously *do* demand a wide set of aesthetic skills, while employment in high-end retail, dining, entertainment, and other service industries in which workers interact with wealthy customers may require cultural competencies and communicative skills that resonate with upper-class style (Grazian 2008b, p. 47).

In the end, Bourdieu's arguments about cultural capital depend on whether differences in cultural tastes and consumer habits persist among social classes in the United States. In fact, it turns out that they do, but only *sort of*. According to surveys conducted in 12 major U.S. cities by the Ford Foundation in the 1970s, professionals and managers were more likely than their blue-collar counterparts to have attended live symphony, ballet, and opera performances in the past year. But social researchers made an interesting discovery: while *relative* attendance among the upper classes was quite high, in fact the *absolute* number of participants was quite low—shockingly low. Among professionals, only 18 percent had attended the symphony in the past year; the ballet, 9 percent; the opera, only 5 percent (Halle 1993, p. 8). As a potential strategy of class domination, this would seem like an especially weak effort on the part of the upper classes.

UCLA sociologist David Halle found that most of the upper-class residents in Manhattan whom he interviewed hung abstract art in their homes, while none of the residents in a lower-middle-class neighborhood in Brooklyn did. What does his research tell us about contemporary elites and class-based taste?

Still, if participation in the arts among the affluent seems tepid, perhaps it can be explained by the vast amounts of cultural capital needed to actually comprehend and experience such highbrow fare in the first place. To find out, UCLA sociologist David Halle (1993) interviewed a variety of people from different neighborhoods in the New York City metropolitan area about their consumption of modern abstract art (i.e., Wassily Kandinsky, Paul Klee, Piet Mondrian, Jackson Pollock), typically regarded as highbrow culture enjoyed by contemporary elites. Sure enough, he discovered that 55 percent of the residents he sampled from Manhattan's ritzy Upper East Side display abstract art on the walls of their homes, while *none* of his respondents from a lower-middle-class urban neighborhood in Brooklyn did. Instead, these less well-off residents tended to decorate their homes with landscapes, and photographs and portraits of family members, and only a quarter of them claimed to even *like* abstract art. Of those who expressed their dislike for it, 30 percent complained that abstract artists are "charlatans" and "frauds," while nearly half said that abstract art was "too complex to understand" (p. 127). Others decried that it is "cold," "harsh," "unemotional," "ugly," and ultimately has no meaning.

Judging from these findings, it would seem that the consumption of abstract art reflects class differences in aesthetic taste, attributable to social inequality on the basis of cultural capital—until the reader learns exactly *why* Halle's affluent respondents collect abstract art. In interviews with Halle on this question, upper-class professionals emphasized the most mundane features of abstract art, like its decorative qualities—its lines, colors, and shapes (p. 129). Some admitted that they liked certain pieces because they matched their furniture, or otherwise improved the décor or even the acoustics of a room in their home. According to one lawyer, "I like the colors. I think of art in semidecorative terms. I think of how it will blend into the room. To me lines and colors are important in themselves. For instance [discussing a large, bright tapestry by Sonia Delaunay] I like the vibrant colors—the dark sinks and recedes. And we wanted a tapestry to absorb sound, since we had taken up the carpets." Another Manhattan resident confessed, "I like them because they're colorful. They brighten up the wall. I aimed for colorful art because of the grayness of the wall and the grayish carpet" (p. 130). As Halle observes, it is hard to imagine why one would need much cultural capital at all to make these kinds of "aesthetic" evaluations; certainly, contrasting a colorful painting to a gray wall does not require an advanced degree in European art history or visual studies. Of course, this hardly means that the consumption of abstract art is *unrelated* to status and distinction—far from it—but it does emphasize the superficial and sometimes flaky character of class-based tastes.

From Cultural Snob to Omnivore

One of Halle's more interesting findings is that while Manhattan professionals are more likely to feature abstract art in their homes than other cultural consumers, they are also much more likely to collect a wider variety of other kinds of art as well. Among Halle's urban elites, 58 percent display non-Western art in their homes, including African, Oceanic, and Native American figurines, masks, weapons, baskets, jewelry, pottery, textiles, musical instruments, and other artifacts, higher than any other group sampled in his research (p. 149). They are also more likely to display painted portraits (45 percent), and landscapes that depict the past (77 percent), or past or present foreign societies (79 percent), or Japan, Britain, or France (38 percent) (pp. 81, 94).

Research on other kinds of cultural consumption suggests similar findings. According to Vanderbilt University sociologist Richard A. Peterson (1992), highly educated professionals are more likely than others to attend opera, jazz and classical music concerts, Broadway musicals and dramatic plays, art museums, ballet and modern dance performances, as we might expect of the stereotypical upper-class snob. (Think Frasier and Niles Crane from the NBC sitcom *Frasier*.) However, they are also more likely to participate in almost *all other* recreational activities than their lower-class counterparts as well, including attending sports events, exercising, gardening, boating, camping, hiking, and photography. (They are also more likely to listen to blues, soul, and big band music.) This suggests that in the context of American life, elite status is signified not only by an

Jay-Z, platinum-selling rapper, entrepreneur, and CEO. How is he an example of Elijah Anderson's concept of code-switching?

affinity for highbrow culture but an appreciation for practically *all* major kinds of leisure activities, creative pursuits, and cultural consumption, highbrow *and* low.

Peterson (1992) calls these affluent consumers *cultural omnivores* because of their far-ranging tastes, as illustrated by well-off suburban teenagers who enjoy hip-hop and punk rock, or the college professor who loves country music. Undergraduate students often display omnivorous consumer tendencies as well. Among those enrolled in my courses at the University of Pennsylvania, in informal surveys students express their simultaneous affinity for radically different pop cultural touchstones. Among movies, the same students seem to like the 1939 epic *Gone with the Wind* as much as *The Lord of the Rings* trilogy; the most recent adaptation of Jane Austen's *Pride and Prejudice* and the Will Ferrell comedy *Talladega Nights: The Ballad of Ricky Bobby.* One student hit a trifecta: *Casablanca, Austin Powers: International Man of Mystery,* and *Hotel Rwanda.* Their music choices are equally omnivorous: folk-rock singer Bob Dylan and R&B pop star Kanye West; jazz artist Miles Davis and pop singer Alicia Keys; country singer Johnny Cash and glam-metal band Guns N' Roses. (And another triple-play: Australian heavy-metal band AC/DC, country music singer Reba McEntire, and the NYC rap group the Wu-Tang Clan.)

Like these students, cultural omnivores rely on their cultural capital not only to consume highbrow fare but also to successfully inhabit several different kinds of social universes, each with a different set of taste expectations, rules of etiquette, and codes of subcultural behavior, language, and style. Yale sociologist Elijah Anderson (1999, p. 36) refers to this ability to negotiate among multiple and varied cultural worlds simultaneously as *code-switching*—a social dexterity famously illustrated by rapper Jay-Z, who moves easily between underground hip-hop clubs and the executive suites of Def Jam Recordings, having served as its president and CEO. (Perhaps Rose, the *Titanic* heroine played by Kate Winslet who smoothly transitions from elegant dining to Irish dancing below deck, provides a suitable fictitious example.) In contemporary American life, the capacity for code-switching and omnivorous consumption signifies class status without necessarily appearing snobbish, which is why so many Facebook members and online daters overload their profiles with dozens of favorite music genres and seemingly contradictory activities that mix highbrow and lowbrow to dizzying effect—motorcycle riding and ballroom dancing, rollerblading and knitting, bullfighting and ballet. In *Bobos in Paradise* David Brooks (2001) similarly argues that the new upper classes combine elite, bourgeoisie tastes with bohemian sensibilities, rejecting traditional luxury goods for Costa Rican fair-trade handicrafts, Ethiopian coffee beans, Malaysian curries, Salvadoran fleece sweaters, and vacations to formerly war-torn countries like Cambodia and Vietnam.

(While the upper classes do not fit the image of the stereotypical snob, working-class consumers do not represent an indiscriminate mass audience either, contrary to most negative depictions of low-income Americans. Peterson (1992) observes that as one moves down the class hierarchy, cultural tastes are extremely varied and more easily explained on the basis of other factors besides class, such as regional background, racial and ethnic identification, age, gender, and religiosity. For instance, note the social differences among "lowbrow" consumers of daytime soap operas, hardcore rap, and Christian rock.)

What can explain the emergence of the cultural omnivore? One might speculate that upwardly mobile Americans who hail from working-class backgrounds never really shed their cultural tastes but merely add to them as they acquire cultural capital. The persistence of working-class tastes among the nouveau riche helps explain why four-star restaurants serve upscale, gentrified versions of otherwise pedestrian foods like meat and potatoes. Barclay Prime, an expensive steakhouse in Philadelphia's ritzy Rittenhouse Square district, serves a $100 Philly cheesesteak prepared with Kobe beef, lobster meat, shaved truffles, caramelized onions, heirloom tomatoes, and melted triple-cream taleggio cheese on a brioche bun; the sandwich comes with a complimentary bottle of Veuve Clicquot champagne (Grazian 2008b, p. 69). (Barclay Prime also serves Kobe "sliders," a refined take on White Castle's mini-hamburgers.) The persistence of formative tastes among upwardly mobile immigrants who carry traditional ethnic and religious customs and cultural practices—Sicilian cooking, Hindu wedding rituals, Mexican folk art, Senegalese dance—into the high-society world of the upper class might also help to explain the omnivorous consumer habits among elite Americans (Peterson 1992, p. 255).

Another possible explanation for the emergence of the omnivore could be the rising commercialization (and thus increased accessibility and acceptance) of numerous types of working-class, folk, ethnic, and non-Western popular culture. In the early 1980s New York art dealers sold samples of the street graffiti common to the city's ghetto walls and subway trains in exclusive downtown galleries (Lachmann 1988). Recent best-selling books include *Reading Lolita in Tehran* by Iranian author Azar Nafisi, *The Kite Runner* and *A Thousand Splendid Suns* by Afghan-born novelist Khaled Hosseini, and *A Long Way Gone*, Ishmael Beah's memoir of growing up in Sierra Leone as a child soldier. Starbucks' Hear Music catalogue promotes CD compilations of a range of folk and world music, including Jamaican ska and rocksteady, Brazilian bossa nova, and Mississippi Delta blues. Starbucks also sells CDs by Matisyahu, a Hasidic Jew turned reggae performer who puts spiritual themes to a dancehall beat.

Finally, we must consider that omnivorous consumption is a product of our national ideals concerning democracy and equality. American ideology emphasizes the importance and value of egalitarianism, as reflected in our typically casual dress and informal norms of etiquette, at least when compared to our European counterparts. In her book *Money, Morals, and Manners* Harvard sociologist Michèle Lamont (1992) shows how disparaging Americans are of "social climbers" and "phonies" who "put on airs" (p. 26). Perhaps because we place so much value on equality in our national culture, a 2008 Pew Research Center report estimated that a majority of Americans (53 percent) identify as being "middle class." If you include those who self-identify as being lower-middle and upper-middle class, the proportion of self-identified "middle class" Americans jumps to over 90 percent, or just about everybody.

Given how Americans so readily identify with the concept of equality as a symbolic ideal, perhaps omnivorous consumption among the affluent classes allows one to perform cultural distinction without appearing overly snobby, pompous, highfalutin' or out of touch with so-called "common" people. In fact, sometimes it seems as though most would just as well forget about seeming highbrow altogether. In American politics, highly stylized candidates often emphasize their working-class tastes, however manufactured. For example, during the 1990s Tennessee Republican Fred Thompson's U.S. senatorial campaign reinvented the wealthy lobbyist "as a good old boy: it leased a used red pickup truck for him to drive, dressed up in jeans and a work shirt, with a can of Red Man chewing tobacco on the front seat" (Krugman 2007). Likewise, although he was a graduate of Phillips Academy, Yale, and Harvard, and the eldest son of a former U.S. president, former President George W. Bush's political career benefited from his handlers' ability to depict the scion as a rough-riding cowboy and all-around "regular guy." During Bush's two terms in office he customarily took his vacations at his ranch in Crawford, Texas—a more ruggedly populist setting than his family's oceanfront retreat in Kennebunkport, Maine:

> President Bush has spent the last three Augusts at his ranch in the scorched flatlands of Crawford, Tex., where he has cleared brush, gone for runs in 105-degree heat and summoned sweaty cabinet members to eat fried jalapeño peppers at the only restaurant in town. No one ever confused the place with that white-wine-swilling island in the Atlantic Ocean, to reprise the president's put-down of Martha's Vineyard, and so Mr. Bush has loved it all the more. (Bumiller 2004, p. A12)

Similarly, after Alaska Governor Sarah Palin's selection as Arizona Senator John McCain's vice presidential running mate in the 2008 election, the campaign and media promoted the conservative Republican's credentials as a middle-class hockey mom, citing her small-town sensibilities, long-standing membership in the National Rifle Association, knack for aerial wolf hunting, and expert ability to properly field dress a moose. Her political fortunes in that campaign began to dwindle when it was discovered that the Republican National Committee spent

$150,000 on clothing, hair styling, cosmetics, and accessories for Palin and her family in a single month, an outlay that included a $75,000 shopping spree at the upscale department store Neiman Marcus. For a time McCain himself had been similarly packaged by his staff and the media as a self-proclaimed "maverick" who named his campaign bus the Straight Talk Express. Late in the campaign he touted the support of an everyman working-class figure called "Joe the Plumber," a fellow who, as it turned out, was not actually a licensed plumber, nor was his name Joe. McCain's act had already begun to sour when it was revealed that, when asked during an interview, he couldn't remember how many houses he owned. (And in the interests of bipartisanship, it bears remembering that the 2004 Democratic presidential nominee John Kerry was ridiculed for windsurfing off the hyper-rich coast of Nantucket, and his running mate, John Edwards, was similarly chastened by the press and public for his $400 haircuts.)

The Blurring of Class Boundaries in American Popular Culture

I began this chapter by suggesting that our national culture today sometimes seems schizophrenic, but the evidence indicates that class boundaries in the United States have always been a bit blurry—in the live entertainment of the nineteenth century, replete with Shakespearean actors, clowns, and acrobats; in the conspicuous if purely symbolic emulation of the wealthy by the working classes through the purchase of designer baby clothes; in the commercialization of graffiti and folk music; and finally, in the cynical masquerading of wealthy politicians and the filthy rich. As historian Michael Kammen (1999) reminds us, the blending of highbrow, lowbrow, and mass culture has been a recognizable quality of American popular culture, entertainment, and art since at least the 1920s. In the late part of that decade, Duke Ellington's harmonious compositions and performances blended together European classical music, ragtime jazz, and the Mississippi blues, as best illustrated by his 1927 record "Black and Tan Fantasy," a song that combines the blues melodies of the Deep South and the muted trumpets and stride piano of Harlem's jazz sound with, of all things, Frédéric Chopin's Funeral March from his Piano Sonata No. 2 in B-flat minor (Grazian 2003, pp. 28—29). In Walt Disney's 1940 film *Fantasia* animated elephants, hippopotamuses, ostriches, and Mickey Mouse are accompanied by selections from the classical music canon: Bach's Toccata and Fugue in D Minor, Tchaikovsky's *Nutcracker Suite*, Beethoven's sixth symphony (the *Pastoral Symphony*), and Stravinsky's *The Rite of Spring*. Starting in the 1950s, Hugh Hefner's *Playboy* magazine began publishing serious short fiction along with its pictorial centerfolds: its authors have included such luminaries as Vladimir Nabokov, Saul Bellow, Norman Mailer, John Cheever, Gabriel García Márquez, John Updike, Joyce Carol Oates, and Philip Roth. Citing creative influences as canonical as Bach, Vivaldi, Paganini, and Pachelbel, progressive rock and heavy metal artists like Rush, Deep Purple, Van Halen, Randy Rhoads, and Yngwie Malmsteen incorporated complex classical music techniques (harmonic progressions, sliding chromatic figures, minor modalities,

A scene from Twyla Tharp's Movin' Out, *a musical based on the songs of Billy Joel.*

fast arpeggios) into their songwriting and performing during the 1970s and 1980s (Walser 1994).

This blurring of class boundaries continues in contemporary American popular culture, especially as elite culture absorbs more popular influences. Choreographer Twyla Tharp's creations include ballet, interpretive modern dance, and theatrical performances set not only to Brahms and Haydn but also the jazz music of Jelly Roll Morton and the pop songs of Frank Sinatra, Bob Dylan, and Billy Joel, just as in 1993 the Joffrey Ballet premiered a rock ballet danced to the recorded music of Prince. Minimalist composer Philip Glass has written symphonies based on the albums of David Bowie. Mainstream film and television similarly borrows from classical and avant-garde sources. The 1995 movie *Clueless* starring Alicia Silverstone is a modernization of the Jane Austen novel *Emma*, just as Gus Van Sant's 1991 drama *My Own Private Idaho* is based on Shakespeare's *Henry IV* plays. The final season of the TV comedy *Seinfeld* included an episode loosely based on the experimental Harold Pinter play *Betrayal:* like the original, the episode's scenes were presented in reverse chronological order, with punch lines delivered before their setups (Johnson 2006, p. 88).

More to the point, one should consider the central attractions of American popular culture consumed by vast audiences whose members hail from all social classes. The longest running and most successful talk show in television history, *The Oprah Winfrey Show* is watched by 30 million American viewers every week; its famous host, the highest-paid personality in television, attracts an enormous base of largely female fans from all walks of life. Late-night TV is similarly inclusive as well as popular: in 2006, NBC's *Tonight Show with Jay Leno* enjoyed nightly ratings of 5.7 million viewers, while CBS's *Late Show with David Letterman* drew in another 4.2 million viewers. Professional men's sports, particularly football, basketball, and baseball, attract fans from all social classes, with games enthusiastically followed on fuzzy TV sets in working-class bars and flat-panel plasma-screen home theaters, in upper-deck bleachers as well as in corporate skyboxes. Of all American sporting events, perhaps the Super Bowl is the most celebrated, watched in 2009 by an estimated 98.7 million American viewers of all social classes, its inclusiveness illustrated by the diversity of pop music stars that have performed during its live halftime shows since 2001: U2, Aerosmith, Britney Spears, Nelly, Shania Twain, P. Diddy, Paul McCartney, Sting, Kid Rock, Jessica Simpson, Mary J. Blige, the Rolling Stones, No Doubt, Prince, Janet Jackson, Tom Petty and the Heartbreakers, Justin Timberlake, and Bruce Springsteen and the E Street Band. Like Shakespeare's comedies and tragedies during the nineteenth century, the sporting event best represents the nationwide reach of our mass entertainment and popular culture.

The grave of Jim Morrison, lead singer of the Doors. Why do visitors attach such significance and meaning to the singer?

the searchers

AUDIENCES AND THE QUEST FOR MEANING IN POPULAR CULTURE

PARIS IS INTERNATIONALLY KNOWN FOR ITS FINE CUISINE, spectacular art museums, fashionable boutiques, lovely cafés, and exuberant street life. Many tourists traveling though the French capital take a detour from the city center to the famous Père Lachaise Cemetery, the final resting place of countless dignitaries of art and intellectual life, including writers Honoré de Balzac, Oscar Wilde, and Marcel Proust; painters Camille Pissarro, Gustave Caillebotte, and Amedeo Modigliani; and even Pierre Bourdieu, the French sociologist discussed in the last chapter. (Auguste Comte, one of the original founders of sociology, is also buried at Père Lachaise: his tombstone features a stone sculpture of an open book.) Yet among the cemetery's crowds of well-wishers, many young Americans bypass the gravesites of these notables on their way toward one of the most visited spots in the cemetery, the tomb of Jim Morrison, lead singer of the 1960s American rock band the Doors. As famous for his charismatic onstage presence (especially as his alter ego, the Lizard King) as for his bluesy psychedelic songs—"Light My Fire," "People Are Strange," "Waiting for the Sun," "The End," "Riders of the Storm," "When the Music's Over"— Morrison died in his Paris apartment bathtub on July 3, 1971, at age 27, possibly of a drug overdose. (No autopsy was ever performed, and speculative rumors and conspiracy theories surrounding his mysterious death abound.)

Morrison's tomb itself is unimpressive, and the headstone is not the original grave marker, which was stolen years ago. So what attracts hordes of tourists to the gravesite? Like religious pilgrims they are on a quest for meaning, only their sacred texts are not biblical but the stuff of popular culture. While some visitors are obviously baby boomers searching for the cultural touchstones of their wild and misspent youth, many others are much younger, born long after Morrison's tragic death. To these fans he exists only in the mediated world of pop culture and myth—the remastered CDs and greatest hits compilations, Oliver Stone's 1991 film *The Doors*, tribute bands like Peace Frog, Wild Child, and the Soft Parade—and yet his significance as an artist, icon, and cultural object is nearly infinite, at least for them. To his followers, Jim Morrison is the Lizard King, and he can do anything.

The last chapter followed the consumer habits of audiences in an attempt to understand the impact of one's social class position on his or her cultural tastes and patterns of consumption. In doing so we discovered the complexities of American popular culture and the frequently shifting boundaries that define identity and status in our society. In this chapter we look beyond consumer preferences and proclivities to assess how people attribute significance and meaning to popular culture. Scholars from a variety of disciplines in the social sciences and the humanities agree that cultural meaning is a product of human engagement and interpretation. While a traditional model of culture might imagine that texts, dramatic plays, sound recordings, film, and visual art are like walnuts, to be cracked open so that their hidden interiors can be revealed and consumed, most social scientists today recognize that cultural meanings are actively created by audiences themselves, albeit in socially patterned ways.

Audiences and Interpretive Communities

If audiences actively construct and attribute meaning and significance to popular culture, it follows that some of their experiences consuming culture will be uniquely singular and intimately personal. Some of those experiences are of a psychological or neurological character. For instance, in his book *Musicophilia* the neurologist and author Oliver Sacks (2007) reports on an epileptic patient whose seizures are provoked by a wildly diverse array of music from operatic Verdi arias to romantic Frank Sinatra tunes to rock music (he must wear earplugs when out of the house), while another patient with a temporal lobe abnormality regularly experiences convulsions after listening to recordings of her favorite Neapolitan songs (pp. 26–27). Even mentally healthy music lovers may swoon over a personally captivating song (as when Elaine's boyfriend has a near-hypnotic reaction to the Eagles' hit "Desperado" during a 1996 episode of *Seinfeld*). Some married couples strongly identify with a featured slow dance number played at their wedding (popular examples include "At Last" by Etta James, "Unchained Melody" by the Righteous Brothers, "Wonderful Tonight" by Eric Clapton, and "You're Beautiful" by James Blunt) while others still wax nostalgic for the song featured as their high school prom theme—"This Is the Time" by Billy Joel, "A Moment Like This" by Kelly Clarkson, "Forever Young" by Alphaville, or, yet again, "Wonderful Tonight" by Eric Clapton.

When attributing meaning and significance to songs, movies, and other kinds of media and popular culture, audiences not only draw on their personal memories or individual psyches but their social circumstances as well. Consumers whose common social identities and cultural backgrounds (whether organized on the basis of nationality, race, ethnicity, gender, sexuality, religion, or age) inform their shared understandings of culture in patterned ways are called *interpretive communities* (Radway 1991; also see Fish 1980). As we discussed in Chapter 1, Native American men tend to be ardent fans of Hollywood Westerns, an enthusiasm that derives in part from the value many place on the principles of hard work and self-reliant country living. Upon viewing the 1956 John Ford film *The Searchers* starring John Wayne, American Indians surveyed by sociologist JoEllen Shively (1992) emphasized the free and independent cowboy lifestyle commonly celebrated in such films: "Westerns relate to the way I wish I could live"; "The cowboy is free"; "He's not tied down to an eight-to-five job, day after day"; "He's his own man"; "Indians today are the cowboys" (pp. 729–30). Similarly, since the narratives of "Bollywood" films produced in Mumbai, India, typically highlight clashes between the traditional world of the settled village and the temptations of the city and its marketplaces, they not only entice regional audiences from South Asia but also like-minded interpretive communities of viewers from developing countries all over the world, including China, Nigeria, South Africa, Kenya, Colombia, Brazil, Peru, and parts of the former Soviet Union (Joshi 2009).

Interpretive communities often share a specific intellectual, religious, or political worldview within a larger institutional context (Fish 1980). For example, Christian organizations greatly differed in their interpretation of director Martin Scorsese's critically acclaimed yet controversial 1988 motion picture *The Last Temptation of Christ,* in which Jesus Christ (played by Willem Dafoe) is presented as a truly human figure tortured by inner demons and grave doubts; in keeping with the 1951 revisionist novel by Nikos Kazantzakis on which the film is based, during his crucifixion Jesus dreams of marrying and making love to Mary Magdalene, impregnating her and going on to lead the life of a normal man. A spokesperson for the National Council of Churches called the movie "an honest attempt to tell the story of Jesus from a different perspective," and the Reverend Michael Himes, a Notre Dame theologian, referred to the film as "fairly distinguished art" (Hunter 1991, pp. 233—34). Meanwhile, conservative Catholic and Evangelical groups were outraged by the film and its depiction of Christ. Focus on the Family attacked the Scorsese film for portraying Jesus "as a confused, lustful wimp who denies his divinity and struggles with his sinful nature," and an organization called Morality in Media proclaimed it "an intentional attack on Christianity" (p. 234).

Interpretive communities materialize during public debates surrounding the value or potential harm of certain types of popular culture. In 1985 the U.S. Senate held hearings on the so-called dangers of heavy-metal rock music lyrics. Led by Tipper Gore (the wife of future vice president Al Gore), the Parents' Music Resource Center (PMRC) demanded that warning labels be placed on metal albums by artists such as Ozzy Osbourne, whose song "Suicide Solution" from the 1980 album *Blizzard of Ozz* had been dubiously blamed for the death of John McCollum, a depressed teenage boy who killed himself with a bullet to the head while listening to the record. At the Senate hearings, one child psychiatrist representing the PMRC attacked the music of Black Sabbath (Osbourne's previous band) and AC/DC for encouraging violent behavior:

> One of the most pathological forms of evil is in the form of the cult killer or deranged person who believes it is OK to hurt others or to kill. The Son of Sam who killed eight people in New York was allegedly into Black Sabbath's music. . . . Most recently, the individual identified in the newspapers as the Night Stalker has been said to be into hard drugs and the music of the heavy metal band AC/DC. . . . Every teenager who listens to heavy metal certainly does not become a killer. [But] young people who are seeking power over others through identification with the power of evil find a close identification. The lyrics become a philosophy of life. It becomes a religion. (quoted in Binder 1993, p. 758)

Meanwhile, an interpretive community made up of a strange mix of music industry executives, newspaper journalists, and musicians from Twisted Sister lead singer Dee Snider to experimental rock guitarist Frank Zappa to acoustic folk and country star John Denver defended the content of contemporary popular music, citing the small minority of songs containing explicit lyrics, the cartoonish and therefore harmless character of heavy metal, and the negligible role that rock lyrics play in the increasing proliferation of images of sex and violence in the media overall (Binder 1993, p. 759).

What spurred interpretive communities to protest the release of Martin Scorsese's film The Last Temptation of Christ?

In later years another public debate emerged among interpretive communities concerning the so-called dangers of popular music, specifically rap and hip-hop. In 1990 the Miami rap group 2 Live Crew's third album *As Nasty as They Wanna Be* was ruled obscene by a U.S. District Court judge in Fort Lauderdale, Florida, and the proprietor of a record store in Broward County was arrested for continuing to sell the album. (The album contains songs with titles such as "Me So Horny," "Put Her in the Buck," "Dick Almighty," "The Fuck Shop," and "Get the Fuck Out of My House." In addition to including over 200 utterances of the word "fuck," the album features over 150 mentions of the word "bitch" and over 80 descriptions of oral sex; see Hunter 1991, p. 232.) On the CBS news program *48 Hours* an attorney accused 2 Live Crew's lead singer Luther Campbell of being "a psychological child molester" (p. 232), while conservative commentator George Will warned in *Newsweek* that the rap group not only threatened young listeners but all of society:

> Fact: some members of a particular age and social cohort—the one making 2 Live Crew rich—stomped and raped [a] jogger to the razor edge of death, for the fun of it. Certainty: the coarsening of a community, the desensitizing of a society will have behavioral consequences. (quoted in Binder 1993, p. 762)

As in the previous controversy surrounding heavy metal, an interpretive community of perhaps uncommon bedfellows came to defend rap music (if not 2 Live Crew itself) from its critics, including African American university professor and ordained Baptist minister Michael Eric Dyson, who writes in an essay on "Gangsta Rap and American Culture" (1996):

At their best, rappers shape the torturous twists of urban fate into lyrical elegies. They represent lives swallowed by too little love or opportunity. They represent themselves and their peers with aggrandizing anthems that boast of their ingenuity and luck in surviving. . . . Before we discard the genre, we should understand that gangsta rap often reaches higher than its ugliest, lowest common denominator. Misogyny, violence, materialism, and sexual transgression are not its exclusive domain. At its best, this music draws attention to complex dimensions of ghetto life ignored by many Americans. Of all the genres of hip-hop—from socially conscious rap to black nationalist expressions, from pop to hardcore—gangsta rap has most aggressively narrated the pains and possibilities, the fantasies and fears, of poor black urban youth. (pp. 177, 184–85)

Likewise, during the 2 Live Crew controversy, pop music journalist Jon Pareles (1990) pointed out in the *New York Times* that "not all rap machismo should be taken entirely at face value. Like other black literary and oral traditions, rap lyrics also involve double-entendre, allegory and parody. Some rap machismo can be a metaphor for pride or political empowerment; it can be a shared joke, as it often is in 2 Live Crew's wildly hyperbolic rhymes." According to anthropologist Philippe Bourgois (whom Pareles interviewed for his *Times* piece):

I see rap as reflective, and what people should be scared about is the extent to which the songs reflect reality. That there is such unbelievable violence in these communities is a national tragedy, while the fact that people express themselves in terms of violence is a part of American culture, a way of thinking that goes back to the Wild West. I wouldn't worry about rap music leading to violence. On the contrary, rap music leads to a productive expression of alienation and oppression, and it's good that it gets channeled into creative outlets rather than drug addiction or physical violence. I see people, high-school dropouts, who carry around notebooks in their back pockets so they can compare their latest rhymes. (quoted in Pareles 1990)

The interpretive communities depicted in the preceding examples are engaged in what James Davison Hunter (1991) refers to as *culture wars*, cultural conflicts fought among ideological adversaries in the public arena. But while interpretive communities may disagree about the fundamental meanings of cultural texts, objects, or events, we need not think of such differences as necessarily combative or even oppositional. For instance, during the 1980s the British rock band the Smiths and its morose lead singer Morrissey attracted an American fan base of shy, pale-skinned white teenagers who identified with the band's melancholic view of life as expressed in morbidly titled songs like "Heaven Knows I'm Miserable Now," "Unhappy Birthday," "Girlfriend in a Coma," "The Boy with the Thorn in His Side," "Still Ill," "Suffer Little Children," "I Want the One I Can't Have," "That Joke Isn't Funny Anymore," "Death of a Disco Dancer," "Barbarism

Begins at Home," and "Meat Is Murder." Today, Morrissey and the Smiths continue to be popular in the United States—but among young Latino men. Reporting in *Spin*, Chuck Klosterman (2006) estimated that at least three-quarters of the 1,400 ticket holders to a 2002 Smiths/Morrissey convention in Hollywood were of Latino origin or descent. Nearly all were under the age of 20 (p. 49).

Interpretive communities rely on common social experiences to frame their collective readings of popular culture, which is why some Latino fans explain their embrace of Morrissey and the Smiths in terms of their shared ethnic heritage and immigrant experience. Gloria Antuez, a 23-year-old junior high school teacher, explains, "Morrissey's family emigrated to England from Ireland, and they were kind of socially segregated from the rest of the country. . . . That is very similar to the Latino experience here in Los Angeles. We see things within his songs that we can particularly relate to. He sings

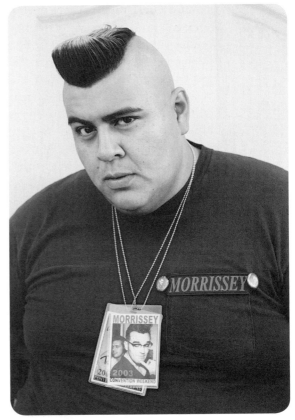

What explains the popularity of British rock singer Morrissey among Latino fans?

about loneliness. He sings about solitude. Those are things any minority group can relate to." According to Martha Barreras, another Latina fan, "We're passionate people. He's passionate like us. . . . The music our parents played when we were growing up was always about love and emotion, and it's the same thing with Morrissey." As Cruz Rubio, a 20-year-old male fan, insists, "He speaks to us, man. As Latinos. He addresses us personally. . . . His music fits our lifestyle" (Klosterman 2006, pp. 49—52). Then again, other Latino fans associate Morrissey's pompadour and rockabilly sensibility with 1950s icon Ritchie Valens, the Mexican-American rock 'n roll pioneer whose hits included "Donna," "Come On, Let's Go," and, most famously, "La Bamba."

Meaning-Making and the Changing Significance of Popular Culture

While interpretive communities may attribute differing meanings and significance to popular culture, often it is the meanings themselves that shift among audiences over time. We have already seen examples of this in earlier chapters, as when contract-based craft production, like Italian Renaissance painting, gains prestige as an art form, or when mass cultural attractions, like Shakespearean drama, are recast as highbrow culture. We have also seen examples of cultural genres once contested among interpretive communities for their so-called threatening and dangerous character rehabilitated in the public imagination, such as the "demoralizing" and "unspeakable" African American jazz music of the 1920s (Appelrouth 2005). Occasionally this reputational augmentation in the national consciousness reaches transformative heights, as in the case of the beloved American folk singer Pete Seeger. The progressive songwriter and performer of songs like "Where Have All the Flowers Gone?" and "If I Had a Hammer," Seeger was demonized as a communist sympathizer during the McCarthyism of the 1950s. He was called to testify before the House Un-American Activities Committee in 1955 and blacklisted for years from performing on prime-time network television. But as a result of the 1960s folk music revival and his subsequent fame as a cultural icon (as well as the eventual discrediting and dissipation of anti-communist hysteria among mainstream Americans), Seeger was selected as an Honoree of the John F. Kennedy Center for the Performing Arts in 1994, its publicity materials identifying him as "arguably the most influential folk artist in the United States" (Bromberg and Fine 2002, p. 1147). Just weeks later, President Bill Clinton awarded Seeger the coveted National Medal of Arts, the highest possible award given to an artist by the U.S. government.

Seeger's gradual transformation from national pariah to official recognition as an American treasure is a testament to the socially constructed character of the interpretive meanings and significance attributed to popular culture. But how common are these kinds of changes in meaning, particularly with regard not simply to individual artists but to entire forms of mass media themselves? In fact, these kinds of shifts occur more frequently than one might think. The reception of film in the United States provides an interesting case. Today we attach great artistic significance to movies, at least those easily recognized by socially conventional standards as worthy of critical praise—recent examples might include Academy Award winners and nominees such as *No Country for Old Men, There Will Be Blood, Michael Clayton, Capote, Sideways, Mystic River, Lost in Translation,* and *Eternal Sunshine of the Spotless Mind.* Yet historically this interpretation of cinema as art is a relatively recent development in American culture and dates back only as far as the 1960s. Earlier in its history, moviegoing was an inexpensive and therefore devalued form of urban entertainment. In New York City, nickelodeons—turn-of-the-century storefront theaters where film screenings could be enjoyed for a nickel—were typically concentrated in blue-collar tenement districts and attracted crowds of predominantly working-class patrons, particularly women and immigrants (Peiss 1986). According to sociologist Shyon Baumann (2007), from its beginnings through the 1930s wealthy and educated cultural snobs looked down upon movies for their "lack of sophistication or aesthetic value," "tackiness," "tastelessness," and "corrupting and immoral" influence, while shunning the theaters themselves for

The Criterion Theater in New York City's Times Square in 1931. Why did many cultural elites in the early twentieth century look down on movies?

attracting audiences of low social status, including ethnic minorities and the poor (pp. 24–25). Movies were considered entertainment for the lowest common denominator of audiences, inferior to more "legitimate" live theatrical performances.

In his book *Hollywood Highbrow*, Baumann (2007) argues that the work of prestige-granting institutions in concert with industry shifts and broader social changes can help explain the rising significance of film among American audiences. Believe it or not, the introduction and rapid popularity of television in American homes during the 1940s and 1950s was a crucial factor. As noted in Chapter 1, in 1953 two-thirds of family households in the U.S. owned at least one television, and by the mid-1960s that figure had grown to 94 percent (Cohen 2003, p. 302). Television's enormous mainstream appeal allowed film to emerge as a more distinctive and status-signaling cultural alternative, and by the 1960s, motion pictures seemed especially smarter and more sophisticated than network television, particularly in light of the formulaic commercial TV programming popularized during the 1940s and 1950s, as represented by shows like *Bozo the Clown, Howdy Doody, Candid Camera,* and *What's My Line*? Meanwhile, the growth of the middle class and the expansion of colleges and universities in the United States after World War II created newly educated audiences who were both hungry for rich cultural experiences and prepared to critically engage with cinema as something more than simply trivial entertainment.

At the same time, a set of legitimating institutions had succeeded in canonizing American films as worthy of intellectual and artistic cultural merit. In 1927 Louis B. Mayer of MGM and other studio heads instituted the Academy of Motion Picture Arts and Sciences as a means of bolstering the industry's image, and in 1929 the organization began nominating and bestowing its Academy Awards—today more popularly known as the Oscars—for achievement in film. By showcasing a small number of films every year, the Academy Awards helped contribute to the creation of a canon of American motion picture "masterpieces," just as prizes like the National Book Award and the Nobel Prize in Literature serve to establish a literary canon over time. The American Film Institute (AFI) was similarly created during the 1960s to recognize achievement in cinema, and in 1998 the AFI established a list of the 100 greatest American movies of all time. (The AFI updates its list every 10 years; in 2007 the AFI 100 top five films were, in descending order, *Citizen Kane* (1941), *The Godfather* (1972), *Casablanca* (1942), *Raging Bull* (1980), and *Singin' in the Rain* (1952). More recent films on the updated list include *Toy Story* (1995), *Titanic* (1997), *Saving Private Ryan* (1998), *The Sixth Sense* (1999), and *The Lord of the Rings: The Fellowship of the Ring* (2001).) The American film canon was also developed during the 1960s by growing numbers of academic departments offering advanced degree programs in film and cinema studies at major colleges and universities such as New York University, Columbia, UCLA, and the University of Southern California. Movies and their directors gained social prestige and scholarly significance as they were gradually incorporated into the university curriculum in courses on film history and theory. The early 1960s also saw the American importation of French auteur theory, which credits the director (rightly or wrongly) with providing the artistic vision for their movies, as if he or she were the sole author of their films. (Well-known examples of the Hollywood director-as-auteur include Spike Lee, Woody Allen, Martin Scorsese, Francis Ford Coppola, Steven Spielberg, Peter Jackson, Steven Soderbergh, and Christopher Nolan.) In addition, by the 1950s and 1960s cosmopolitan American cities—Chicago, San Francisco, New York, Boston, Seattle—began hosting international film festivals showcasing new films as worthy of critical and intellectual consideration.

These changes helped reshape the heightened meaning and artistic significance that American audiences today attach to popular film. Baumann (2007) cleverly illustrates this interpretive shift by examining the differences between movie reviews published before and after the 1960s. Whereas earlier film reviews were short write-ups with little more than plot summaries and consumer recommendations, starting in the mid-1960s movie critics began employing an increasingly sophisticated language in lengthier discussions of films. Contemporary reviewers characterize film using an analytic voice featuring a critical terminology usually reserved for dissecting great works of literature and art—"composition," "irony," "metaphor," "symbol," "tone." Critics today make references to the creative vision and authorial control of the director by using laudatory adjectives such as "art," "brilliant," "genius," "inspired," and "master," and modifiers like Hitchcockian or Tarantinoesque when comparing the cinematographic styles of different directors (pp. 119–20).

Of course, one could (incorrectly, I think) argue that contemporary critics are more likely to describe films as artistic and intellectually significant simply because movies *are* actually more artistic and culturally significant today—except that Baumann also discovered these differences among earlier and later reviews of *the same movies,* including *Casablanca, Gone with the Wind,* and *The Wizard of Oz* (pp. 128–33). As an illustrative example, Baumann presents early and more recent reviews of the Disney animated classic *Snow White and the Seven Dwarfs.* As *The New Yorker* told readers in 1938, shortly after the film's premiere:

> He has perhaps overdone the wicked stepmother, and just for a moment or two has tinted the film with too lurid a touch. In one other element, too, I think Mr. Disney's judgment has erred. The language of the dwarfs is funny, but it must be called a little tough. It smacks too much of the language of the streets, and in a film like this it should be most literate, punctilious, and polite. No nice dwarf, Mr. Disney, ever says "ain't." (quoted in Baumann 2007, pp. 131–32)

Note the differences between this recap from the late 1930s, and a more recent *Village Voice* review from 1973:

> Disney is for children as much as Chaplin and Keaton are, by which I mean that children understand the broadest aspects of these artists—the lowest slapstick comedy and, in the case of Disney, the terror—but little else. "Bambi," for example, with its subtle mood studies, its deliberate lack of story-line and identification figures, left the largely children's audience I saw it with restless. . . . On a narrative level this sense of the past and emphasis on family relationships make the films, like fairy tales, fertile ground for Freudian analysis. As in the Grimm original, "SNOW WHITE AND THE SEVEN DWARFS" centers around a sexual jealousy between an overweeningly vain queen and her innocent step-daughter. (quoted in Baumann 2007, p. 132)

In this latter review from the 1970s, the *Village Voice* compares Disney's work to that of Charlie Chaplin and Buster Keaton (both directors as well as comedic actors) and draws on terminology like "Freudian" and "narrative." Since then, *Snow White and the Seven Dwarfs* has been added to the U.S. National Film Registry (founded in the 1980s to honor and preserve "culturally, historically or aesthetically significant films"), named by the American Film Institute as the

Snow White and the Seven Dwarfs *(1937)*.

34th greatest American film of all time, and the *greatest* animated movie ever. (So much for Mr. Disney's "erred" judgment.)

In today's popular cultural environment, few American audiences would deny that filmmakers possess the potential to create transcendent works of artistic import and significance, and in hindsight the success of cinema's socially engineered shift from entertainment to art almost seems inevitable, a foregone conclusion. A less prestigious brand of popular culture, such as rock 'n roll music, may better emphasize the conflicts and contestation surrounding these kinds of transformations in cultural meaning-making. During its emergence in the 1950s cultural authorities vilified rock 'n roll, calling it juvenile, simplistic, and coarsely sexual, but in the last several decades rock critics and the remaining major record labels have worked tirelessly to increase its prestige as a respectable American art form, in part by relying on the same strategies as the Hollywood film industry and its institutional enablers. The National Academy of Recording Arts and Sciences annually honors rock artists with its Grammy Awards. Founded in 1983, the Rock and Roll Hall of Fame and Museum canonizes rock artists much in the same way that the American Film Institute attributes significance to Hollywood movies. (Inductees have ranged from Chuck Berry and Elvis Presley to more contemporary acts like U2, Madonna, Aerosmith, R.E.M., and Metallica.)

Rock magazines such as *Rolling Stone* and *Spin* also engage in canon formation by generating lists of classic CDs and singles; for example, in December 2003 *Rolling Stone* released its list of "The 500 Greatest Albums of All Time." Artists included in its top 10 included the Beatles (whose *Sgt. Pepper's Lonely Hearts Club Band* was honored with the coveted No. 1 spot on the list), the Beach Boys, Bob Dylan, Marvin Gaye, the Rolling Stones, and the Clash. College professors at Columbia and Northwestern University teach courses with titles such as "Issues in Rock Music and Rock Culture" and "Special Topics: The Music of Radiohead," while Liverpool Hope University now offers a Master of Arts degree in "The Beatles, Popular Music and Society" (Kozinn 2009). Academics and journalists organize scholarly conferences around the intellectual study of rock music as well. At the 2006 annual Pop Conference of the Experience Music Project in Seattle, participants presented papers that included these titles:

- "Gwen Stefani is the New Dracula and Beyoncé Makes a Great Ghost: The Shame of Appropriation and 'Passing' as Attributes to the Success of Gwen Stefani and Beyoncé Knowles"
- "10 Reasons Why the Monkees Should Be in the Rock and Roll Hall of Fame"
- "Boldly Gone: A Personal Trek into the Shameless, Sincere Music of Leonard Nimoy"
- "Swashbucklers of Agitproptic Burnbabydom: George Clinton and the Radical Poetics of P-Funk"
- "Take a Look at Me Now: Phil Collins and the Great Generational Divide"
- "Nickelback Appreciation Syndrome: How Shame Becomes Pride across the Racial Divide"
- "Is that Cultural Capital in Your Pocket, or Are You Just Glad to See Me?"

Finally, today's music critics lionize canonical rock albums by relying on the same critical terminology and intellectualizing discourse employed by contemporary film reviewers, as illustrated in the above examples. In his book *It Ain't No Sin to Be Glad You're Alive: The Promise of Bruce Springsteen,* Eric Alterman (1999), a columnist for the *Nation* as well as a professor of journalism and English, writes:

> *Born to Run* exploded in my home and my mind and changed my life, just as Elvis and the Beatles had done for Bruce a decade earlier. I never could have articulated it at the time, but *Born to Run* offered me an alternative context for my life, a narrative in which hopes and dreams that felt ridiculous were accorded dignity and, no less important, solidarity. . . . The poetry and power of *Born to Run* lie in its unwillingness to compromise, in the refusal of its protagonists to accept passively the hand dealt to them by circumstance. . . . The album's stories are internal monologues and dramatic renderings of Springsteen's own personal struggles with his parents, with authority, with

women, and with the expectations of the world, universalized and ennobled through the language of the radio. . . . It is an album about the unsung heroism of everyday life, the quiet glory of unflinching personal integrity in a world where virtue is deemed to be its own reward. (pp. 73—76)

Note the language Alterman employs to characterize *Born to Run,* Springsteen's celebrated 1975 album: he emphasizes its "narrative," "poetry and power," and "internal monologues and dramatic renderings," all "universalized and ennobled," just as if he were dissecting Fyodor Dostoyevsky's *Crime and Punishment* or William Faulkner's *The Sound and the Fury.* This artistic and literary characterization of rock among music journalists and critics, along with the formation of a classic rock canon, university courses and scholarly conferences, an endowed museum, and award-granting institutions, all shape the heightened meaning and artistic significance that American audiences today attach to rock 'n roll music.

However, unlike cinema, rock has had more than its fair share of dissenters and party-poopers, and not just among the psychiatrists and politicians' wives associated with the Parents' Music Resource Center of the 1980s culture wars. In *The Closing of the American Mind,* the renowned University of Chicago philosophy and classics professor Allan Bloom (1987) writes:

Though students do not have books, they most emphatically do have music. . . . This is the significance of rock music. I do not suggest that it has any high intellectual sources. But it has risen to its current heights in the education of the young on the ashes of classical music. . . . Ministering to and according with the arousing and cathartic music, the lyrics celebrate puppy love as well as polymorphous attractions, and fortify them against traditional ridicule and shame. . . . Picture a thirteen-year old boy sitting in the living room of his family home doing his math assignment while wearing his Walkman headphones or watching MTV. He enjoys the liberties hard won over centuries by the alliance of philosophic genius and political heroism, consecrated by the blood of martyrs; he is provided with comfort and leisure by the most productive economy ever known to mankind; science has penetrated the secrets of nature in order to provide him with the marvelous, lifelike electronic sound and image reproduction he is enjoying. And in what does progress culminate? A pubescent child whose body throbs with orgasmic rhythms; whose feelings are made articulate in hymns to the joys of onanism or the killing of parents; whose ambition is to win fame and wealth in imitating the drag-queen who makes the music. In short, life is made into a nonstop, commercially prepackaged masturbational fantasy. . . . People of future civilizations will wonder at this and find it as incomprehensible as we do the caste system, witch-burning, harems, cannibalism and gladiatorial combats. (pp. 68—75)

Bloom's vitriol betrays a wide generational gap as well as his inability to code-switch between classical and pop music worlds. But while he launches his attack on the significance of rock from outside its cultural universe, plenty of rock musicians *themselves* fight against the emergent production of prestige surrounding popular music as well, arguing that attempts to fabricate its critical and canonical "legitimacy" deprives rock of its rebelliousness and subcultural cool. British rock vocalist and guitarist Elvis Costello has been quoted as asserting that "writing about music is like dancing about architecture—it's a really stupid thing to want to do." And in February 2006, the surviving members of the 1970s punk band the Sex Pistols reacted to their upcoming induction into the Rock and Roll Hall of Fame by posting the following announcement (replete with grammatical and spelling errors) on their Web site, explaining their refusal to attend the induction ceremony at New York's Waldorf-Astoria Hotel:

> Next to the SEX PISTOLS rock and roll and that hall of fame is a piss stain. Your museum. Urine in wine. Were not coming. Were not your monkey and So what? Fame at $25,000 if we paid for a table, or $15000 to squeak up in the gallery, goes to a non-profit organisation selling us a load of old famous. Congradulations. If you voted for us, hope you noted your reasons. Your anonymous as judges, but your still music industry people. Were not coming. Your not paying attention. Outside the shit-stem is a real SEX PISTOL.

By refusing to donate thousands of dollars for a table at the black-tie event, the Sex Pistols railed at what many consumers recognize as the worst excesses of the rock music industry: the prohibitive cost of stadium and arena concerts, the endless celebration of passé or otherwise forgotten musicians, the commoditization of beloved rock songs, and, most of all, the lack of rabble-rousing authenticity among millionaire rock stars.

Popular Culture and the Search for Authenticity

Perhaps no other desire motivates consumers of contemporary popular culture more than the search for authenticity. In recent years reality television has proliferated not only because it is very inexpensive to produce (as we discussed in Chapter 6) but also for its

The note from the Sex Pistols declining to attend the ceremony inducting them into the Rock and Roll Hall of Fame.

brazen attempts to capture "ordinary" people in unscripted moments of everyday life, warts and all (Grindstaff 2002). African American hip-hop music artists sell millions of CDs on the basis of their ability to "keep it real" by remaining "true" to "the street," even when they hail from middle-class suburbs (McLeod 1999). Television news anchors and on-air media personalities go so far as to downgrade their résumés for fear of seeming inauthentic and insufficiently populist. On Fox News, cable TV host Bill O'Reilly has asserted that "I understand working-class Americans. I'm as lower-middle-class as they come," even though he hails from the decidedly well-off neighborhood of Westbury, Long Island, and earned advanced degrees from Harvard and Boston University without financial aid (Murphy 2002).

Since the onslaught of the Industrial Revolution in the nineteenth century, the search for authenticity has been a middle-class reaction to the soulless-ness of monopoly capitalism and the ravaging of the countryside, whether as expressed by Karl Marx's critique of alienated labor or Walt Whitman's and Henry David Thoreau's pastoral odes to the natural landscape. Today, as contemporary media and popular culture grow evermore processed and manufactured, many consumers place increasing value on those things that appear less prone to manipulation and thus more authentic. For instance, in our postmodern age of high-tech frivolity—as exemplified by the proliferation of Botox and online shopping malls, Big Macs and iMacs, email scams and edge cities, Hollywood artifice and boy-band pop, MySpace and virtual reality—consumers nostalgically seek out the authenticity suggested by symbols of agrarian simplicity (organic beets, world music) or the gritty charms of proletarian life (Pabst Blue Ribbon beer, trucker hats).

Authenticity can refer to a variety of desirable traits: credibility, original-ity, sincerity, naturalness, genuineness, innateness, purity, or realness. Like a badge of honor, authenticity connotes legitimacy and social value, but like honor itself it is also a social construct with moral overtones rather than an objective and value-free appraisal. Given its socially constructed and thus elusive nature, authenticity *itself* can never be authentic but must always be performed, staged, fabricated, crafted, or otherwise imagined (MacCannell 1976; Peterson 1997; Fine 2003; Grazian 2003). The performance of authentic-ity always requires a close conformity to the expectations set by the cultural context in which it is situated. For instance, in American politics authenticity is marked by straight talk, plain speech, and working-class cultural sensibilities, whereas foodies evaluate the authenticity of ethnic cuisine according to its closeness to national, local, or regional sources of tradition (Lu and Fine 1995; Johnston and Baumann 2007).

Consumers attribute authenticity to cultural objects and symbols as a means of creating distinction, status, prestige, or value; it is therefore ironic that authenticity is so often associated with hardship and disadvantage. Collectors assign legitimacy to the childlike artwork of uneducated, self-taught artists on the basis of its unmediated purity, its expression of the wild but innocent creativity of an unrefined mind (Fine 2003). Music fans and ethnomusicologists romanticize the Mississippi Delta blues melodies of poor sharecroppers as rural expressions of African American primitivism and Anglo-Saxon folk ballads for their association with working-class country living (Roy 2002). For similar reasons, international tourists and consumers delight in their purchases of indigenous crafts handmade in developing countries such as Thailand and Costa Rica (Wherry 2008).

While these examples illustrate how the search for authenticity can serve as an exercise in snobbery or condescension, other cases reveal how consumers and cultural authorities can establish distinction through a more democratizing discourse of authenticity attribution. Gourmet food writers, cooks, and diners alike validate ingredients, recipes, and dishes as authentic by associating them with a particular geographic region, whether in the case of Tuscan wild boar stew, Vietnamese beef wraps, Maryland crab cakes, or Nashville hot chicken. (The specificity of place also serves as a marker of authenticity among consumers of globally popular music from Punjabi bhangra to Jamaican reggae.) Other consumers legitimate food as authentic by emphasizing the rustic quality of homegrown or organic produce—heirloom tomatoes, handpicked cilantro, shaved truffles—or else the modesty of handmade dishes such as black beans and rice, or mint cucumber salad (Johnston and Baumann 2007).

Considering their invented quality, attributions of authenticity must often be passionately defended if they are to masquerade as actual facts, occasionally to ridiculous ends. Many locals insist that a truly authentic Philadelphia cheesesteak must be prepared with one of three kinds of cheese—American, provolone, or Cheez Whiz, even though the latter is perhaps the most artificial and synthetic of all foodstuffs, invented in a laboratory in 1952 (two decades after the introduction of the "original" Philly cheesesteak), and in Canada, no less. (When in 2003 U.S. presidential hopeful John Kerry accidentally ordered a cheesesteak in South Philadelphia with Swiss cheese, local reporters suggested that it may have marked the "unraveling" of his campaign.) Food companies liberally draw on ideologies surrounding authenticity to euphemize the use of flavor additives and extracts as "natural flavors" (Schlosser 2002). Meanwhile, national supermarket chains such as Whole Foods market their most highly processed foods from frozen burritos and pizzas to TV dinners as "organic" as if such dishes were grown on small family farms rather than manufactured in industrial laboratories and packing plants (Pollan 2006).

Given that the authentic experiences American consumers value are inevitably rooted in stereotypical and fanciful images of reality rather than the messiness (and sometimes unpleasantness) of everyday life as it is actually lived, the search for authenticity can prove to be a risky balancing act. After all, few contemporary home buyers on the market for a "historically preserved" nineteenth-century Victorian carriage house are likely to desire one lacking indoor toilets. American diners at ethnic restaurants may crave exotic dishes from faraway lands, but not those foods so far removed from their customary palates that they deem them inedible, such as Swiss horsemeat, or Malaysian webbed duck feet, or *bosintang*, a Korean soup prepared with dog meat. In fact, the representation of cultural authenticity in dining and other entertainment

Tenry Johns Blues Band with Claudette playing at Blue Chicago, one of the Windy City's most popular downtown blues venues. Why do blues clubs in Chicago almost exclusively hire African American bandleaders?

settings almost always relies on a somewhat imaginary and aesthetically pleasing simulation of reality. In mainstream Chinese restaurants in the United States, dishes like Mongolian Beef are prepared with lots of sugar to appeal to American tastes; soup is served as an appetizer course rather than at the end of the meal (as it would be in China); and traditional Chinese dishes such as beef tripe, ox's tail, and pig's tongue are excluded from most menus (Lu and Fine 1995). Feigning authenticity, Mexican restaurants in the United States serve tortilla chips before the meal and burritos as a main course—not because traditional Mexican folkways demand it (they do not), but because Anglo customers do (Gaytan 2008, pp. 325–26).

Within the media and culture industries, the production of popular music relies on similarly strategic methods of representing authenticity. In the early era of country-western music, record companies portrayed their actual artists as authentic old-timers, hillbillies, and cowboys (Peterson 1997). Contemporary recording labels rely on racially charged stock characters to market their rap and hip-hop acts as gang-bangers, street thugs, pimps, convicted felons, ex-cons, and drug users. Pop bands take their fashion cues from once-underground punk and skateboarding scenes in order to camouflage themselves in the symbolic authenticity of alienated youth and independent rock. In spite of the popular success of talented white blues artists such as Eric Clapton, Stevie Ray Vaughan, and the Allman Brothers Band, blues club owners in Chicago almost exclusively hire African American bandleaders for profitable weekend gigs in response to audience demand for the authenticity that affluent white consumers usually attribute to black blues performers (Grazian 2003). According to one local guitarist:

> It's because white audiences and owners are ignorant. The owners know that tourists will ask at the door, "Well, is the band playing tonight a *black* band, or is it a *white* band?" Because the tourists only want to hear black bands, because they want to see an authentic Chicago blues band, and they think a black band is more *real*, more *authentic*. When they come to Chicago, it's like they want to go to the "Disneyland of the Blues." You know, it's like this: people want German cars, French chefs, and well, they want their bluesmen black. It's a designer label. (quoted in Grazian 2003, p. 36)

Adventures in the Quest for Meaning in Popular Culture

While the search for authenticity among consumers has perhaps never been stronger, others embrace an alternative set of pop cultural pursuits that devalue, deconstruct, or otherwise challenge such explorations as tradition-bound, humorless, or else pretentious. For example, in the quest for meaning in popular culture, many postmodern consumers seek out exemplars of *hybridity* in which otherwise disparate cultures are melded together in a self-conscious manner to generate new possibilities for creative expression. In many ways the entire history of American popular music in the twentieth century was marked by attempts at synthesis and fusion. Blues and jazz developed as a mélange of African and European musical traditions, while early rock 'n roll pioneers developed the genre by blending together urban blues with country music. Such experiments in hybridity are also evident in Bob Dylan's mid-1960s development of electric folk-rock (which signaled his supposed *lack* of authenticity among more traditional folk music adherents, including the aforementioned Pete Seeger); Miles Davis's forays into free jazz, funk, and psychedelic rock on albums like *Bitches Brew* and *On the Corner*; the appropriation of classical music techniques in 1970s and 1980s progressive rock and heavy metal; and the emergence of rap rock, an amalgam of punk, hard rock, and hip-hop music exemplified by 1980s and 1990s acts such as the Beastie Boys, the Red Hot Chili Peppers, and Rage Against the Machine. (Meanwhile, the rap-rock artist Kid Rock manages to unite rap with heavy metal, rhythm and blues, and country music.)

Like the pursuit of authenticity, adventures in cultural hybridity are popular among foodies, as evidenced by the pervasiveness of global fusion cooking in fine-dining establishments worldwide. In New York, San Francisco, Chicago, and other cosmopolitan cities, three- and four-star restaurants prepare fashionable exemplars of hybrid cuisine that combine French cooking with a mixture of ingredients from Japan, Italy, Cuba, Mexico, and Morocco, among other locales.

The Village People performing in 1979.

In downtown Philadelphia restaurants, fusion dishes include seared Kobe beef carpaccio, truffle-scented edamame ravioli, and chocolate mousse with fresh grated wasabi (Grazian 2003, p. 233). By playfully combining culinary traditions common to regional cuisines, chefs and dining patrons alike reject the social construction of authenticity in favor of global fusion.

If the pursuit of hybridity represents a challenge to tradition, adventures in *irony* reject authenticity performances for their often humorless pretentions, as cultural creators and consumers playfully mock what they regard as the self-importance of such displays. Since the early 1990s it has become fashionable for indie rock bands to rerecord pop hits as ironic jokes, as faithless covers that satirize rather than emulate the typically overwrought tone of their original versions. (Examples include Dinosaur Jr.'s 1990 cover of the Cure's "Just Like Heaven," Cake's 1996 rerecording of Gloria Gaynor's "I Will Survive," and Fountains of Wayne's 1999 remake of Britney Spears's ". . . Baby One More Time.") Similarly, as discussed in earlier chapters, disc jockeys and recording renegades have built a cottage industry out of mash-ups, typically unauthorized remixes that combine the vocals from one recording with the instrumental track from another; the resultant cacophony serves a satirizing function by announcing itself as a kind of anti-authentic performance. Examples include Destiny's Child singing "Bootylicious" over Nirvana's grunge-rock anthem "Smells Like Teen Spirit," and Christina Aguilera's "Genie in a Bottle" laid over the rock guitar tracks of the Strokes' "Hard to Explain."

Similarly, the ironic embrace of kitsch, or *camp*, has long remained a staple of pop cultural consumption, especially among gay and lesbian audiences. Colorful examples from the world of gay camp include drag queens and drag kings; the bizarre films of John Waters and Russ Meyer; the revival of hopelessly dated 1970s and 1980s hairstyles, dances, television shows, and other fads and fashions; and the disco group the Village People, whose hits include "Macho Man," "In the Navy," and, most famously, "Y.M.C.A."

More mainstream iterations of camp abound as well. Tribute bands (or "mock stars") such as Strutter (KISS), Bjorn Again (ABBA), Planet Earth (Duran Duran), and Paradise City (Guns 'N Roses) call attention to the stylized artifice and ostentatious theatricality of pop music and celebrity culture (Klosterman 2004)—as do the dead-on song parodies and music videos of Weird Al Yankovic, who has sold more than 12 million albums, more than any other comedy act ever. Meanwhile, cult movies with demonstrable camp appeal among winking audiences include *The Rocky Horror Picture Show* (1975), a low-budget musical parody that today boasts the longest theatrical run in motion picture history, and *Showgirls* (1995), a box-office bomb that went on to gross over $100 million in the video rental market. Even certifiably awful films and other pop cultural duds can entertain audiences, and in doing so can be made meaningful, and even significant.

What do shopping centers such as the Mall of America tell us about the centrality of cultural consumption in everyday life?

scenes
from a mall

CULTURAL CONSUMPTION
AND STYLE IN EVERYDAY LIFE

AT 4.2 MILLION SQUARE FEET, THE MALL OF AMERICA IN BLOOMING-ton, Minnesota, is a pop cultural marvel by any measure. The Mall attracts 40 million visitors a year; it boasts 520 stores, an indoor NASCAR motor speedway, and a four-story LEGO Imagination Center. Its Nickelodeon Universe, where kids can meet Dora the Explorer, Diego, SpongeBob SquarePants, and the Backyardigans, is a seven-acre theme park that features over 27 rides, including five roller coasters. If that is not enough, there is also an A.C.E.S. Flight Simulation, an Underwater Adventures Aquarium stocked with 4,500 sharks and other sea creatures, a Moose Mountain 18-hole miniature golf course, and a 14-screen multiplex movie theater. The Mall's themed restaurants, which include Famous Dave's BBQ, Rainforest Café, Ruby Tuesday, Johnny Rockets, and Hooters, are as well known as its four anchors: Bloomingdale's, Macy's, Nordstrom's, and Sears.

There are few places quite like the Mall of America, but its uniqueness in the American cultural landscape is only a matter of degree rather than kind. There are 28,500 malls in North America, and almost all of them rely on similar formulas to generate the most profitable mix of retail, dining, entertainment, and services (Crawford 1992, p. 7). Their flashy designs, bright lights, and abundant variety draw shoppers from many walks of life, and their relative cleanliness and safety make them attractive to senior citizens as well as families with small children. Mega-suburban malls serve as virtual downtowns for residents living on the periphery of metropolitan centers, while shopping plazas and their food courts have colonized urban downtowns themselves, replacing the sidewalk streetscapes of the city with gold-trimmed glass towers that offer indoor access to parking, public transportation, office space, hotel rooms, and in some cases even high-priced residences. This configuration is especially prominent in Asia, home to eight of the ten largest shopping malls in the world. (The most capacious is the South China Mall in Dongguan, China, which features over 1,500 stores and 7.1 million square feet of leasable retail space.) In *The Global Soul*, travel writer Pico Iyer (2001) describes the inclusiveness of a mall complex in Hong Kong:

> We could order room service, I was told, from a hotel with 565 rooms next door, or from one with 604 rooms next to it; we could order food from the other hotel in the complex, which had 512 rooms. . . . Beneath us, in the area known as Admiralty, were the trappings of the new Empire—a four-story shopping mall (called simply—definitely—the Mall), where shiny signs pointed towards the Atrium, The United Center, One Pacific Place and Two. "The thing about this place," Richard said to me as I slipped in and out of time zones, "is that you've got a miniairport on the ground floor, where

you can check in for all Cathay flights. There's a Seibu department store on Level Two, where you can buy everything you want. My bank's next to the elevator, and the Immigration Office is next to my office. You never really have to leave the building."

There were four cinemas in the Mall where we were sleeping, more than twenty places in which to eat, and fully ninety-seven boutiques (Gucci, Guess, Valentino, Vuitton; Boss, Hugo Boss, the Armani Exchange). There was access to the MTR subway, to the Far East Finance Center, and to a car park. There were the great department stores of Britain, Hong Kong, and Japan. "A world of delights," as the literature announced, "under one roof." (pp. 81–82, 85)

The proliferation of highly stylized and all-inclusive shopping malls both in the United States and abroad highlights two recent shifts in the organization of social life in the contemporary world. The rapid growth of malls, along with the rise of retail outlets within an array of public spaces from museums to zoos to airports, illustrates the *centrality of cultural consumption in everyday life*. At the same time, the ubiquity of shopping malls and their creative architectural forms and designer brands points to an even more consequential social development, *the rise of aesthetics and the triumph of style*, especially given how in the past few decades the most mundane aspects of our everyday lives have become extraordinarily design-intensive, from our detergent bottles and toothbrushes to the offices where we work. In this chapter we will explore the rise of theatricality and style in popular culture and everyday life and the accompanying growth in landscapes of cultural consumption, with an emphasis on spaces of high-end retail and entertainment. After describing this brave new cultural terrain, we will examine exactly how such landscapes of consumption are staged in order to produce the experience of pleasure, or at least its illusion. We will conclude with an accounting of the human costs of creating and sustaining these landscapes, as well as what happens to society as a whole when style conquers all, even substance itself.

The Triumph of Style in Everyday Life

The second its opening scene floods the screen, Floria Sigismondi's vision as a director is unmistakable. A lithe blonde model awakens in a room bathed in blue light, stretches next to her white cat as the sun rises behind her, and stows away her Murphy bed, revealing a wall of blue packages of bathroom tissue stacked up like Andy Warhol's famous silkscreen paintings of Campbell's soup cans. Dancing to Devo's 1981 song "Beautiful World," she enters the washroom and pulls back the mirrors of the medicine cabinet to reveal perfect stacks of blue boxes containing bars of soap, while across the corridor, another blonde model slides open an illuminated closet filled with nothing but translucent bottles of peppermint mouthwash. Sigismondi's Pop Art world is one of modernist furniture, chrome baby strollers, and turquoise parking meters, but it is not a movie. It isn't even a music video, although she has directed videos for Marilyn Manson, Tricky, Fiona Apple, Christina Aguilera, Interpol, David Bowie, the White Stripes,

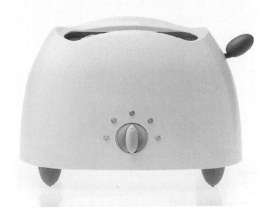

A toaster designed by Michael Graves.

and the Raconteurs. It is a television commercial, for Target; it features cross-promotional appearances by Charmin Ultra, Zest, Scope, Windex, and Pampers (all in blue packaging); and it is gorgeous.

Our postmodern age is marked by the triumph of style and the proliferation of aesthetics in everyday life. *Aesthetics* refers to how we communicate and express through the senses, through sight and sound, taste and touch. The sensations produced through aesthetics are immediate and emotional, much like the arousal we experience from beauty or sexual attraction. We also react strongly to novelty and humor in design, and the excitement of aesthetic change, which explains the success of business strategies like planned obsolescence (as we discussed in Chapter 3), in which the introduction of freshly redesigned products, such as automobiles, women's shoes, blue jeans, handbags, and other fashionable commodities, generates sales while devaluing last season's styles. It also explains why people associate ultra-new design (or refurbished vintage fashion) with high status; as *Atlantic* columnist Virginia Postrel (2004) argues in *The Substance of Style,* "sensory pleasure works to commercial and personal advantage because aesthetics has intrinsic value" (p. 75). Of course, this does not necessarily mean that there are universal standards of aesthetic beauty or attractiveness—radical differences in fashion and music throughout history and among world civilizations clearly deny the existence of such agreed-upon standards—only that within any given social or cultural context, style *matters*.

At the same time, our global and technological age provides opportunities for the individual expression and consumption of popular style unavailable at any other time in human history. Once upon a time, everyday fashionable attire was enjoyed only by royalty and the aristocracy, whereas today almost anyone can afford inexpensive yet durable clothing in a brilliant range of bold colors, styles, fabrics, and textures. Digital word processing allows writers to compose in virtually any typeface that graphic designers can imagine, while personalized ringtones allow cell phone users to have their calls announced by wind chimes, or aliens, or Justin Timberlake's singing, or anything else. Crate and Barrel and Pottery Barn bring high-concept design to the middle classes, and thanks to Target and IKEA, even *low*-end home furnishings come in a variety of fabulous styles from modernist to funky.

These last examples illustrate the way playful style has triumphed even in the most mundane areas of everyday life. The architect Michael Graves designs toasters and blenders for Target. OXO sells models of its kitchen tools ranging from tongs to vegetable peelers to measuring cups manufactured with sculpted nylon and polished plastic for extra comfort, handling, and a streamlined look.

Dyson vacuum cleaners are noted for their design and have been exhibited in museums in New York, London, Paris, Sydney, and Zurich. Television commercials selling the most boring of products—toilet paper, window cleaner, bar soap— rely on the same innovative filming and editing techniques used in music video production. Today's cutting-edge commercials also feature indie rock songs and retro-pop classics that may not otherwise get played on MTV—"Signal in the Sky" by the Apples in Stereo (for the Samsung Instinct), "New Slang" by the Shins (for McDonald's), "Mr. Blue Sky" by the Electric Light Orchestra (for the Volkswagen Beetle), "I'm Not Like Everybody Else" by the Kinks (for IBM).

The everyday environments in which we ensconce ourselves are similarly design-intensive. Starbucks does not necessarily owe its success to the superiority of its coffee (which McDonald's has beaten in independent taste tests) as much as it depends on what Postrel (2004) calls its "multisensory aesthetic experience"; as she explains, "the company employs scores of designers to keep its stores' 'design language'—color palettes, upholstery textures, light fixtures, brochure paper, graphic motifs—fresh and distinctive" (p. 20). In a variety of industries, particularly in the areas of media and cultural production, interior office spaces are designed to precise specifications to heighten the functionality of the work environment as well as project a desirable aesthetic image to the public. Hollywood talent agencies emphasize sleekness and a minimalist orderliness in their workspaces (Zafirau 2008, p. 111), whereas the offices of Internet development companies and advertising agencies often rely on a more youthful look that emphasizes bright colors and features skateboarding or biking ramps, as well as areas that encourage creative play. As for urban residences, the most coveted interior designs mimic that of industrial loft conversions, with exposed piping and brickwork, hardwood floors, and high timber ceilings.

Finally, no matter how one finds their coffee, the Starbucks example illustrates the heightening of aesthetic standards in everyday eating and drinking. Among middle-class Americans, lattes and cappuccinos are enjoyed as frequently as drip coffee, while scones and almond croissants have replaced cheese and cherry Danish. Grilled panini sandwiches and rosemary-and-olive flatbreads compete with hoagies and pizza; Italian prosciutto is the new bologna; arugula and mixed baby greens have replaced wedges of iceberg lettuce; and sushi rolls are today's on-the-go snacks. Nor is this a matter of taste simply becoming upscale—witness the explosive popularity of Krispy Kreme glazed doughnuts. As best illustrated by the pop art commercials produced for discount chain stores like Target, the recent rise of aesthetics and the triumph of style have been surprisingly democratic.

Landscapes of Cultural Consumption

The rise of quirky art installations in American cities illustrates the extent to which popular culture and whimsical style have invaded even the most public spaces of everyday life. In front of the Philadelphia Museum of Art stands a much-photographed statue of Rocky Balboa, the fictitious boxer played by Sylvester Stallone in *Rocky* and its many sequels. Behind Philadelphia's dignified City Hall,

What is the strategy behind creating new urban entertainment districts such as Chicago's Navy Pier?

Thomas Paine Plaza features giant-size steel and fiberglass reproductions of Monopoly board pieces (specifically the hat, wheelbarrow, and iron), chessmen, dominoes, and bingo card markers, while around the corner stands Claes Olden-burg's 45-foot, 10-ton replica of a clothespin. In 1999 the streets of Chicago were invaded by 300 life-size fiberglass cows, each painted by a different local artist, architect, photographer, or designer: the bovine collection included "Incowgnito," painted in black-and-white zebra stripes; a cubist "Pi-COW-so" designed as a parody of a Picasso painting; and "Cowch Potato" featuring a black-spotted cow lazing on a sofa, bottles of milk at her side. Today, Chicago's Millennium Park features Cloud Gate, a three-story, 110-ton steel sculpture shaped like a giant kidney bean, and the Crown Fountain, which features two 50-foot transparent glass-brick towers that project LED video images of the faces of ordinary local residents, a thousand people in all.

The last decades of the twentieth century marked a tremendous shift in the organization of urban life, particularly as cities formerly known for industrial manufacturing like Chicago and Philadelphia were transformed into centers of retail, entertainment, tourism, and leisure. Downtown areas and their public spaces strongly reflect the urban renaissance experienced by many American cities during the 1990s, as illustrated by the rise of flagship stores, gaming arcades, multiplex theatres, and tourist attractions. The new urban landscape evokes a notable overindulgence in branding among franchised outposts—Nike, Polo, Toys 'R' Us, Dave & Buster's, Kenneth Cole, Foot Locker, Old Navy, Williams-Sonoma. (In fact, many such outposts do little more than celebrate trademarked popular culture itself—ESPN Zone, Coyote Ugly, the Bubba Gump Shrimp Company.)

These sites of popular cultural consumption often are clustered in *urban entertainment districts* developed as part of a larger strategy of city growth and renewal (Hannigan 1998). The revitalization of once decrepit ports represents a major effort to sanitize the American city of its blue-collar past by replacing its now-defunct shipbuilding, fishing, and transport industries with shopping malls and museums that romanticize the backbreaking labor of dockworkers, longshoremen, and lobstermen. Baltimore's Inner Harbor today features Oriole Park at Camden Yards, the National Aquarium, the American Visionary Art Museum, and shopping and dining at Harborplace and the Gallery (which, like the Mall of America, includes Johnny Rockets and Hooters, each offering their own particular brand of nostalgia). Chicago's Navy Pier features the Chicago Shakespeare Theater, Chicago Children's Museum, a Build-a-Bear Workshop, a 150-foot-high Ferris wheel, an IMAX Theater, the Bud Light Stage and Pepsi Skyline Stage, and a life-size statue of Dr. Robert Hartley, the psychologist played by TV comedian Bob Newhart on *The Bob Newhart Show* in the 1970s. As a tourist attraction, New York's South Street Seaport relies on refurbished architectural and exterior aesthetic details (cobblestones, brickwork, lampposts, wagons) to present itself as a living testament to its former nineteenth-century self, although once inside, the Seaport resembles almost any other shopping mall: its tenants include Abercrombie & Fitch, Ann Taylor, Coach, The Gap, Express, Aerosoles, J. Crew, Sunglass Hut, Talbots, The Body Shop, and Victoria's Secret (Boyer 1992).

The rise of urban entertainment districts reflects how cities and regions attempt to position themselves favorably within the global tourism economy. This often requires locales to market themselves in ways that emphasize their singularity and thus attractiveness in the public imagination as places of authenticity and prestige (Grazian 2003). Memphis promotes itself on the basis of its music legacy, which draws tourists to the former recording studios of Sun Records and Stax Records, Elvis Presley's Graceland estate, and the blues clubs that line the city's famous Beale Street. Nashville similarly draws on its pop cultural heritage as the nation's capital of country music production to attract tourists and their dollars—they flock to the Country Music Hall of Fame Museum, the record companies along Music Row, the Grand Ole Opry and the Ryman Auditorium, the CMA Music Festival Fan Fair, and rowdy honky-tonks like Tootsie's Orchid Lounge. Even post-Hurricane Katrina, New Orleans still draws visitors to its raucous Bourbon Street, Mardi Gras parades, and annual springtime Jazz and Heritage Festival.

Amid this consumerist landscape in cities across the globe lurks the spectacle of the new urban nightlife, a bonanza of gentrified entertainment zones, velvet-roped nightclubs, and high-concept restaurants. These places tend to be highly stylized, demonstrating a concern with aesthetic imagery and playful design, and the restaurants of Philadelphia's emergent nightlife scene provide an excellent case study. The Old City section of downtown Philadelphia features a set of commercial blocks lined with hip restaurants and nightclubs with alluring names like Glam, Bleu Martini, and Swanky Bubbles. At the intersection of Second and Market Streets sits the neighborhood's crown jewel, the Continental Restaurant and Martini Bar, its interior lit by halogen lamps shaped like giant Spanish olives. At Continental, attractive female servers present guests with fusion dishes splashed with curry, lime, coconut, and soy, and a limitless array of designer cocktails, including the White Chocolate Martini sprinkled with white crème de cacao and a Hershey's Kiss, and the Dean Martini served with a Lucky Strikes cigarette and matchbook (Grazian 2008b, p. 11).

A few blocks away at Buddakan, an extravagantly ornamented Pan-Asian restaurant, a foreboding 16-foot gilded statue of the great Buddha himself overlooks all patrons, emphasizing the relationship between decadent gastronomy and dramatic style in the postmodern global city. At Tangerine, a fashionable French-Moroccan restaurant and cocktail lounge, diners enter a candlelit Mediterranean dreamscape adorned with red fabrics and pillows, each room draped with velvet curtains, providing pleasure seekers with their very own Arabian nights. Patrons gush over North African-inspired selections that include king salmon poached in olive oil and served with potato tortelloni and hazelnut-basil mousse, and chicken tagine, a Moroccan stew prepared with green olives and preserved lemons (p. 1). Elsewhere in Philadelphia's Old City, restaurants prepare fashionable exemplars of hybrid cuisine and cosmopolitan chic, whether lobster empanadas and fried plantains at Cuba Libre Restaurant and Rum Bar, or tobiko-crusted scallops with spinach risotto and lemongrass sauce at the appropriately named World Fusion (pp. 11–12).

Many of Philadelphia's most glamorous restaurants evoke a theatrical spectacle of global cosmopolitanism and myth. Morimoto features a cavernous dining room that beckons all comers like an ethereal banquet hall, a palace of dreams. Named for its executive chef and part-owner Masaharu Morimoto—better known as one of the culinary stars of cable television's *Iron Chef*—the most renowned Japanese restaurant in the city is bathed in light, from its 3-D lenticular hologram that greets patrons at the door to the sprightly lit dining booths that turn various shades of Technicolor neon as the evening progresses (Grazian 2005). Conceived by industrial designer Karim Rashid, the interior décor features a rolling ceiling of compressed bamboo rods: a larger-than-life-sized sushi mat built from 70 tons of wood (Quinn 2002). Across town at Pod, a pan-Asian hideaway near the University of Pennsylvania campus, the space-age interior evokes the futuristic chill of Stanley Kubrick's *2001: A Space Odyssey* and *A Clockwork Orange*. Mechanized conveyor belts transport sashimi and spring rolls around the bar while customers fiddle with the fluorescent lights in their groovy booths that recall the Orgasmatron from Woody Allen's *Sleeper*.

The many allusions to pop culture, cinema, and the theater in these nightlife spaces are not accidental. A former nightclub owner and concert promoter, *Bon Appétit* magazine's 2005 Restaurateur of the Year Stephen Starr—the creator of Continental, Buddakan, Tangerine, Morimoto, and Pod—specializes in branding high-concept dining as a theatrical event to be enjoyed as a total experience, a heady concoction of sight and sound, buzz and light. In this regard, he is as much a showman and entertainer as a businessperson: in fact, he refers to his dining customers as his "audience." As he told *Philadelphia* magazine, "I want people to feel like they're not in Philadelphia or near their home . . . when they come to one of my places. Let's face it—life is pretty mundane, for you, for me, or Cindy Crawford. So I want their night out to feel like they're getting away. I'm selling the experience" (Platt 2000). Built as elaborate stage sets, each of Starr's stylized restaurants conjures up an imaginative fantasy world of trendy eclecticism and exotic delight.

Morimoto, a Japanese restaurant in downtown Philadelphia, emphasizes theatricality and imaginative style.

For young consumers, these kinds of urban restaurants and cocktail lounges evoke particularly fantastic images from the mediated world of popular culture, especially MTV reality shows like *The Hills* and *The City*, and the HBO hit *Sex and the City*. When Indrajit, a 19-year-old University of Pennsylvania freshman from Gladstone, New Jersey, compares Alma de Cuba (another Starr restaurant in Philadelphia) to the imaginary universe presented as contemporary New York in *Sex and the City,* she reveals a wide-eyed sense of excitement common to many college-aged suburbanites upon discovering the extravagance of the new urban nightlife:

> I pushed open the heavy door and was at once overwhelmed by the scene. I really didn't think such places existed outside of Carrie Bradshaw's world in a glamorous New York, and even then, on a TV sitcom. The exhilarating beat of Spanish music, similar to the Gypsy Kings, boomed out of powerful surround-sound speakers and below the elevated bar area was a seating area sprinkled with white couches and coffee tables. Large black fans whirled overhead, and the mahogany and dark wood décor really gave the place an exotic feel. Alma de Cuba was packed. I half-expected to turn around and see the four females of the often-quoted show seated behind me. [My friend] Steven went off to the bathroom and told me to order him whatever I was having. I took a breath, told myself to be confident, that I didn't look like I belonged in middle school on this evening, and edged into the crowd surrounding the bar. . . . That half-hour at Alma de Cuba was the closest to the epitome of a real night out on the town that I'd ever experienced. Everyone looked so young, beautiful, carefree and fun; it was right out of a movie. I'm glad I savored the experience because it will be a very long time before I'm back. The whole scene was "fabulous," as my hero, Carrie Bradshaw, would say. (quoted in Grazian 2008b, pp. 231–32)

The Staging of Cultural Commerce

If Pod makes the diner feel enveloped by a Tokyo sci-fi dreamworld, then Cuba Libre Restaurant and Rum Bar evokes the sultry paradise of 1950s Havana and its beach resorts and sidewalk cafés—or at least the Havana longingly conjured up in nostalgic films like *The Godfather, Part II* and *Before Night Falls.* The dining mezzanine is designed as a tiled rooftop garden overlooking a faux outdoor streetscape, replete with hanging flora, stained-glass windows, iron railings, and terra-cotta balconies. Yet according to Danny Lake, a local publicist for various nightspots around Philadelphia, the cinematic metaphor is more than fitting to describe Cuba Libre. Its fabricated interior was constructed by a movie set designer and inspired by stock images of Cuba culled from various Web sites. As Lake explains in my book *On the Make: The Hustle of Urban Nightlife* (Grazian 2008b):

> Cuba Libre decided to build their brand to look like buildings in Cuba, to look old. And, you know, we had really serious issues. . . . Do we want to disclose how we made this brand look aged when it was brand-new? Because we used some interesting building materials: *Styrofoam.* The destination's built by a guy who owns a company called Dynamic Imagineering, and he builds movie sets. And it looks like a movie set (especially if you go back in, and now that I have told you that, you can see how it does), or like, I hate to use this word, but maybe like something you'd see in Disney—the street scene, the images, the crumbling planters, and the lush palms. . . . We went to salvage yards to find the wrought-iron gates that we had used for both the railings and part of the décor. And we did it this way because our research primarily on the Internet showed us images that looked just like this. (pp. 32—33)

It is no coincidence that Lake invokes the magic of Disney to describe Cuba Libre, because through its many famous themed environments (Magic Kingdom, Epcot's World Showcase, Disney's Hollywood Studios, Animal Kingdom, Celebration), the Disney Corporation has led the way in creating artificially produced entertainment landscapes that prioritize simulated realities over seemingly authentic experiences (Zukin 1991, 1995; Sorkin 1992). But while the Disneyfication of urban downtowns has characterized the development of themed restaurant chains such as the Rainforest Café, Planet Hollywood, and ESPN Zone (itself a Disney-owned franchise), the high-concept interiors of more exclusive restaurant and nightclub spaces like Morimoto and Cuba Libre are similarly shaped by the aesthetic theatricality of the stage and cinema. For example, among dominant design elements, complicated lighting schemes make up perhaps the most significant décor component of urban nightlife establishments. According to Jason, a photographer who works on lighting effects for a variety of reality TV programs in addition to laboring as a server and bartender in numerous Philadelphia hotspots since 1988, nightlife venues employ lighting strategically to create shadow and aura rather than bright illumination. In many nightclubs, glowing light is emitted from underneath or within the bar fixtures themselves, rather than cast from directly overhead. In *On the Make,*

Jason observes that at Tangerine, one of his former bartending posts, "The most important thing is the lighting. . . . You can't see by it—it is just a visual pattern that you get, and that's what pretty much every place does with the lighting. You are not supposed to see by the lighting, but it adds flourishes, or highlights some architectural feature" (quoted in Grazian 2008b, pp. 35–36).

On the other hand, the muted lighting of nightclubs and restaurants also hides the weaknesses inherent in aesthetically pleasing designs featuring low-grade materials such as Styrofoam. As Jason explains, "The bars, when you see them with the lights on, they are nothing special. You are seeing behind the curtain at that point, because nobody is spending a lot of money on real quality construction or anything. . . . It's exactly like a movie set; so when you dim the lights, you are also hiding some of the flaws." According to Jason, flimsy construction materials are not the only imperfections that remain hidden in the dimmed glow of dance clubs and cocktail lounges:

> Well, you are hiding the flaws. That's why you don't do direct lighting in the first place. You don't want to show off flaws in the location *or the people who are there*. So bars are dark. You get an *impression* of someone; you don't get an actual look at someone. That's why anybody who has been at a bar when they turn the lights on has seen that it is not as pretty as it was ten minutes ago. . . . You do it for effect. (p. 36)

Of course, the so-called flaws of an unattractive clientele pale in comparison to the unsanitary conditions concealed behind the facades of Philadelphia's hottest restaurants and nightclubs. As a rule, restaurants try to keep the messy work of food preparation out of their patrons' line of sight, and even dining establishments with exhibition-style kitchens keep their dry-goods closets, staff locker rooms, roach spray, and mousetraps out of view—and much more, as it turns out. According to the Philadelphia Department of Health, in 2004 local restaurants and nightclubs that received health code violations included Alma de Cuba (fly infestation), Bleu Martini (mouse infestation and feces contamination), Pod (uncovered/unprotected food in walk-in refrigerators), and Continental (fly infestation, contaminated ice, excessive mold, and inadequate frequency of employee hand-washing).

Shopping mall retailers adopt similarly tactical staging and lighting techniques, including a strategy of *adjacent attraction* in which dissimilar objects are placed next to each other so consumers might identify them as parts of a whole (Crawford 1992, p. 14). At Urban Outfitters, old-school Atari 2600 video game machines and cheap couches are placed next to skateboarding shoes, retro bell-bottom jeans, bike-messenger shoulder bags, and snarky T-shirts, conjuring up a stage set of a super-hip teenager's room. Starbucks surrounds its packages of coffee beans with posters of the African landscape and other exotic climes. Borders and Barnes and Noble rely on espresso bars and plush armchairs to add an ambience of luxury and sophistication to their bookstores. In many ways, the book-lined walls themselves serve as little more than a backdrop for the main attraction: the

Why does the book industry refer to most of the books displayed in this Barnes and Noble as "wallpaper"?

best-sellers promoted on tables placed prominently at the front of their stores. As for the great majority of titles on display (of which most superstores sell fewer than two copies a year), the book industry disparagingly refers to the bulk of its merchandise as "wallpaper," as mere scenery (Miller 2007, p. 78).

Retail chains also use in-store music soundtracks to associate their merchandise with hi-fidelity style. Brooks Brothers plays elegant jazz ballads by Billie Holiday, Ella Fitzgerald, Dinah Washington, and Sarah Vaughan to give customers the feel of a cocktail soirée where their new blazers and ties will be the hit of the party. The Gap in-store playlist includes songs by Amy Winehouse, John Mayer, Sara Bareilles, and Feist. American Apparel has its own Internet radio station, Viva Radio, which provides all its in-house selections from indie rock to dance music. Of course, major corporate brands take adjacent attraction out of the store entirely, sponsoring hip-hop concerts (Sprite), BMX races (Red Bull), and the annual Lollapalooza music festival (Budweiser, Vitamin Water, XM Satellite Radio, Dell).

Retailers additionally rely on an entire science of shopping and consumption that consultants like Paco Underhill have spent the last several years developing by drawing on intensive fieldwork and human observation in shopping environments all over the world. In his eye-opening book *Why We Buy,* Underhill (2009) reveals how malls and other retail spaces can be engineered to deliver their optimum purchasing potential. It begins outside the store itself, where retailers hope to attract passersby. Pedestrians typically move at a quick clip down the street, and in order to stop they must downshift to a lower speed, much like a car does. Once a customer enters a store, it takes them a few seconds to slow down and become fully acclimated to the lighting, temperature, and scale of its interior, which means that anything on display in the area that Underhill calls the "decompression zone" immediately inside the front door usually goes completely unnoticed by the consumer. Also, in part because Americans drive on the right side of the road, we almost always reflexively turn to the right when we enter a place of business. Retailers familiar with these behavioral patterns typically organize their shop floors accordingly by placing their most impor-tant merchandise, or at least those goods that require "100 percent shopper exposure" just beyond the decompression zone, on the right-hand side of the doorway (Underhill 2009, p. 80).

Underhill also observes that the longer customers spend shopping, the greater their chances of making a purchase. As a result, retailers rely on all sorts of tricks to increase the duration of time consumers spend in their stores. Supermarkets keep their dairy cases against the back wall, which forces consumers to walk past aisles of groceries and back again during even quick trips to the store for milk (p. 85). For the same reason, chain drugstores place their pharmacy counters toward the back area of their stores. In the interests of pulling (or trapping) con-sumers deeper into their cavernous spaces packed with merchandise, department stores often hide their restrooms in isolated corners, away from entrances and exits, and ascending and descending escalators are frequently kept at opposite ends of shopping mall corridors—all to ensure ever more foot traffic past yet another Banana Republic, another Burberry, another Jamba Juice.

The Hidden Costs of Cultural Consumption

Among the staging techniques designed to woo cultural consumers in shopping malls, restaurants, and nightclubs, none are nearly as problematic as those involving human labor. At retail stores like Abercrombie & Fitch, much of this work is handled backstage in stock rooms, sometimes until two o'clock in the morning. Clothing retailers usually invite consumers to fondle their tactile fabrics because when they interact with merchandise in a sensuous manner they are more likely to purchase it (Underhill 2009, p. 172). Consequently, store workers—typically young people in their teens or twenties—spend their days and often late nights painstakingly refolding, straightening, and stacking up brightly colored sweaters and T-shirts on easy-to-reach counters. Socio-logist Sharon Zukin (2004, p. 202) compares these irresistibly attractive piles of pink, violet, and crimson cashmere and cotton to "gumdrops in a candy store"— they are the product of excessive and tedious workloads performed largely by adolescents for little pay.

One strategy for easing the workload is to stack sweaters in darker shades on top of lighter ones, making it easier to mask their grubbiness after hours of customer abuse (Underhill 2009, p. 190.) Still, these notoriously unstable retail jobs require employees to stand on their feet for entire shifts, all for low-paying wages and limited work hours without benefits. In fact, most brand-name companies in the retail service sector pay only minimum wage or else slightly more (Klein 2002, p. 236). (As of July 24, 2009, the U.S. federal minimum wage was $7.25 per hour.) While Borders can afford to expand into new markets with its growing superstores, it cannot seem to pay its employees a livable income. Addressing this very issue in a 1997 letter to Borders workers, company president Richard L. Flanagan chided, "While the concept is romantically appealing . . . it ignores the practicalities and realities of our business environment" (p. 239). Similarly, during a period when Starbucks was both doubling its profits and opening 350 stores a year, in British Columbia the company actually *decreased* the wages of its new workers. According to a Starbucks employee Naomi Klein (2002) interviews in her book *No Logo,* "They expect us to look like a Gap ad, professional, clean and neat all the time, and I can't even pay to do laundry. . . . You can buy two grande mocha cappuccinos with my hourly salary" (p. 239).

This last remark—"They expect us to look like a Gap ad"—points to the peculiar nature of retail work. The youthful employees of branded companies like Urban Outfitters, Diesel, American Apparel, and Juicy Couture not only fold clothes and ring up packages: they are the embodied representatives of the brand itself. The clothier Abercrombie & Fitch requires its workers to adhere to the guidelines catalogued in its Look Book regarding personal appearance, and demotes employees who fail to live up to such standards. According to an exposé in the *Dallas Morning News,* "Employees: 'Hierarchy of hotness' rules at Abercrombie & Fitch":

There's no in between. You're either Abercrombie hot—or you're not.

Kristen Carmichael discovered she didn't fit the clothing store's self-described "sexy, effortless style" when she was pulled from a sales position on the floor of the North Park Center store and shoved back to the stockroom to fold clothes.

This was after they'd rated her face.

The college student who was in Dallas for the summer and her female co-worker had received a 0 ranking on a district manager's monthly audit. The report, posted on a wall in the office, included the question, "Do all female models currently working have beautiful faces?"

There were two choices, 0 and 5, with the higher number signifying an approval rating for the models—an Abercrombie & Fitch term for sales representatives. The same question for the male models had both 0 and 5 marked—a mix.

"It's so subjective how they judge you," said Ms. Carmichael, a 19-year-old brunette with sharp blue-green eyes and a trim, athletic build, who was told by one manager that she wasn't attractive enough to work on the floor.

Sales people function as the store's advertising and are handpicked by current employees, said Joshuah Welch, a 26-year-old Dallas resident, was hired two weeks ago as a manager and told to recruit people who walked into the store looking "all-American, clean, wholesome, or the girl or boy next door." He said stocking employees, on the other hand, are told not to speak to customers.

"It's a hierarchy of hotness," he said.

Cory Payne thought he reached the upper tier when he was recruited as a "model," or salesman, at the Dallas store. Then he found himself in the back storeroom. "It wasn't the job we signed up for," said the tall 22-year-old blond athlete. "We showed up on time and we felt we were being punished for being good employees."

A weekly "secret shopper" evaluation posted in the back room also focuses on appearance. Employees receive one point for a "yes" to the questions, "Was the person in the women's front room attractive?" and "Was the cashier attractive?"

These rating systems remain legal as long as they don't discriminate based on race or gender. (Meyers 2008)

Perhaps not surprisingly, the expectations of service personnel in nightlife settings are prefigured within commonplace ideals of beauty and sexual magnetism as well, particularly among women. According to Jason, the aforementioned bartender, "With women, as long as you are hot, that's the only requirement." Allison, a hostess and cocktail waitress at Tangerine, reports that female job applicants are often immediately flagged by the staff on the basis of their attractiveness and on-the-spot demeanor. "As a hired hostess, if someone fills out an application, we are permitted to write 'NRL' on the top—*Not Right Look*," she reveals. "They have to have the right look, everything from what you wear when you walk in to how you approach" (Grazian 2008b, p. 54). The mandatory uniforms worn by young cocktail waitresses at Tangerine emphasize their sexuality as well, even to the point of discomfort:

Abercrombie & Fitch has been accused of evaluating its young employees on the basis of their looks.

> We have tight, black, long-sleeved crewneck shirts. . . . You wear your own black skirt. It has to be a skirt, no pants. . . . At first, I just wore the short skirt like everyone else did, and opaque tights, and that was fine. In the lounge at Tangerine, the tables are really low, like, less than two feet off the ground. And it gets really busy, like standing-room only almost, and you have to fight to get through the crowds with your tray of these martini glasses. I mean, you don't want to spill all over everybody, so what you have to do is either bend over and wear shorts underneath your skirt or just squat like a catcher, put your drinks down, and then pick them back up. . . .

> One of my biggest issues is having to squat down and serve someone, and there are some people that really eat it up. Like they just know you are serving them and they are in love with it. . . . So at first I started with the short skirt, and then I didn't like the way that people would look at me and watch. . . . I would see guys leering . . . or guys would, you know . . . you see people looking at you and talking. And guys would try and talk to me. . . . They were always asking if I had a boyfriend, and then you are trying to remain professional and keep walking. . . . I switched to a skirt that went below my knees, and I made a lot less money. (quoted in Grazian 2008b, pp. 48—49)

As Allison's experience makes clear, worker-unfriendly dress codes often place heavy burdens on female service personnel by pigeonholing them into sexualized roles that invite ogling and unwanted attention from boorish men.

As embodied brand representatives, both retail and nightlife workers also engage in what sociologist Arlie Russell Hochschild (1983) refers to as *emotional labor*, in which workers manage and manipulate the outward display of their feelings as a controlled performance, all for the benefit of paying customers or clients. In retail settings, emotional labor involves greeting shoppers with a cheerful smile, complimenting their selections with enthusiasm—"That looks *fabulous* on you!"—and begging for their quick return. In nightlife settings, the emotional labor required of typically female servers and hostesses includes handling rude and suggestive comments from slobbering male patrons with playful come-ons and tactful wit, all while balancing unwieldy cocktails on small trays for hours on end (Grazian 2008b, p. 86). The nature of service work demands that employees negotiate the ever-present boundaries between their public and backstage personalities. As Jason recalls from his years of bartending, "I can't necessarily say everything that's popping into my head. . . . Like I could be pissed off at the bar back for not getting me beer, but that's not going to come out onstage—that's behind the stage." Caitlin, a former restaurant server, shares Jason's experience: "There was definitely a performance aspect to it. The worst is people that tell really dumb jokes and you have to laugh. You have to—you as a waiter can't even pretend that their joke wasn't funny. You have to tap-dance for it, and you do . . . and then you go in the back and you are like, *'I hate you, I hate myself, I hate you—I hate this business. Does anybody have any wine?'"* (p. 46).

The emotional labor required of nightlife workers also includes adherence to scripted guidelines for interacting with customers. Some restaurants have a "two-foot rule" that requires all personnel to greet any patron within a two-foot perimeter, no matter how inconvenient it might be. According to the employee manual used by one Philadelphia restaurant, "Smile easy and often. Smiling is a very big part of our business. Be ready with that smile at all times. Smile whenever you make eye contact." "Do not discuss money or tips during service or in front of the kitchen." Workers are also reminded to "avoid the word 'I'—use words like 'Our,' 'We,' and 'Us,'" and to offer guests a "genuine" farewell upon their departure (p. 50). Managers routinely give service workers quizzes on directives from the employee manual, just as restaurants employ teams of "secret shoppers" who spy on their servers while pretending to be legitimate customers. Again, according to Caitlin:

> They [the restaurant's management company] hired this firm. . . . They pay them to come in and they pretend that they are regular customers and they grade everything: what the door looks like; are there fingerprints on the door; how the hostess greeted them; if they asked for them to check their coats. Did they want to sit at the bar? How did the bartender act? What kind of drinks? What was the drink like? Was it over-poured or under-poured? I mean, the reports that they give are *this big* [gestures with hands to indicate enormity of size], and they are all graded like a term paper. You get like an A or a 91 percent on this or that or the other thing. They have the lapel recorder; they tape everything. . . . They have to write down the times of everything, from how long it took you to get to the table and greet them, to how long it took for their food to get to the table. . . . They're offensive. Nobody likes them. It's like *1984,* you know? (p. 52)

Secret shoppers in restaurants achieve worker control through fear; of course, as illustrated by the Abercrombie & Fitch news story above, shopping-mall retailers routinely hire secret shoppers to spy on their employees as well. They are a reminder that although malls have taken on many of the functions of public downtowns, they are nevertheless private spaces under constant surveillance, whether from secret shoppers, closed-circuit video cameras, or armed security guards. It is worth remembering that while American citizens maintain their constitutional right to free speech, assembly, political protest, and collective organizing on public city streets, none of these rights are guaranteed under the roof of a privately owned shopping mall, no matter how many roller coasters it may have.

When Style Conquers Substance

These last examples of the labor required to create the entertainment landscapes that we enjoy need not shame us into monasticism, but they ought to induce a greater self-awareness of the human costs of our consumer-oriented way of life, as well as the consequences of the triumph of aesthetics and style in our contemporary world.

For example, to what extent should we rely on attractiveness as a sign of intelligence, leadership, or artistic ability? The facts are fairly disturbing. A 2004 study found that tall people make (on average) more money than their shorter counterparts, with every extra inch of height amounting to an additional $789 increase in annual wages, after controlling for education and experience. In 2005 researchers at the Federal Reserve Bank of St. Louis found that above-average-looking people tend to earn 5 percent more per hour than their less attractive colleagues. Meanwhile, literary writers with good-looking author's photos are thought to have more promising careers in book publishing than their less attractive counterparts. The *Guardian* reported that "literary success is now as much about looks as the quality of your books. The "gorge factor"—whether a new author is seen as gorgeous or not—has become a key criterion in deciding whether a book gets the kind of marketing push that will give it a chance of selling" (Gibbons 2001). According to an article in the *Washington Post*, "Looks sell books. It's a closed-door secret in contemporary American publishing, but the word is leaking out. Not that you have to resemble Denzel Washington or Cameron Diaz, but if you can write well *and* you possess the haute cheekbones of Susan Minot, the delicate mien of Amy Tan or the brooding ruggedness of Sebastian Junger, your chances are much greater" (Weeks 2001).

At her 2001 commencement address at Yale University, no less a powerful figure than Hillary Rodham Clinton bitterly remarked on society's exaggerated attentiveness to personal appearance with a joke, of sorts:

> The most important thing that I have to say today is that hair matters. . . . This is a life lesson my family did not teach me, Wellesley and Yale failed to instill in me: the importance of your hair. Your hair will send very important messages to those around you. It will tell people who you are and what you stand for. What hopes and dreams you have for the world . . . and especially what hopes and dreams you have for your hair. Likewise, your shoes. But really, more your hair. So, to sum up. Pay attention to your hair. Because everyone else will. (quoted in Postrel 2004, p. 72)

Best-selling author Sebastian Junger. Why would an author's appearance matter to book publishers?

In fact, from her early years as first lady during the 1990s to her Senate career to her Cabinet post as U.S. secretary of state in the Obama administration, Clinton's hair has been a much-discussed matter in the American popular press, and her rebuke is worth considering. At what point do we as a society begin to elevate style over substance, and at what cost? Given that beautiful people are paid more than mere normal-looking Average Joes (like myself), should our universities offer credit-bearing courses on grooming and personal hygiene, or hair care, or aerobics and weight training?

Whatever the answer, it is clear that our emphasis on looks has never been made more of a public sport than today. Web sites like Hotornot.com allow viewers to evaluate the relative attractiveness of total strangers and compare their scores to the responses of an audience of thousands. Undergraduates spend in-class time checking out their fellow students' racy digital photo albums on Facebook. Internet dating sites emphasize the photogenic looks of would-be suitors, and online participants regularly lie about their physical appearance—which is why men report heights that are one inch taller than the national average on such

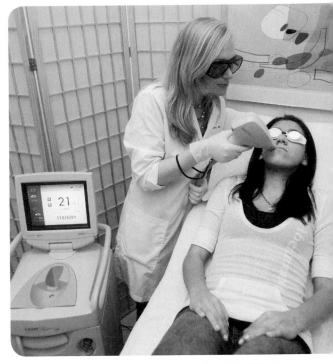

A doctor at a cosmetic surgery clinic uses a laser to remove a teenager's facial hair.

sites, while women are far more likely than men to identify their hair color as blonde or auburn (Hitsch, Hortacsu, and Ariely 2004).

One also wonders what physical and mental health consequences our current obsessions with aesthetics, beauty, and style may bring. Truly, we live in an age of miracle and wonder: as Postrel points out, "Spared not only the disfiguring diseases and malnutrition of earlier centuries but the crooked teeth, acne scars, and gray hair of our parents and grandparents, the people of the industrialized countries are arguably the best-looking people in history" (2004, p. 26). And yet, again, the facts are fairly disturbing. It is estimated that between seven and ten million women suffer from eating disorders such as anorexia and bulimia in the United States, as do one million men. And as noted in Chapter 3, according to the American Society of Plastic Surgeons, in 2007 Americans spent over $12.4 billion on cosmetic procedures. In that year, doctors performed 11.8 million procedures, a 59 percent increase from 2000. (The vast majority, 10.7 million procedures, were performed on women.) Of those procedures, 224,658 were performed on adolescents ages 13 to 19 years old. One wonders whether the benefits of these attempts at hyperstylizing the self can ever truly exceed the costs.

What is the role of digital technology in our everyday lives? Did Mark Zuckerberg, Facebook CEO and co-founder, transform how we relate to each other when he created the site?

10

strange days

POPULAR CULTURE AND
MASS MEDIA IN THE DIGITAL AGE

EVERY FEW WEEKS OR SO I RECEIVE AN EMAIL FROM A BANKER, government official, businessperson, or heir asking for help diverting temporarily inaccessible funds from Nigeria to the United States, of which I am promised a generous portion. All I am asked for in return is to send ahead the necessary transaction and transfer costs, attorney fees and taxes, along with all of my personal banking information. My correspondent assures me that I will be doing his family and perhaps justice itself a great service by assisting him. He flatters me, yes he does. But this deal is too good to be true.

Of course, the Nigerian email scam is notorious by now; most readers have received several such entreaties in the past few months, if not days. Two things about the scam are less well known, however. The first is that although it sounds impossibly ludicrous, in fact it is based on a confidence game dating back to the sixteenth century, the Spanish Prisoner. The setup is different in its particulars every time, but it essentially remains the same con as its centuries-old predecessor in which the mark, typically a member of the English gentry, is told a fantastic story about a prince unfairly imprisoned somewhere in Spain. The mark is asked to cover the costs of bribing the guards and financing his escape, after which the prince himself will reward him handsomely with his newly accessible riches. (Often there is a beautiful sister involved as well, with dropped hints and suggestions that if all goes according to plan, the mark will win her love as well.) Of course, once the mark has taken the bait and volunteered to front a small stake for the enterprise, numerous problems ensue: the guards demand additional bribes for their accomplices, a wayward conspirator steals the money in reserve, the prisoner is moved to a more impenetrable site—all of which requires more and more of the mark's money until he has been sapped bone dry. The brilliance of the Spanish Prisoner is that when it has been performed correctly, the mark need not ever know that he has, in fact, been scammed, that such a prisoner never existed in the first place. He is left empty-handed, cursing his bad luck that the prince's escape has been foiled, yet again.

The second thing most people do not know about the Nigerian email scam is that very shrewd, college-educated professionals fall for it all the time. In 2006 Mitchell Zuckoff reported in *The New Yorker* on one such victim, a Massachusetts psychotherapist named John W. Worley, whom online con artists swindled for at least $40,000. (Even after Worley was sentenced to federal prison for passing their bad checks, he maintained his confidence in the legitimacy of the scammers and their money-transfer scheme.) In 2005 the U.S. Federal Trade Commission received 55,000 complaints about such email scams, also known as "419" schemes, named after the anti-fraud section of the criminal code in Nigeria. Occasionally American victims actually travel to Nigeria to conduct the transactions in person. A recent FTC consumer alert warns, "According to

State Department reports, people who have responded to these 'advance-fee' solicitations have been beaten, subjected to threats and extortion, and in some cases, murdered."

While 419 schemes have proliferated since Nigeria's economic upheaval in the mid-1980s, clearly the Internet has made such crimes infinitely easier to pull off. Email is a practically costless method of communication on a truly mass scale, which is what makes it so easy to fish among millions for an eventual victim. (This is also why the proliferation of spam is so intractable: if service providers were to charge even a ridiculously low fee for sending emails, say one-twentieth of one cent per message, we would put a serious dent in email fraud as well as all other spam.) Email communication is also faceless and nearly untraceable, unlike phone calls or handwritten letters, which is why so few Internet swindlers are ever apprehended (Zuckoff 2006). But the Nigerian email scam also works because we have grown so reliant on today's digital technology to communicate with friends and family, express intimate opinions, and even romantic desire. We open our hearts and minds to perfect strangers online all the time, and so it should hardly surprise us that even the shadiest of deals can seem so tantalizing when processed through the familiar interface of our laptops and iPhones, machines equipped with our cherished photos and favorite songs.

This chapter is about the role that digital technology plays in our everyday lives, as a mediator of interpersonal communication and social interaction. Like the Nigerian email scam, not all of the news is upbeat, or even all that new—just think about how long con men have kept the Spanish Prisoner in operation. Much of it is still open to debate and conjecture; all of it is subject to revision. Unlike the American popular culture of the nineteenth century, the story of the digital age is still being written, by all of us. Going forward, how should we think about the impact of the Internet on our cognitive capacity to concentrate for extended periods of time? How will the future of American journalism and the news media be impacted by the digital revolution? How much can we trust MySpace or online dating sites? How does the rise of YouTube and easy-to-use recording and editing hardware and software complicate the distinction between the pop cultural creator and consumer in the digital age? Turn down your iPods, and let us begin the conversation.

The Medium is the Message

Over forty years ago communications theorist Marshall McLuhan (1967) developed a pathbreaking idea—media not only pass along messages from sender to receiver but actively reshape how we process information, knowledge, and text. While much has changed since McLuhan's time, the relationship between our media environment and its impact on how we perceive the world around us has rarely been more thoroughly debated than in our current digital age. In his recent book provocatively titled *Everything Bad Is Good for You,* Steven Johnson (2006) argues that unlike past iterations of arcade fun, new generations of video games like the *Call of Duty* and *Grand Theft Auto* series are uniquely capable of teaching young people to develop intellectual thinking abilities and problem-solving

According to Steven Johnson, why might playing Grand Theft Auto *actually be good for you?*

skills. While reading textbooks may provide a kind of *explicit learning* by facilitating the absorption of crystallized knowledge like dates, facts, and figures, playing video games contributes to what the great American philosopher John Dewey called *collateral learning* by facilitating the development of cognitive skills and competencies among energized participants. According to Johnson, this skill set includes pattern recognition, task prioritization, decision making, and most of all, how to find order and meaning in chaos.

One explanation for how games like *Grand Theft Auto* contribute to one's cognitive development relates to their fundamental architecture: they are goal-oriented and therefore require players to constantly make decisions on the basis of available evidence and reasoned analysis. But perhaps more important, this decision making is made under an unusual set of circumstances for a friendly game, because unlike poker, chess, or baseball, the actual rules of play are intentionally withheld from the players. Therefore, part of the challenge lies in figuring out the game's multiple and hierarchically nested objectives, its density of rules and regulations, and how to maneuver within its confusing universe—all of which can be learned only by playing the game in frustrating fits and starts, relying on analytic logic and creative hunches, hypothesis development and theory testing, trial-and-error and discovery. Unlike fast-paced distractions with quick rewards (like CGI-laden blockbuster thrillers), modern video games can be tedious and difficult. They require patient experimentation and teach players to delay gratification as they probe what Johnson calls the *physics* of the game's complex virtual world—how far across a canyon a character can jump while wearing armor; the relative amounts of blood one loses if wounded in the legs or the chest; from which direction the robot is most likely to invade (Johnson 2006, p. 44). Along the way, these intellectual demands exercise and sharpen the mind, augmenting how the brain functions not only during jarring rounds of play but in more common place settings as well.

Others suggest that sophisticated digital games help participants develop crucial organizational and decision-making skills ideal for the professional world. For instance, *massively multiplayer online role-playing games* (or MMORPGs) like *World of Warcraft* and *EverQuest* allow players to adopt virtual identities or *avatars* to communicate and interact with one another through the game's visual and audio interface. Through their avatars, participants form guilds, clans, and other social alliances and collectively solve problems and achieve complex goals (Castronova 2005). Management gurus like Stanford communication professor Byron Reeves argue that familiarity and experience navigating MMORPGs provide superior training for positions of leadership in business. In *Virtual Worlds, Real Leaders* (2007), a "Global Innovation Outlook 2.0 Report" prepared for IBM employees, Reeves proclaims, "If you want to see what business leadership may look like in three to five years, look at what's happening in online games." According to the IBM report:

> Online games, and specifically massively multiplayer online role-playing games (MMORPGs), offer a glimpse at how leaders develop and operate in environments that are highly distributed, global, hyper-competitive, and virtual. Hundreds of thousands of players—sometimes millions—interact daily in highly complex virtual environments. These players self-organize, develop skills, and settle into various roles. Leaders emerge that are capable of recruiting, organizing, motivating, and directing large groups of players toward a common goal. And decisions are made quickly, with ample, but imperfect, information. Sound familiar?

> "MMORPGs mirror the business context more than you would assume," says Reeves. "They presage one possible future for business—one that is open, virtual, knowledge-driven, and comprised of a largely volunteer or at least transient workforce." Of course, online games do not provide a perfect analog for the business world of the future. The stakes in the real world are obviously much higher. But it's easy to see how some of the qualities of gifted gaming leaders could translate into a corporate setting. The collaborative influence that online leaders exhibit is extraordinary in some cases. Gaming leaders are more comfortable with risk, accepting failure, and the resulting iterative improvement, as part of their reality. Many of these leaders are able to make sense of disparate and constantly changing data, translating it all into a compelling vision. And the relationship skills of the best gaming leaders would put many Fortune 500 managers to shame. (pp. 4–5)

Of course, we experience digital media in a variety of platforms that may impact our social and cognitive capacities in contradictory ways. In an essay for the *Atlantic*, "Is Google Making Us Stupid?" Nicholas Carr (2008) argues that if video games like *Call of Duty* make us smarter, then how we surf online—"reading and writing emails, scanning headlines and blog posts, watching videos and listening to podcasts, or just tripping from link to link"—may have a more deleterious effect on our mental faculties (p. 57). Carr and others wonder if latter-day Internet habits have impaired our ability to read deeply and contemplatively, to absorb texts critically with a sufficient degree of concentration. Already, other media are adapting to the Internet's frenetic visual norms. Magazines and newspapers feature shorter articles and capsule summaries, and the *New York Times* now includes article abstracts in every edition (p. 60). Television networks clutter

A college student plays roulette online. How do gaming sites put consumers in "the zone"?

the screen with distracting banners, news crawls, promotional icons and ads, mini-trailers, quick weather updates, and stock quotes (Lee 2007). As TV soundtracks and commercials become the primary medium for introducing pop songs to mass audiences, even our attention span for music listening diminishes as our exposure to new recordings is increasingly confined to 10-, 15-, and 30-second snippets of sound.

If Internet surfing makes us prone to distraction, then for some the debilitating effects of digital media can be quite costly indeed. For instance, about $60 billion is illegally gambled in Internet poker games each year, a pursuit that draws in an estimated 1.6 million U.S. college students. As Mattathias Schwartz (2006) reported in the *New York Times Magazine*, in 2005 Lehigh University sophomore class president Greg Hogan, Jr., lost $7,500 playing online poker, and out of desperation, in December of that year he held up a Wachovia bank for $2,871 in cash. With no casino dealers, card shuffling, or friendly table partners to distract him, Hogan found the seamless, fast-paced action of digital poker "paralyzing" and "narcotic," a familiar sensation among addicts, men and women alike. According to Schwartz, "Many, like Lauren Patrizi, a 21-year-old senior at Loyola University in Chicago, have had weeks when they're playing poker during most of their waking hours. Rarely leaving their rooms, they take their laptops with them to bed, fall asleep each night in the middle of a hand and think, talk and dream nothing but poker."

According to cultural anthropologist Natasha Dow Schull (2005, p. 73), digital technologies succeed in creating what consumers call *the zone,* a dissociated subjective state marked by a suspension of normative parameters—monetary, bodily, temporal, and spatial. Gambling sites rely on cashless transactions (performed with credit and debit card numbers) in which financial stakes are transformed into pixilated "chips" that no longer seem like real money. Unlike dorm-lounge poker games in which classmates eventually get tired, punch-drunk, or else lose their shirts, online casinos never close, but consistently and relentlessly maintain a steady rhythm of play that keeps addicts glued to their screens alone for hours, nights, and weeks on end. With only computer keys to depress, players never drop their cards; moreover, gambling software allows gamers to bet multiple hands simultaneously, further increasing the hypnotic speed and tempo with which one gains and (more often) loses.

Eventually, one relinquishes all proper sense of time until, as one of Schull's informants admits, "It's not about *winning*: it's about *continuing to play*" without interrupting the "illusion of control," the experience of total flow (pp. 74–75).

The departure from conventions of temporal reality experienced by Internet gamblers is not sufficiently different from the heightened states known to other video game players. In a piece for *Harper's* magazine fittingly titled "The Perfect Game," Joshua Bearman (2008) reports that according to Walter Day, founder and proprietor of Twin Galaxies, an online organization for video game fanatics, "'Top gamers have yogic concentration,' he says, 'combining utter focus with extreme relaxation, like what I've studied with the Maharishi.' Walter says the players, like all great athletes, can enter flow states when navigating Pac-Man or marathoning on games like Nibbler. And many players do in fact report moments, deep into the hours, when everything but the game recedes" (p. 69).

While admittedly extreme, this dissociation from reality is merely illustrative of the increased levels of loneliness and alienation experienced by many young people, and their condition is perhaps only exacerbated by digital technologies. Writing in the British journal *Biologist*, Aric Sigman (2009, p. 15) argues, "The rapid proliferation of electronic media is now making private space available in almost every sphere of the individual's life. Yet this is now the most significant contributing factor to society's growing physical estrangement. Whether in or out of the home, more people of *all* ages in the UK are physically and socially disengaged from the people around them because they are wearing earphones, talking or texting on a mobile telephone, or using a laptop or Blackberry." This loss of face-to-face interpersonal contact has been associated with a variety of physiologically debilitating conditions and an increased incidence of a number of illnesses, including diabetes, cardiovascular disease, and rheumatoid arthritis (p. 17).

What Happens Online Doesn't Always Stay Online

The Hogan bank robbery illustrates that while the online universe may be virtual, it is nevertheless severely consequential for what happens here in the real world. In *Synthetic Worlds,* telecommunications professor Edward Castronova (2005) explores the porous quality of the barrier (or what he calls the *membrane*) separating the imaginary realm of cyberspace from the material world of everyday life. As he argues, "we find human society on either side of the membrane, and since society is the ultimate locus of validation for all our important shared notions—value, fact, emotion, meaning—we will find shared notions on either side as well" (pp. 147–48).

Nowhere is this blurred boundary more apparent than in the online economies of MMORGs such as *World of Warcraft* (*WOW*) and 3D virtual worlds like *Second Life* (*SL*). In warehouses packed with computer terminals throughout China, thousands of young "digital sweatshop" workers play *WOW* seven days a week in 12-hour shifts, developing high-status avatars and collecting virtual gold coins, magic wands, and weapons that American gamers buy on eBay and Yahoo! for actual U.S. dollars (Barboza 2005). (According to the *New York Times*, in 2005 game players could expect to pay $9.99 on eBay for 100 grams of *WOW* gold, and $269 to be transported to Level 60, the game's highest level at that time.) In *Second Life,* the 10 million-plus registered users of the Web site can

Chinese workers playing World of Warcraft *in a "digital sweatshop."*

trade real U.S. dollars for Linden dollars (*SL*'s fluctuating online currency) and purchase conceptual "real estate" for their online home or business; lingerie, formalwear, puppies, and sports cars for their avatars; and even animated oral sex from virtual prostitutes and escorts. (According to sources, cyber-brothels in *SL* charge customers anywhere from 2,000 to 3,000 Linden dollars—or about $9 to $13—for an online "avatar-on-avatar" sexual encounter.)

How much does the economy and social life circulating within online games and synthetic environments impact the material world? As Castrovona (2005, p. 148) points out, for all intents and purposes the distinction between "real" and "virtual" in this context is practically nonexistent. Online gamers spend over $1 billion a year on flashy virtual assets made up of little more than digital ones and zeroes. In June 2007, $6.8 million changed hands on *SL*'s Lindex in a single month: the exchange rate was about 270 Linden dollars to one U.S. dollar (Dell 2007). Through her avatar "Anshe Chung," in 2006 virtual real estate developer and broker Ailin Graef became the first person to earn $1 million in *SL*.

Meanwhile, the social lives perpetuated in synthetic worlds reverberate offline as well. Flesh-and-blood lovers frequently meet in *SL,* just as adulterous extramarital affairs that occur online often lead to real-life divorces. In recent years *SL* has provided a virtual environment where elite universities offer inter- active classes, businesses run professional conferences, and corporations hold shareholders meetings. Virtual worlds like *SL* even offer simulated contexts lifelike enough to prepare emergency workers to erect medical facilities in the event of a dangerous crisis. And lest we forget, according to the authorized edition of the *9/11 Commission Report* (National Commission on Terrorist Attacks 2004), the al-Qaeda terrorists responsible for the September 11 attacks on the World Trade Center and the Pentagon in 2001 relied on digital entertainment software—in their case, flight-simulator computer games—for their training as well (pp. 157—58).

How else do goings-on within the virtual world impact our everyday lives offline? Certainly, the ease with which information flows online among otherwise discrete interpersonal networks has obvious consequences for how we maintain control over our reputations and identities. As George Washington University law professor Daniel Solove (2007) observes in *The Future of Reputation*, since anyone with an Internet connection can post intimate photographs, juicy gossip, or vicious rumors on the Web for a potential worldwide audience of billions, personal reputations can easily be maligned within hours. In 2003 Kelley D. Parker, a partner at the elite New York law firm of Paul, Weiss, Rifkind, Wharton and Garrison, allegedly ordered a paralegal to conduct research on nearby sushi restaurants after eating some bad takeout. The underling wrote up a three-page memo replete with interview quotes, footnotes, and exhibitions, and the scanned document later appeared on the Web site Gawker for her colleagues to mock (Glater 2003). (The memo memorably ends, "I would hope you find the attached helpful in choosing the restaurant from which your dinner will be ordered on a going-forward basis.") While it was never determined whether the infamous "sushi memo" was a hoax or a prank, it presumably hardly matters to Ms. Parker, whose reputation has been forever marred by the online posting.

Of course, rumors of bad behavior among celebrities likely travel faster online than any other kind of hearsay. Web sites like Gawker, The Smoking Gun, TMZ, and YouTube are veritable clearinghouses for such gossip, as actor Christian Bale learned after he cursed out the director of photography on the movie set of *Terminator: Salvation* in 2008 for nearly four minutes, and a full-length audio recording of his tantrum resurfaced on YouTube the following year. (Bale has since apologized for the outburst, but notably did so only after its public airing.) The Web site Bitter Waitress provides an ongoing list of celebrity (as well as civilian) diners who have stingily tipped less than 15 percent of their check: famous cheapskates shamed by the site include actresses Lindsay Lohan and Helena Bonham Carter, former Miami Dolphins quarterback Dan Marino, rock singer David Lee Roth, and reality TV figure Dog the Bounty Hunter. In March 2009, People for the Ethical Treatment of Animals (or PETA) published an online list of celebrities who unabashedly wear fur, including Madonna, Maggie Gyllenhaal, Kanye West, Elizabeth Hurley, Kate Moss, Demi Moore, Ashton Kutcher, Mary J. Blige, and Mary-Kate and Ashley Olsen.

A very different kind of online clearinghouse for the airing of grievances, Rate My Professors (RMP) sells itself as an unscientific *Consumer Reports* for undergraduates and an Internet forum for shaming university instructors of ill repute. A Web site that empowers college students by allowing them to anonymously post ratings (on the basis of easiness, clarity, overall quality, helpfulness, and "hotness") as well as descriptive evaluations of their professors for the world to read, RMP reverses the power dynamic otherwise inherent in teacher-student relationships by establishing a semipermanent public record of ridicule and complaint often built entirely out of vengeance, deserved or not (Solove 2007, p. 98). "Andy," a writing instructor from the University of Massachusetts-Lowell, reveals on his blog some of the more colorful online postings written about him by former students:

- Andy is impossible to please and he can be a wicked jackass. He writes really mean comments on students' papers. I do not recommend him. Find someone else!!!
- He does not know how to teach nor does he like his job. He grades really hard and expects way too much. . . . Nothing is ever good enough for this man.
- Impossible. . . . I would be surprised if you get above a 75 on any of the 4 essays. He discusses your grade with other students in your absence. . . . Complains about his other class to us; I'm sure he complains about us to them. Kills any self esteem you may have had in your writing: not helpful at all. Do anything to avoid this class!!
- He's not a good writing teacher at all!! He's not even a real teacher, he grades essays by putting them in a pile from best to worst (he said this to my class). Very hard grader, the highest grade I got was a 78. He's not helpful: when he tries to help, he makes things worst. He came to class dressed like he just got out of bed, every class!!
- The guy is a teacher only to inflate his ego, which is why he checks this Web site to see what people think of him.

In retaliation for this public pillorying, "Andy" attacks his students on his blog:

- I don't know what this person is talking about with regards to discussing grades with other students. I'm pretty sure I never did that. But I do talk about the other classes to each other, in a general sense. And while I'll concede that maybe I shouldn't, I don't feel that bad about it. I never say anything about another class that I haven't already said to their faces. The greater point here is that I kill their fragile self-esteem. These kids have never been told they're anything less than wonderful. They were all the best writers in their high-school class. They are all brilliant. Yet most of them wouldn't know a comma if it spliced them between the eyes. I have no idea what's going on in high school English classrooms, but the system is broken if you can get a diploma without the most basic of basic skills. Teaching two 8 AM sections my first semester probably didn't help matters. These kids love to sleep, but not when they should be sleeping. During those hours, they are binge drinking or playing Guitar Hero. That may be unfair, as many of them are also paying their way through school and working part-time jobs. But regardless, the majority is sleep-deprived, and in no condition to learn at 8 AM.

- It's pretty reflective of the sense of entitlement felt by some of these kids. They deserve an A simply because (a) they're God's special creatures and (b) writing is no more important than gym class.
- I'm always amazed by how hard these students think they're trying. Sometimes they'll ask me questions about their papers, but generally when you strip away the bullshit, their questions all amount to: "How can I get an A on my paper without doing any actual work?" I've had about 100 students, and despite their complaints about grades, maybe five or six have actually come to my office hours to discuss how to improve their writing. I've probably put more time and effort into this blog post than some of them put into their papers.

The difference between "Andy's" blog posts and RMP is that the latter is an extraordinarily well-known and heavily networked Web site, and its impact sometimes goes far beyond the university quad. For instance, Miriam Gershow is a writing instructor in the English Department at the University of Oregon, and although she has received many positive evaluations on Rate My Professors from satisfied students over the years, an equal number of posted comments have been mean and nasty: "Do not take her class!!" "I NEVER GIVE ADVICE, BUT THIS ONE IS THE WORST TEACHER IN THE UNIVERSE. IF YOU REALLY VALUE YOUR LIFE, THEN DO NOT THINK ABOUT TAKING HER CLASSES. A SUICIDE DECISION. HORRIBLE, HORRIBLE, HORRIBLE!" "I got a good grade in the class, but simply put this teacher is garbage." "Worst . . . teacher . . . ever." But while RMP is presumably designed to help university students choose courses and instructors, anyone can access the site, including potential employers, divorce lawyers, and book reviewers from the *New York Times.* When Janet Maslin of the *Times* reviewed Gershow's 2009 novel *The Local News,* which features an anxious yet smug teenager named Lydia Pasternak as its lead character, she drew on the author's online student evaluations to explain Lydia's social status:

> Ms. Gershow has been a teacher at the University of Oregon, where some students' online ratings of her sound like a continuation of Lydia's high school nightmare. Being regarded as neither popular nor hot seems to be territory that Ms. Gershow knows well, maybe in the classroom and certainly on the pages of her unusually credible and precise novel. (Maslin 2009, p. C7)

Does Maslin's use of Rate My Professors (and its "hotness" ratings scale) represent a violation or ethical breach? What if a job interviewer relies on an applicant's Facebook profile (replete with their odd musical tastes and suggestive photographs) when rendering judgment about their professional qualifications? Given the far-ranging uses of Internet networking and dating sites like Facebook, MySpace, and Match, it is no wonder that subscribers strategically design their online profiles and behaviors in self-interested ways. Among Facebook users, young people augment their social standing by linking to high-status or especially attractive friends; bald men refer to their heads as "shaved"; restaurant servers and retail workers list their aspirational careers (e.g., fashion modeling, acting, screenwriting, guitar playing) as their actual occupations; college professors avoid posting photos of themselves playing beer pong (Rosenbloom 2008). According to an unpublished paper by economists at MIT and the University of Chicago on Internet courtship (Hitsch, Hortacsu, and Ariely 2004), less than 1 percent of both men and women who use dating sites like Match describe themselves as having "less than average looks." As noted in Chapter 9, men report heights that are one inch taller than the national average, while women underreport their weight (again, compared to the national average) by a difference of 20 pounds for women in the 30–39 and 40–49 age ranges. As Jennifer Egan (2003) reports in the *New York Times Magazine*, "most online daters have at least one cranky tale of meeting a date who was shorter or fatter or balder or generally less comely than advertised. Small lies may even be advisable; by dropping a year or two off her age, a 40-year-old woman will appear in many more men's searches, and the same is true for a man shorter than 5-foot-11 who inflates his height even slightly."

Tina Meier shows pictures of her daughter Megan, who committed suicide after receiving cruel messages on MySpace.

Of course, lying about one's online identity can be more consequential than simply suffering through a disappointing date. In 2006 Megan Meier, a 13-year-old girl from Dardenne Prairie, Missouri, began emailing with Josh Evans, an adorable boy who befriended her on MySpace. Josh was 16 years-old, six-foot-three, and had blue eyes and wavy brown hair. He owned a pet snake, liked pizza, and preferred Coke to Pepsi (Collins 2008). To any 13-year-old girl, he would have been a perfect boyfriend if not for his one flaw—he wasn't actually real but an online cipher invented and animated by Lori Drew, a 47-year-old mother; her 13-year-old teenage daughter Sarah, a former friend of Megan's; and Ashley Grills, an 18-year-old family friend (Steinhauer 2008). They created a MySpace profile for "Josh Evans" to spy on Megan and eventually bully her as a form of emotional torture, knowing she had a history of depression for which she was taking prescribed medication. On October 15 of that year, after their online courtship had lasted several weeks, Megan received a strangely hostile message from the imaginary boy: "I don't like the way you treat your friends, and I don't know if I want to be friends with you" (Maag 2007). After school the next day, she continued fighting online with "Josh," who called her names before sending her a final message—"The world would be a better place without you"—and she responded, "You're the kind of boy a girl would kill herself over" (Steinhauer 2008). Later that afternoon, Megan was found dead in her bedroom closet, where she had hanged herself with a belt.

Digital Technology and the Media Industries

One notable element of the MySpace Suicide Hoax (as the Meier case would come to be known) is that MySpace is a free Web site, as are most popular media sites, including YouTube, Comcast, CNN, Hulu, and ESPN. Although all forms of online mass media cost money and require expert talent to produce and maintain, in the last decade the overriding economic model for the Internet has emphasized payments upfront to an online service provider (like Comcast or Verizon) in return for unlimited access to largely free content from a seemingly infinite variety of sources. With Web advertising revenue shrinking, many wonder what will come of the media industries that rely on capital investments to produce the kinds of popular culture that we have grown used to consuming online for free. With the help of Apple's iTunes, the music industry has succeeded in convincing consumers to pay for downloaded music at 99 cents per song, rather than simply share pirated recordings on peer-to-peer networks like LimeWire. In 2008 consumers downloaded just over a billion songs from iTunes, a 27 percent increase from 2007, while compact disc sales were down nearly 20 percent from the year before (Sisario 2005).

The online market for newspaper content has not been as lucrative, and many papers around the country are expected to go under in the next few years, even to the point that some big cities may be left without a major newspaper (Pérez-Peña 2009). This is ironic, since newspapers have more readers today than ever before, especially among young people—yet only a small portion of those readers pay for the privilege, given the availability of free newspaper content online (Isaacson 2009). In truth, past efforts to persuade Internet readers to pay for newspaper content (like the *New York Times*) have largely failed, in part because of extreme competition from an abundance of free online news sites. As Michael Kinsley (2009), founding editor of the online magazine *Slate*, wisely observes, whereas in the past readers were beholden to their local newspaper (if for no other reason than it was prohibitively expensive to have papers, like *Le Monde* or the *Jerusalem Post*, delivered from another country every day), today "every English-language newspaper is in direct competition with every other. Millions of Americans get their news online from the *Guardian*, which is published in London. This competition, and not some kind of petulance or laziness or addled philosophy, is what keeps readers from shelling out for news." Meanwhile, other sources of newspaper revenue like classified ads have shrunk dramatically due to the greater efficiency of online sites like eBay and Craigslist.

The solution is far from obvious; in fact, many hardly recognize that there is much of a problem, given the seemingly excessive sources of news available online. But although many of us rely on myriad bloggers and news-digest Web sites for the day's headlines—the *Huffington Post, Politico, Salon*—few of their writers actually go out into the world to honestly *report* on the news, and instead rely on the hard-nosed journalists who work for the newspapers most jeopardized by the digital revolution. Meanwhile, few bloggers or online pundits have the professional journalistic experience, interviewing and fact-checking skills, financial resources, or institutional power to conduct long-term investigations that reveal government corruption or corporate malfeasance. As Andrew Keen (2007) observes in *The Cult of the Amateur*, the democratization of the Internet, "despite its lofty idealization, is undermining truth, souring civic discourse, and belittling expertise, experience, and talent" (p. 15).

> It is threatening the very future of our cultural institutions. I call it the great seduction. The Web 2.0 revolution has peddled the promise of bringing more truth to more people—more depth of information, more global perspective, more unbiased opinion from dispassionate observers. But this is all a smokescreen. What the Web 2.0 revolution is really delivering is superficial observations of the world around us rather than deep analysis, shrill opinion rather than considered judgment. The information business is being transformed by the Internet into the sheer noise of a hundred million bloggers all simultaneously talking about themselves.
>
> Moreover, the free, user-generated content spawned and extolled by the Web 2.0 revolution is decimating the ranks of our cultural gatekeepers, as professional critics, journalists, editors . . . and other purveyors of expert information are being replaced . . . by amateur bloggers [and] hack reviewers. . . . For the real consequence of the Web 2.0 revolution is less culture, less reliable news, and a chaos of useless information. One chilling reality in this brave new digital epoch is the blurring, obfuscation, and even disappearance of truth. (pp. 15—16)

Again, the solution needed to fix the current implosion of the newspaper industry is far from obvious. Kinsley thinks that once the herd is thinned down to a half dozen national papers like the *New York Times* and the *Washington Post*, these elite news-gathering organizations will emerge stronger and more competitive than ever, able to keep growing ranks of war journalists in Baghdad and Kabul, and hard-hitting investigative reporters in Beijing and at the Pentagon. Of course, this will not do very much for smaller cities across the country from Sacramento to Cleveland to Tulsa, where citizens rely on their local papers and news bureaus to serve as watchdogs that ensure the integrity of local and state legislatures, government agencies, school boards, and judicial bodies.

Others suggest alternate funding arrangements for online news and other media. Walter Isaacson (2009), a former managing editor of *Time*, recommends instituting an easy-to-use automatic system for collecting micropayments (similar to the iTunes Store) for inexpensive but immediate access to online media content (TV newscasts, short videos and films, blogs, newspaper articles, magazine profiles), sort of like an E-Z Pass for the information superhighway. This could provide the necessary financial incentives and support for citizen-journalists and creative artists to produce media deemed worthy and valuable by the public—all without relying solely on the unpredictability of advertising revenue. Another workable strategy is for journalists to develop media partnerships with private universities and other nonprofit organizations. A successful example of this model in action includes the Medill Innocence Project established by David Protess, a Northwestern journalism professor who directed a team of students whose collective investigative reporting contributed to the exoneration of 11 innocent and falsely imprisoned men and women, including five death row inmates. Similarly, in his book *Fighting for Air: The Battle to Control America's Media,* New York University sociologist Eric Klinenberg (2007) reports on the work of the Citizens Union Foundation, a nonprofit research,

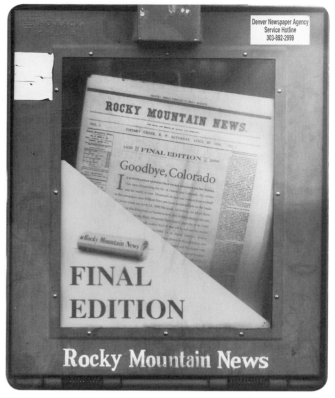

The final edition of Colorado's oldest newspaper, the Rocky Mountain News, which was nearly 150 years old when it shut down in 2009.

education, and advocacy group in New York that launched the *Gotham Gazette,* an online publication, in September 1999. Funded by grants and pledge drives, the *Gazette* provides "original reporting on a broad range of civic, cultural, and political issues" germane to local city residents: an example includes its award-winning coverage following the 9/11 terrorist attack on the World Trade Center in 2001 (pp. 182–84).

The Future of Online Media and the Digital Age

As this last discussion illustrates, the future of online media is unknown. According to Henry Jenkins (2006), the founder and director of the Comparative Media Studies Program at MIT, the digital age is marked by the rise of three interrelated phenomena: the *convergence* of content across multiple mass media platforms and industries; the active *participation* of audiences that coproduce their own media experiences, often by digitally manipulating the raw materials of popular culture; and the harnessing of *collective intelligence* as an emergent form of media power in which consumers draw on the networking faculties of the Internet to pool their resources and skills with the goal of either challenging traditional media forms or else producing something altogether new. Each presents a unique set of opportunities as well as reasons for tempering expectations. Let us take each in turn.

First, the *convergence* of media content across platforms promises the development of exciting and dynamic new forms of cultural production. Jenkins (2006) points to *The Matrix* juggernaut as a prime example. After the runaway success of the 1999 feature film (which grossed over $170 million at the U.S. box office), its creators, Andy and Larry Wachowski, leveraged the film's concept, characters, and rich aesthetic across numerous media and art-making enterprises, including two sequels (*The Matrix Reloaded* and *The Matrix Revolutions*); three DVDs packed with documentaries, interviews, and other special features; two video games (*Enter the Matrix* and the MMORG *The Matrix Online*); a collection of short animated films (*The Animatrix*); and a series of comics (*Déjà Vu, I Kant*) by cult artists and illustrators such as Dave Gibbons (*Watchmen*) and Bill Sienkiewicz (*Elektra: Assassin*). Unlike most tent-pole franchises in which movie stars, characters, and logos are licensed for endless McDonald's Happy Meals, cheap toys, and soda cups devoid of truly creative content, the strategy of convergence employed for *The Matrix* combines cross-promotion with "synergistic storytelling," with each additional multimedia platform providing new narrative experiences and insights for its audiences (Jenkins 2006, pp. 104–5).

If convergence represents a top-down model of digital pop cultural production created by profit-seeking industries, other examples suggest how consumers themselves *participate more actively* in the coproduction of their own new media experiences. As we have discussed in earlier chapters, popular culture fans create their own spoofs through the emergent medium of the mash-up, in which two or more media are sampled, manipulated, and juxtaposed together to ironic effect. Armed with Photoshop, political junkies create an array of sight gags to be distributed via the Internet: Barack Obama as a Vulcan, George W. Bush as Elvis Presley (in his 1970s Las Vegas period), Dick Cheney as Shrek. A three-and-a-half-minute mock movie trailer, *Tom Hanks Is James Bond* intercuts shots of recent Bond films with scenes from Hanks's many box-office hits, including *Splash, Bachelor Party, The Money Pit, The Man with One Red Shoe,* and *The Da Vinci Code.* A shorter mash-up features Miss Piggy, Scooter, and the felt-headed gang from *The Muppets Take Manhattan* lip-synching the dialogue from the opening diner scene in Quentin Tarantino's *Reservoir Dogs.* (The lovable Kermit the Frog and Fozzie Bear argue over the merits of restaurant tipping, in the tough voices of actors Steve Buscemi and Harvey Keitel.) Other enthusiastic fans simply film *themselves* lip-synching to pop songs and post their homemade videos online, as 19-year-old Gary Brolsma from Saddle Brook, New Jersey, did in 2004 when he recorded himself dancing to "Dragostea din tei," a techno track by the Moldovan pop group O-Zone. (Relatively unknown in the United States, the song was a No. 1 hit single in at least 12 European countries that year, including Germany, Switzerland, Denmark, Portugal, and Romania.) Gary submitted the finished product to a Web site, and he became an overnight sensation: his video, which he dubbed the "Numa Numa Dance," has been downloaded from the Internet at least seven million times, and he has appeared on *Good Morning America*, NBC's *Tonight Show*, and CNN (Solove 2007, p. 42).

The creators of the popular YouTube mash-up Reservoir Dogs Take Manhattan *layered the famous diner scene from Tarantino's crime drama over footage from* The Muppets Take Manhattan.

If individuals can create their own mash-ups while working alone on their home desktops, other kinds of participatory culture employ the *collective intel-ligence* of networked contributors working collaboratively toward a common creative objective. For example, Linux is a computer operating system based on free open source software, and anyone is permitted to use, modify, and redistribute its source code. Originally developed by a Finnish hacker, Linus Torvalds, while he studied computer science at the University of Helsinki, Linux steadily improves year after year because of the aggregate knowledge and diverse expertise of its untold thousands of programmers. Moreover, each participant relies on his or her own particular brand of proficiency to contribute not only to the functionality, reliability, and robustness of the software but also to a larger and perhaps more ideologically satisfying goal—to challenge the market and institutional dominance of privately owned, profit-generating operating systems such as Unix, Mac OS, and Microsoft Windows. The collective intelligence of those thousands of Linux programmers, or what *New Yorker* business columnist James Surowiecki (2005) refers to as "the wisdom of crowds," best illustrates how the Internet can connect individuals whose shared ingenuity often proves more advantageous in the pursuit of cultural creativity and innovation than the solitary labors of even the greatest thinkers, isolated in their studio or laboratory. Of course, it should be noted that while the system is decentralized it is hardly anarchic since a small group of elite programmers (including Torvalds himself) vet all alterations to the source code (p. 74). (One senses that the Linux brain trust holds a tighter grip on its content than other Internet sites that rely on collective intelligence, such as the consistently fallible Wikipedia.)

Obviously, a pop cultural landscape marked by the convergence of content across media platforms, the active participation of audiences that coproduce their own entertainment experiences, and the harnessing of collective intelligence as a resource for creativity and innovation suggests an exciting future for online media and the digital age. Still, at least two general caveats are in order. First, cultural convergence across platforms can drive the production of media content in rather insidious ways. If serious journalists are expected to generate entertaining news stories that easily travel from print to television to the Internet, less flashy issues of critical substance may not get the coverage they deserve. Likewise, the increased duties among reporters who are increasingly required to find and incorporate digital photography, streaming video, and interactive graphics into their stories may find they have less time to do the actual newsgathering necessary for producing high-quality investigative journalism (Klinenberg 2005). As Hollywood studios seek out computer-animated film projects that can be seamlessly translated into online role-playing games and fully loaded DVD box sets, perhaps fewer art-house movies, costume dramas, or war documentaries will receive adequate financing.

Second, the rising participatory culture in which American consumers coproduce their own media experiences will require fundamental changes in our nation's outdated approach to intellectual property and copyright law. Currently, intellectual property law and the litigious impulses of a consolidated media industry with unlimited financial resources and political influence prevent cultural innovators from borrowing corporate-controlled images and reproductions, even for seemingly "fair use" purposes. Merely the *threat* of litigation restricts many contemporary artists who choose self-censorship over sinking into debt to fight off lawsuits from multinational giants like Sony, Time Warner, Viacom, and Disney, even winnable ones. In such cases, what is *technically* considered fair use by legal definition and thus protected by statute can hardly be acknowledged as permissable in any real or *practical* sense.

In his spirited manifesto *Free Culture*, Stanford law professor Lawrence Lessig (2005) warns that the rise of new media technologies only exacerbates this problem by choking the options of consumers and creators. According to current copyright law, it is within one's rights as the purchaser of a compact disc, paperback novel, or newspaper to lend it to multiple friends, sell it to a secondhand shop, or give it a third and fourth listen or read oneself, as these activities constitute fair use. In a digitized format, however, doing any of these things with a cultural object under copyright protection can technically be considered illegal, since using even a fragment of a digitized text (such as a downloaded photograph or an excerpt from an electronically published book or journal article) almost always involves making a *new* electronic copy of the material in question. In fact, in certain cases each use can constitute an entirely separate alleged offense, as Jesse Jordan, a freshman at Rensselaer Polytechnic Institute, learned the hard way when he modified a preexisting search engine built for his school's network, allowing students to access one another's publicly available computer files, including those containing music. The following year the

Recording Industry Association of America (RIAA) sued Jordan for "willfully" violating copyright law and demanded statutory damages of $150,000 per infringement. RIAA alleged that each use of a music file constituted a separate infringement and cited more than 100 individual acts of illegality. According to RIAA, Jordan owed $15 million in damages (Lessig 2005, pp. 48–51).

While the recording industry claims that it no longer targets individuals who use peer-to-peer software to download music illegally, cases such as Jordan's illustrate the profiteering behavior of the culture industries in the digital age. Although the rise of new media promises cultural creators the autonomy to produce innovative or critical artworks that sample or borrow from preexisting pop cultural films, television shows, recordings, or brands, in many instances it can be infuriatingly challenging to procure permission to use logos, cartoon characters, and other kinds of corporate-controlled intellectual property. While digital technologies may allow for an unprecedented abuse of preexisting copyright law—as the proliferation of mash-ups on YouTube clearly demonstrates—the tools provided by Web-based search engines like Google and Yahoo! allow major media companies to efficiently monitor the Internet landscape and

College students are not the only consumers being sued by the RIAA. Jammie Thomas, a mother of four from Minnesota, was taken to trial by the recording industry for sharing 1,702 songs online.

identify violators for harassment and legal action, a practice seemingly driven by spite as much as by greed. As Naomi Klein (2002, p. 178) argues in *No Logo,* even in the wake of the digital age "the underlying message [from the media industries] is that culture is something that happens to you. You buy it at the Virgin Megastore or Toys 'R' Us and rent it at Blockbuster Video. It is not something in which you participate, or to which you have the right to respond."

But as Lessig reminds us, the health of any democratic society requires that its cultural products and ideas be available for unfettered distribution, commentary, and eventual innovation and appropriation to ensure their rejuvenation and evolution over time. After all, the availability of unprotected cultural objects contributed to the richness of twentieth-century American popular culture, from Walt Disney's appropriation of classic fairy tales to the modern rise of free open-source software like Linux. Just as we place limitations on the extension of patents in order to promote scientific progress, the fecundity of our cultural landscape requires similar guarantees. As students and scholars of media and popular culture as well as devoted fans, we should demand nothing less.

Bibliography

Adorno, Theodor W. "On the Fetish-Character in Music and the Regression of Listening," in *The Essential Frankfurt School Reader,* Andrew Arato and Eike Gebhardt, eds. (New York: Continuum, 1997).

Adorno, Theodor W. "Perennial Fashion—Jazz," in *Critical Theory and Society,* Stephen Eric Bronner and Douglas MacKay Kellner, eds. (New York: Routledge, 1989).

Adorno, Theodor, and Max Horkheimer. "The Culture Industry: Enlightenment as Mass Deception," in *The Cultural Studies Reader,* Simon During, ed. (London: Routledge, 1993).

Albini, Steve. "The Problem with Music," in *Commodify Your Dissent: Salvos from the Baffler,* Thomas Frank and Matt Weiland, eds. (New York: Norton, 1997).

Alterman, Eric. *It Ain't No Sin to Be Glad You're Alive: The Promise of Bruce Springsteen* (Boston: Back Bay, 2001).

Anderson, Benedict. *Imagined Communities: Reflections on the Origin and Spread of Nationalism* (London: Verso, 1991).

Anderson, Elijah. *Code of the Street: Decency, Violence, and the Moral Life of the Inner City* (New York: Norton, 1999).

Anderson, Elijah. *Streetwise: Race, Class, and Change in an Urban Community* (Chicago: University of Chicago Press, 1990).

Appelrouth, Scott. "Body and Soul: Jazz in the 1920s," *American Behavioral Scientist* 48 (2005): 1496–1509.

Appelrouth, Scott. "Constructing the Meaning of Early Jazz, 1917–1930," *Poetics* 31 (2003): 117–131.

Arndt, Johan. "Role of Product-Related Conversations in the Diffusion of a New Product," *Journal of Marketing Research* 4 (1967): 291–295.

Atkins, E. Taylor. "Can Japanese Sing the Blues? 'Japanese Jazz' and the Problem of Authenticity," in *Japan Pop! Inside the World of Japanese Popular Culture,* Timothy J. Craig, ed. (Armonk, NY: M. E. Sharpe, 2000).

Barboza, David. "Ogre to Slay? Outsource It to Chinese," *New York Times* 9 December 2005: C4.

Baumann, Shyon. *Hollywood Highbrow: From Entertainment to Art* (Princeton, NJ: Princeton University Press, 2007).

Baxandall, Michael. *Painting and Experience in Fifteenth-Century Italy* (Oxford: Oxford University Press, 1972).

Bearman, Joshua. "The Perfect Game," *Harper's,* July 2008: 65–73.

Becker, Howard S. *Art Worlds* (Berkeley: University of California Press, 1982).

Becker, Howard S. *Outsiders: Studies in the Sociology of Deviance* (New York: Free Press, 1963).

Beisel, Nicola. "Morals versus Art: Censorship, the Politics of Interpretation, and the Victorian Nude," *American Sociological Review* 58 (1993):145–162.

Bennett, Andy. *Cultures of Popular Music* (Philadelphia: Open University Press, 2001).

Bennett, Andy. *Popular Music and Youth Culture: Music, Identity and Place* (New York: St. Martin's Press, 2000).

Bennett, Andy, and Richard A. Peterson, eds. *Music Scenes: Local, Trans-local, and Virtual* (Nashville, TN: Vanderbilt University Press, 2004).

Bielby, William T., and Denise D. Bielby. "'All Hits Are Flukes': Institutional Decision-Making and the Rhetoric of Network Prime-Time Program Development," *American Journal of Sociology* 99 (1994): 1287–1313.

Binder, Amy. "Constructing Racial Rhetoric: Media Depictions of Harm in Heavy Metal and Rap Music," *American Sociological Review* 58 (1993): 753–767.

Bissinger, H. G. *Friday Night Lights: A Town, a Team, and a Dream* (Reading, MA: Addison-Wesley, 1990).

Bloom, Allan. *The Closing of the American Mind* (New York: Simon and Schuster, 1987).

Bloom, Harold. *The Western Canon: The Books and School of the Ages* (New York: Riverhead, 1994).

Boorstin, Daniel J. *The Image: A Guide to Pseudo-Events in America* (New York: Vintage, 1961).

Borer, Michael Ian. *Faithful to Fenway: Believing in Boston, Baseball, and America's Most Beloved Ballpark* (New York: NYU Press, 2008).

Bourdieu, Pierre. *Distinction: A Social Critique of the Judgment of Taste,* Richard Nice, trans. (Cambridge, MA: Harvard University Press, 1984).

Bourgois, Philippe. *In Search of Respect: Selling Crack in El Barrio,* 2nd ed. (Cambridge: Cambridge University Press, 2002).

Boyer, M. Christine. "Cities for Sale: Merchandising History at South Street Seaport," in *Variations on a Theme Park: The New American City and the End of*

Public Space, Michael Sorkin, ed. (New York: Hill and Wang, 1992).

Brewster, Bill, and Frank Broughton. *Last Night a DJ Saved My Life: The History of the Disc Jockey* (New York: Grove, 2000).

Bromberg, Minna, and Gary Alan Fine. "Resurrecting the Red: Pete Seeger and the Purification of Difficult Reputations," *Social Forces* 80 (2002): 1135–1155.

Brooks, David. *Bobos in Paradise: The New Upper Class and How They Got There* (New York: Touchstone, 2001).

Bryson, Bethany. "Anything but Heavy Metal: Symbolic Exclusion and Musical Dislikes," *American Sociological Review* 61 (1996): 884–899.

Bumiller, Elisabeth. "White House Letter: When a Campaign Intrudes on Vacation," *New York Times* 19 July 2004: A12.

Carr, Nicholas. "Is Google Making Us Stupid?" *Atlantic* July/August 2008: 56–63.

Carter, Bill. "On TV, Timing Is Everything at the Olympics," *New York Times* 25 August 2008: C1.

Castronova, Edward. *Synthetic Worlds: The Business and Culture of Online Games* (Chicago: University of Chicago Press, 2005).

Champion, Sarah. "Fear and Loathing in Wisconsin," in Steve Redhead, ed., *The Clubcultures Reader: Readings in Popular Cultural Studies* (Oxford: Blackwell, 1997).

Chen, Shu-Ching Jean, "McDonald's Quietly Raises Prices in China," *Forbes.com*, 25 February 2008.

Chevalier, Judith A., and Dina Mayzlin. "The Effect of Word of Mouth on Sales: Online Book Reviews." Working Paper, National Bureau of Economic Research, 2003.

Clifford, Stephanie. "A Product's Place Is on the Set," *New York Times* 22 July 2008, http://www.nytimes.com/2008/07/22/business/media/22adce.html.

Cohen, Lizabeth. *A Consumers' Republic: The Politics of Mass Consumption in Postwar America* (New York: Knopf, 2003).

Collins, Lauren. "Friend Game," *New Yorker* 21 January 2008: 34–41.

Collins, Patricia Hill. *Black Sexual Politics: African Americans, Gender, and the New Racism* (New York: Routledge, 2005).

Collins, Randall. *Interaction Ritual Chains* (Princeton, NJ: Princeton University Press, 2004a).

Collins, Randall. "Rituals of Solidarity and Security in the Wake of Terrorist Attack," *Sociological Theory* 22 (2004b): 53–87.

Collins, Randall. *The Sociology of Philosophies: A Global Theory of Intellectual Change* (Cambridge, MA: Belknap, 1998).

Cooley, Charles Horton. "The Social Self—the Meaning of 'I,' " in *On Self and Social Organization*, Hans-Joachim Schubert, ed. (Chicago: University of Chicago Press, [1902] 1998).

Crawford, Margaret. "The World in a Shopping Mall," in *Variations on a Theme Park: The New American City and the End of Public Space*, Michael Sorkin, ed. (New York: Hill and Wang, 1992).

Currid, Elizabeth. *The Warhol Economy: How Fashion, Art, and Music Drive New York City* (Princeton, NJ: Princeton University Press, 2007).

Dargis, Manohla. "Showdown in Gotham Town," *New York Times* 18 July 2008.

Davis, Michael. *Street Gang: The Complete History of Sesame Street* (New York: Viking, 2008).

Dell, Kristina. "Second Life's Real-World Problems," *Time* 9 August 2007: 49–50.

DeVeaux, Scott. *The Birth of Bebop: A Social and Musical History* (Berkeley: University of California Press, 1997).

Dichter, Ernest. "How Word-of-Mouth Advertising Works," *Harvard Business Review* (1966): 147–166.

DiMaggio, Paul. "Cultural Entrepreneurship in Nineteenth-Century Boston: The Creation of an Organizational Base for High Culture in America," *Media, Culture & Society* 4 (1982): 33–50.

DiMaggio, Paul, and Francie Ostrower. "Participation in the Arts by Black and White Americans," *Social Forces* 68 (1990): 753–778.

Douglas, Mary. *Purity and Danger: An Analysis of the Concepts of Pollution and Taboo* (London: Routledge, 1991).

Durkheim, Emile. *The Elementary Forms of Religious Life*. Karen E. Fields, trans. (New York: Free Press, [1912] 1995.)

Dyson, Michael Eric. *Between God and Gangsta Rap: Bearing Witness to Black Culture* (New York: Oxford University Press, 1996).

Ebert, Roger. "The Shawshank Redemption," *Chicago Sun-Times* 17 October 1999, http://regerebert.suntimes.com/apps/pbcs.dll/article?AID=/19991017/REVIEWS08/910170301/1023.

Ebert, Roger. "The Year's Ten Best Films and Other Shenanigans," *Chicago Sun-Times* 20 December 2007.

Egan, Jennifer. "Love in the Time of No Time," *New York Times Magazine* 23 November 2003: 66–128.

Ellison, Ralph. "The Golden Age, Time Past," in *Shadow and Act* (New York: Vintage, [1964] 1995).

Erickson, Bonnie. "Culture, Class, and Connections," *American Journal of Sociology* 102 (1996): 217–251.

Farrell, Michael P. *Collaborative Circles: Friendship Dynamics and Creative Work* (Chicago: University of Chicago Press, 2001).

Fatsis, Stefan. *Word Freak: Heartbreak, Triumph, Genius, and Obsession in the World of Competitive Scrabble Players* (New York: Penguin, 2001).

Faulkner, Robert R. *Hollywood Studio Musicians: Their Work and Careers in the Recording Industry* (Chicago: Aldine, 1971).

Faulkner, Robert R., and Andy B. Anderson. "Short-Term Projects and Emergent Careers: Evidence from Hollywood," *American Journal of Sociology* 92 (1987): 879–909.

Feick, Lawrence, and Linda L. Price. "The Market Maven: A Diffuser of Marketplace Information," *Journal of Marketing* 51 (1987): 83–97.

Fine, Gary Alan. "Crafting Authenticity: The Validation of Identity in Self-Taught Art," *Theory and Society* 32 (2003): 153–180.

Fine, Gary Alan. "The Culture of Production: Aesthetic Choices and Constraints in Culinary Work," *American Journal of Sociology* 97 (1992): 1268–1294.

Fischer, Claude S. "Toward a Subcultural Theory of Urbanism," *American Journal of Sociology* 80 (1975): 1319–1341.

Fischer, David Hackett. *Paul Revere's Ride* (New York: Oxford University Press, 1994).

Fish, Stanley. *Is There a Text in This Class? The Authority of Interpretive Communities* (Cambridge, MA: Harvard University Press, 1980).

Foer, Franklin. *How Soccer Explains the World: An Unlikely Theory of Globalization* (New York: Harper Perennial, 2004).

Frank, Thomas. "Why Johnny Can't Dissent," in *Commodify Your Dissent: Salvos from the Baffler*, Thomas Frank and Matt Weiland, eds. (New York: Norton, 1997).

Frederick, Jim. "The Intern Economy and the Culture Trust," in *Boob Jubilee: The Cultural Politics of the New Economy*, Thomas Frank and David Mulcahey, eds. (New York: Norton, 2003).

Gabler, Neal. *Life the Movie: How Entertainment Conquered Reality* (New York: Vintage, 2000).

Gamson, Joshua. *Claims to Fame: Celebrity in Contemporary America* (Berkeley: University of California Press, 1994).

Gans, Herbert J. *The Urban Villagers: Group and Class in the Life of Italian-Americans* (New York: Free Press, 1962).

Gaytan, Marie Sarita. "From Sombreros to *Sincronizadas*: Authenticity, Ethnicity, and the Mexican Restaurant Industry," *Journal of Contemporary Sociology* 37 (2008): 314–341.

Geertz, Clifford. "Deep Play: Notes on the Balinese Cockfight," in *The Interpretation of Culture* (New York: Basic, 1973).

Gelder, Ken, and Sarah Thornton. *The Subcultures Reader* (London: Routledge, 1997).

Gertner, John. "Box Office in a Box," *New York Times Magazine*, 14 November 2004, http://www.nytimes.com/2004/11/14/movies/14DVD.html.

Gibbons, Fiachra. "The Route to Literary Success: Be Young, Gifted, but Most of All Gorgeous," *Guardian* 28 March 2001: 3.

Gibbs, Nancy. "Lessons from the Spirit World," *Time* 21 August 2008, http://www.time.com/time/magazine/articles/0,9171,1834677,00.html.

Gitlin, Todd. *The Sixties: Years of Hope, Days of Rage* (New York: Bantam, 1987).

Gladwell, Malcolm. *Blink: The Power of Thinking without Thinking* (New York: Little, Brown, 2005).

Gladwell, Malcolm. "The Coolhunt," *New Yorker* 17 March 1997: 78–88.

Gladwell, Malcolm. *The Tipping Point: How Little Things Can Make a Big Difference* (Boston: Back Bay, 2002).

Glater, Jonathan D. "Legal Research? Get Me Sushi, with Footnotes," *New York Times* 22 October 2003: A1.

Gluckman, Max. *Order and Rebellion in Tribal Africa* (New York: Free Press, 1963).

Godes, David, and Dina Mayzlin. "Using Online Conversations to Study Word-of-Mouth Communication," *Marketing Science* 23 (2004): 545–560.

Goffman, Erving. *The Presentation of Self in Everyday Life* (New York: Anchor, 1959).

Gramsci, Antonio. *Selections from the Prison Notebooks*, Quitin Hoare and Geoffrey Nowell Smith, eds. and trans. (New York: International Publishers, 1971).

Granovetter, Mark S. "The Strength of Weak Ties," *American Journal of Sociology* 78 (1973): 1360–1380.

Grazian, David. *Blue Chicago: The Search for Authenticity in Urban Blues Clubs* (Chicago: University of Chicago Press, 2003).

Grazian, David. "I'd Rather Be in Philadelphia," *Contexts* 4 (2005): 71–73.

Grazian, David. "The Jazzman's True Academy: Ethnography, Artistic Work and the Chicago Blues Scene," *Ethnologie française* 38 (2008a): 49–57.

Grazian, David. *On the Make: The Hustle of Urban Nightlife* (Chicago: University of Chicago Press, 2008b).

Grazian, David. "Opportunities for Ethnography in the Sociology of Music," *Poetics* 32 (2004): 197–210.

Grindstaff, Laura. *The Money Shot: Trash, Class, and the Making of TV Talk Shows* (Chicago: University of Chicago Press, 2002).

Griswold, Wendy. "American Character and the American Novel: An Expansion of Reflection Theory in the Sociology of Literature," *American Journal of Sociology* 86 (1981): 740–765.

Griswold, Wendy. *Cultures and Societies in a Changing World*, 2nd ed. (Thousand Oaks, CA: Pine Forge, 2004).

Griswold, Wendy. "The Fabrication of Meaning: Literary Interpretation in the United States, Great Britain, and the West Indies," *American Journal of Sociology* 92 (1987): 1077–1117.

Griswold, Wendy. *Regionalism and the Reading Class* (Chicago: University of Chicago Press, 2008).

Griswold, Wendy. *Renaissance Revivals: City Comedy and Revenge Tragedy in the London Theatre, 1576–1980* (Chicago: University of Chicago Press, 1986).

Gross, Daniel. "What's Wrong with Payola?" *Slate* 27 July 2005, http://www.slate.com/id/2123483.

Halle, David. *Inside Culture: Art and Class in the American Home* (Chicago: University of Chicago Press, 1993).

Hannigan, John. *Fantasy City: Pleasure and Profit in the Postmodern Metropolis* (New York: Routledge, 1998).

Hebdige, Dick. *Subculture: The Meaning of Style* (London: Routledge, 1979).

Hemingway, Ernest. *A Moveable Feast* (New York: Bantam, 1965).

Hesse-Biber, Sharlene, Margaret Marino, and Diane Watts-Roy. "A Longitudinal Study of Eating Disorders among College Women," *Gender and Society* 13 (1999): 385–408.

Higie, Robin A., Lawrence F. Feick, and Linda L. Price. "Types and Amount of Word-of-Mouth Communications about Retailers," *Journal of Retailing* 63 (1987): 260–278.

Hirsch, Paul M. "Processing Fads and Fashions: An Organization-Set Analysis of Culture Industry Systems," *American Journal of Sociology* 77 (1972): 639–59.

Hitsch, Guenter, Ali Hortacsu, and Dan Ariely. "What Makes You Click? An Empirical Analysis of Online Dating." Unpublished manuscript, University of California, Santa Cruz, 2004.

Hochschild, Arlie Russell. *The Managed Heart: Commercialization of Human Feeling* (Berkeley: University of California Press, 1983).

Hodos, Jerome, and David Grazian. "The Philadelphia Sound," *Footnotes* July/August 2005: 1, 7.

Hunter, James Davison. *Culture Wars: The Struggle to Define America* (New York: Basic, 1991).

Isaacson, Walter. "How to Save Your Newspaper," *Time* 5 February 2009: 30–33.

Iyer, Pico. *The Global Soul: Jet Lag, Shopping Malls, and the Search for Home* (New York: Vintage Departures, 2001).

Jenkins, Henry. *Convergence Culture: Where Old and New Media Collide* (New York: New York University Press, 2006).

Johnson, Steven. *Everything Bad Is Good for You: How Today's Popular Culture Is Actually Making Us Smarter* (New York: Riverhead Books, 2006).

Johnston, Josee, and Shyon Baumann. "Democracy versus Distinction: A Study of Omnivorousness in Gourmet Food Writing," *American Journal of Sociology* 113 (2007): 165–204.

Joshi, Priva. "Bollylite in America." Paper presented to the Penn Humanities Forum, University of Pennsylvania, 3 March 2009.

Kammen, Michael. *American Culture, American Tastes: Social Change and the 20th Century* (New York: Knopf, 1999)

Katz, Jack. *How Emotions Work* (Chicago: University of Chicago Press, 1999).

Kaufman, Jason, and Orlando Patterson. "Cross-National Cultural Diffusion: The Global Spread of Cricket," *American Sociological Review* 70 (2005): 82–110.

Keen, Andrew. *The Cult of the Amateur: How Today's Internet Is Killing Our Culture* (New York: Doubleday, 2007).

Kinsley, Michael. "You Can't Sell News by the Slice," *New York Times* 10 February 2009: A27.

Klein, Bethany. *As Heard on TV: Popular Music in Advertising* (Surrey: Ashgate, 2009).

Klein, Naomi. *No Logo: No Space, No Choice, No Jobs* (New York: Picador, 2002).

Klinenberg, Eric. "Convergence: News Production in a Digital Age," *Annals of the American Academy of Political and Social Science* 597 (2005): 48–64.

Klinenberg, Eric. *Fighting for Air: The Battle to Control America's Media* (New York: Henry Holt, 2007).

Klosterman, Chuck. *Sex, Drugs, and Cocoa Puffs: A Low Culture Manifesto* (New York: Scribner, 2004).

Klosterman, Chuck. "Viva Morrissey!" in *Chuck Klosterman IV: A Decade of Curious People and Dangerous Ideas* (New York: Scribner, 2006).

Kozinn, Allan. "A Master's in Paul-Is-Definitely-Not-Dead," *New York Times* 8 March 2009: WK3.

Krugman, Paul. "Authentic? Never Mind," *New York Times* 11 June 2007.

Lachmann, Richard. "Graffiti as Career and Ideology," *American Journal of Sociology* 94 (1988): 229-250.

Lamont, Michele. *Money, Morals, and Manners: The Culture of the French and the American Upper-Middle Class* (Chicago: University of Chicago Press, 1992).

Lee, Steven S., and Richard A. Peterson. "Internet-based Virtual Music Scenes: The Case of P2 in Alt.Country Music," in *Music Scenes: Local, Trans-local, and Virtual*, Andy Bennett and Richard A. Peterson, eds. (Nashville, TN: Vanderbilt University Press, 2004).

Lee, Wendy A. "As the Fall Season Arrives, TV Screens Get More Cluttered," *New York Times* 24 September 2007: C1.

Leland, John. "For Rock Bands, Selling Out Isn't What It Used to Be," *New York Times Magazine* 11 March 2001, http://www.nytimes.com/2001/03/11/magazine/11SELLOUT.html?pagewanted=all.

Lessig, Lawrence. *Free Culture: The Nature and Future of Creativity* (New York: Penguin, 2005).

Levine, Lawrence W. "William Shakespeare and the American People: A Study in Cultural Transformation," in *Rethinking Popular Culture*, Chandra Mukerji and Michael Schudson, eds. (Berkeley: University of California Press, 1991).

Lieberson, Stanley. *A Matter of Taste: How Names, Fashions, and Culture Change* (New Haven, CN: Yale University Press, 2000).

Liu, Yong. "Word of Mouth for Movies: Its Dynamics and Impact on Box Office Revenue," *Journal of Marketing* 70 (2006): 74-89.

Lofland, Lyn H. *A World of Strangers: Order and Action in Urban Public Space* (New York: Basic, 1973).

Long, Elizabeth. *Book Clubs: Women and the Uses of Reading in Everyday Life* (Chicago: University of Chicago Press, 2003).

Lopes, Paul D. "Innovation and Diversity in the Popular Music Industry, 1969 to 1990," *American Sociological Review* 57 (1992): 56-71.

Lu, Shun, and Gary Alan Fine. "The Presentation of Ethnic Authenticity: Chinese Food as a Social Accomplishment," *Sociological Quarterly* 36 (1995): 535-553.

Maag, Christopher. "A Hoax Turned Fatal Draws Anger but No Charges," *New York Times* 28 November 2007, http://www.nytimes.com/2007/11/28/us/28hoax.html.

MacCannell, Dean. *The Tourist: A New Theory of the Leisure Class* (New York: Schocken, 1976).

MacDonald, Dwight. "A Theory of Mass Culture," in *Mass Culture: The Popular Arts in America*, Bernard Rosenberg and David Manning White, eds. (New York: Free Press, 1957).

Marek, Angela. "Fifteen Minutes: The Beautiful and the Damned: Enforcing 'the Look' at Abercrombie & Fitch," *Harvard Crimson* 24 February 2000, http://www.thecrimson.com/article.aspx?ref=100196.

Maslin, Janet. "With a Disappearance, Life Turns Upside Down," *New York Times* 16 February 2009: C7.

Massey, Douglas, and Nancy Denton. *American Apartheid: Segregation and the Making of the Underclass* (Cambridge, MA: Harvard University Press, 1993).

McCormick, Lisa. "New Fish on the Block," *Contexts* 8 (2009): 62-64.

McLeod, Kembrew. "Authenticity within Hip-Hop and Other Cultures Threatened with Assimilation," *Journal of Communication* 49 (1999): 134-150.

McLuhan, Marshall. *The Medium Is the Massage* (New York: Random House, 1967).

Mead, Rebecca. *One Perfect Day: The Selling of the American Wedding* (New York: Penguin, 2007).

Meredith, Robyn. *The Elephant and the Dragon: The Rise of India and China and What It Means for All of Us* (New York: Norton, 2007).

Meyers, Jessica. "Employees: 'Hierarchy of Hotness' Rules at Abercrombie & Fitch," *Dallas Morning News*, 27 August 2008, http://www.dallasnews.com/sharedcontent/dws/dn/latestnews/stories/082708dnmetabercrombie.4027698.html.

Miller, Laura J. *Reluctant Capitalists: Bookselling and the Culture of Consumption* (Chicago: University of Chicago Press, 2007).

Milstein, Denise. *Protest and Counterculture under Authoritarianism: Uruguayan and Brazilian Musical Movements in the 1960s.* Unpublished dissertation, Department of Sociology, Columbia University, 2007.

Mishkind, Marc E., Judith Rodin, Lisa R. Silberstein, and Ruth H. Striegel-Moore. "The Embodiment of Masculinity: Culture, Psychological, and Behavioral Dimensions," *American Behavioral Scientist* 29 (1986): 545-562.

Morgenson, Gretchen. "Given a Shovel, Americans Dig Deeper into Debt," *New York Times* 20 July 2008: A1.

Murphy, Cullen. "Lifosuction," *Atlantic* February 2002, http://www.theatlantic.com/doc/200202/murphy.

National Commission on Terrorist Attacks upon the United States. *The 9/11 Commission Report: Final Report of the National Commission on Terrorist Attacks upon the United States* (New York: Norton, 2004).

Neff, Gina, Elizabeth Wissinger, and Sharon Zukin. "Entrepreneurial Labor among Cultural Producers: 'Cool' Jobs in 'Hot' Industries," *Social Semiotics* 15 (2005): 307-334.

Negus, Keith. "Cultural Production and the Corporation: Musical Genres and the Strategic Management of Creativity in the US Recording Industry," *Media, Culture and Society* 20 (1998): 359-379.

Ohmann, Richard, ed. *Making and Selling Culture* (Hanover, NH: University Press of New England, 1996).

Pareles, Jon. "An Album Is Judged Obscene; Rap: Slick, Violent, Nasty and, Maybe Hopeful," *New York Times* 17 June 1990: sec. 4, p. 1.

Pareles, Jon. "Songs from the Heart of a Marketing Plan," *New York Times* 28 December 2008: AR1.

Peiss, Kathy. *Cheap Amusements: Working Women and Leisure in Turn-of-the-Century New York* (Philadelphia: Temple University Press, 1986).

Peterson, Richard A. *Creating Country Music: Fabricating Authenticity* (Chicago: University of Chicago Press, 1997).

Peterson, Richard A. "Understanding Audience Segmentation: From Elite and Mass to Omnivore and Univore," *Poetics* 21 (1992): 243-258.

Pérez-Peña, Richard. "As Cities Go from Two Papers to One, Talk of Zero," *New York Times* 12 March 2009: A1.

Platt, Larry. "The Reincarnation of Stephen Starr," *Philadelphia Magazine* (September 2000): 82, 83.

Pollan, Michael. *The Omnivore's Dilemma: A Natural History of Four Meals* (New York: Penguin, 2006).

Postman, Neil. *Amusing Ourselves to Death: Public Discourse in the Age of Show Business* (New York: Viking, 1984).

Postrel, Virginia. *The Substance of Style: How the Rise of Aesthetic Value Is Remaking Commerce, Culture, and Consciousness* (New York: Perennial, 2004).

Pressler, Jessica. "Philadelphia Story: The Next Borough," *New York Times* 14 August 2005: Sunday Styles sec., p. 1.

Pressler, Jessica. "The Philly School," *Philadelphia Magazine*, May 2006.

Putnam, Robert D. *Bowling Alone: The Collapse and Revival of American Community* (New York: Simon and Schuster, 2000).

Quinn, Jim. "The Making of Morimoto," *Philadelphia Magazine* January (2002): 72.

Radway, Janice A. *Reading the Romance: Women, Patriarchy, and Popular Literature* (Chapel Hill: University of North Carolina Press, 1991).

Reynolds, Simon. *Generation Ecstasy: Into the World of Techno and Rave Culture* (New York: Routledge, 1999).

Rosenbloom, Stephanie. "Putting Your Best Cyberface Forward," *New York Times* 3 January 2008,

Rosenfeld, Michael. "Celebration, Politics, Selective Looting and Riots: A Micro Level Study of the Bulls Riot of 1992 in Chicago," *Social Problems* 44 (1997): 482-502.

Roy, William G. "Aesthetic Identity, Race, and American Folk Music," *Qualitative Sociology* 25 (2002): 459-469.

Sacks, Oliver. *Musicophilia: Tales of Music and the Brain* (New York: Knopf, 2007).

Schlosser, Eric. *Fast Food Nation: The Dark Side of the All-American Meal* (New York: Perennial, 2002).

Schor, Juliet B. *Born to Buy* (New York: Scribner, 2005).

Schor, Juliet B. *The Overspent American: Why We Want What We Don't Need* (New York: Harper Perennial, 1998).

Schwartz, Barry. "Memory as a Cultural System: Abraham Lincoln in World War II," *American Sociological Review* 61 (1996): 908-927.

Schwartz, Barry. "Postmodernity and Historical Reputation: Abraham Lincoln in Late Twentieth-Century American Memory," *Social Forces* 77 (1998): 63-103.

Schwartz, Barry, and Howard Schuman. "History, Commemoration, and Belief: Abraham Lincoln in American Memory, 1945-2001," *American Sociological Review* 70 (2005): 183-203.

Schwartz, Mattathias. "The Hold-'Em Holdup," *New York Times Magazine* 11 June 2006, htt p://www.nytimes.com/2006/06/11/magazine/11poker.html.

Schull, Natasha Dow. "Digital Gambling: The Coincidence of Desire and Design," *Annals of the American Academy of Political and Social Science* 597 (2005): 65-81.

Sey, Jennifer. *Chalked Up* (New York: William Morrow, 2008).

Shales, Tom, and James Andrew Miller. *Live from New York: An Uncensored History of Saturday Night Live* (Boston: Little, Brown, 2002).

Shively, JoEllen. "Cowboys and Indians: Perceptions of Western Films among American Indians and Anglos," *American Sociological Review* 57 (1992): 725-734.

Sigman, Aric. "Well Connected? The Biological Implications of 'Social Networking,'" *Biologist* 56 (2009): 14-20.

Simmel, Georg. "The Metropolis and Mental Life," in *On Individuality and Social Forms*, Donald N. Levine, ed. (Chicago: University of Chicago Press, [1903] 1971).

Simon, Richard Keller. *Trash Culture: Popular Culture and the Great Tradition* (Berkeley: University of California Press, 1999).

Sisario, Ben. "Music Sales Fell in 2008, but Climbed on the Web," *New York Times* 1 January 2009: C1.

Solove, Daniel J. *The Future of Reputation: Gossip, Rumor, and Privacy on the Internet* (New Haven, CT: Yale University Press, 2007).

Sorkin, Michael. "See You in Disneyland," in *Variations on a Theme Park: The New American City and the End of Public Space*, Michael Sorkin, ed. (New York: Hill and Wang, 1992).

"Starbucks Wars," *Consumer Reports*, March 2007, http://www.consumerreports.org/cro/food/beverages/coffee-tea/coffee-taste-test-3-07/overview/0307_coffee_ov_1.htm.

Steinhauer, Jennifer. "Verdict in MySpace Suicide Case," *New York Times* 27 November 2008: A25.

Surowiecki, James. *The Wisdom of Crowds* (New York: Anchor, 2005).

Taylor, John. "Word of Mouth Is Where It's At," *Brandweek*, 2 June 2003: 26.

Thompson, Hunter S. *Hell's Angels: A Strange and Terrible Saga* (New York: Ballantine, 1967).

Tocqueville, Alexis de. *Democracy in America*, J. P. Mayer, ed., George Lawrence, trans. (New York: Harper Perennial, 1988).

Tucker, Robert C., ed., *The Marx-Engels Reader*, 2nd ed. (New York: Norton, 1978).

Underhill, Paco. *Why We Buy: The Science of Shopping* (New York: Simon and Schuster, 2009).

Veblen, Thorstein. *The Theory of the Leisure Class* (New York: Penguin, [1899] 1994).

Virtual Worlds, Real Leaders: Online Games Put the Future of Business Leadership on Display. IBM Global Innovation Outlook 2.0 Report (2007).

Walker, Rob. *Buying In: The Secret Dialogue between What We Buy and Who We Are* (New York: Random House, 2008a).

Walker, Rob. "Enterprising," *New York Times Magazine* 28 December 2008b: 14.

Walker, Rob. "Mash-Up Model," *New York Times Magazine* 20 July 2008c, http://www.nytimes.com/2008/07/20/magazine/20wwln-consumed-t.html.

Walser, Robert. "Highbrow, Lowbrow, Voodoo Aesthetics," in *Microphone Fiends: Youth Music and Youth Culture*, Andrew Ross and Tricia Rose, eds. (New York: Routledge, 1994).

Wareham, Dean. *Black Postcards: A Rock & Roll Romance* (New York: Penguin, 2008).

Weeks, Linton. "Judged by Their Back Covers: Writing Well Helps Sell a Book, and Photographing Well Doesn't Hurt," *Washington Post* 2 July 2001: C1.

Weil, Elizabeth. "A Swimmer of a Certain Age," *New York Times Magazine* 29 June 2008, http://www.nytimes.com/2008/06/29/magazine/29sorres-t.html.

Wherry, Frederick F. *Global Markets and Local Crafts: Thailand and Costa Rica Compared* (Baltimore, MD: Johns Hopkins University Press, 2008).

Whyte, William Foote. *Street Corner Society: The Social Structure of an Italian Slum* (Chicago: University of Chicago Press, 1943).

Williams, Raymond. *Keywords: A Vocabulary of Culture and Society* (New York: Oxford University Press, 1983).

Wirth, Louis. "Urbanism as a Way of Life," *American Journal of Sociology* 44 (1938): 1–24.

X, Malcolm. *The Autobiography of Malcolm X* (New York: Ballantine, 1964).

Yuen, Nancy Wang, "Performing Authenticity: How Hollywood Working Actors Negotiate Identity." Unpublished dissertation, Department of Sociology, UCLA, 2008.

Zafirau, Stephen. "Reputation Work in Selling Film and Television: Life in the Hollywood Talent Industry," *Qualitative Sociology* 31 (2008): 99–127.

Zengerle, Jason. "The State of the George W. Bush Joke," *New York Times* 22 August 2004: sec. 2, p. 2.

Zolberg, Vera L. "Conflicting Visions in American Art Museums," *Theory and Society* 10 (1981): 103–125.

Zuckoff, Mitchell. "The Perfect Mark," *New Yorker* 15 May 2006: 36–42.

Zukin, Sharon. *The Cultures of Cities* (Cambridge, MA: Blackwell, 1995).

Zukin, Sharon. *Landscapes of Power: From Detroit to Disney World* (Berkeley: University of California Press, 1991).

Zukin, Sharon. *Point of Purchase: How Shopping Changed American Culture* (New York: Routledge, 2004).

Credits

Chapter 1
pp. 2–3 Diane Bondareff/Bloomberg News/Landov; **p. 5** (top left), Skip Bolen/WireImage/Getty Images; **p. 5** (top right), Fin Costello/Redferns/Retna Ltd.; **p. 5** (middle), Archive Photos/Getty Images; **p. 5** (bottom left), Michael Ochs Archives/Getty Images; **p. 5** (bottom right), Keith Morris/Redferns; **p. 10**, Columbia/Courtesy Everett Collection; **p. 12**, Excerpt from "The Problem with Music" by Steve Albini, from COMMODIFY YOUR DISSENT: THE BUSINESS OF CULTURE IN THE NEW GILDED AGE, edited by Thomas Frank and Matt Weiland. Copyright © 1997 by The Baffler Literary Magazine, Inc. Used by permission of W. W. Norton & Company, Inc.; photograph © Brad Miller/Retna Ltd.; **p. 13**, (left), Charles Trainor/Time & Life Pictures/Getty Images; **p. 13** (right), Tom Copi/Michael Ochs Archives/Getty Images **p. 15**, Bob Levey/WireImage/Getty Images; **p. 16**, Lyle A. Waisman/FilmMagic/Getty Images; **p. 18**, Courtesy Everett Collection; **p. 20**, Mark Leong, 2006, Redux.

Chapter 2
pp. 22–23, Peter Turnley/Corbis; **p. 26** (left), Mohamed Messara/epa/Corbis; **p. 26** (right), Sitton/zefa/Corbis; **p. 28**, Jeff Greenberg/Photo Edit; **p. 29**, AP Photo/ Joseph Kaczmarek; **p. 32**, Justin Sullivan/Getty Images; **p. 34**, PEOPLE © 2009 Time Inc. All rights reserved; **p. 35**, Fred Duval/FilmMagic/Getty Images; **p. 37**, Allan Grant/Time Life Pictures/Getty Images; **p. 39**, William Thomas Cain/Getty Images; **p. 41**, Joe McNally/Getty Images; **p. 42**, Courtesy Everett Collection.

Chapter 3
pp. 44–45, *Adbusters*; **p. 47**, Contemporary Films Ltd./Photofest; **p. 49**, The Kobal Collection; **p. 50**, Fox Searchlight/Everett Collect; **p. 53**, Dmitry Krasny/ Deka Design; **p. 55**, Fox/Photofest; **p. 57**, Marc Asnin/ Corbis; **p. 58** (left), Warner Bros./Everett Collection; **p. 58** (right), Tommy Baynard/NBC/Everett Collection; **p. 60**, AP Photo; **p. 62**, Nhat V. Meyer/MCT/Landov; **p. 64**, Laura Dwight/Photo Edit.

Chapter 4
pp. 66–67, Rolf Bruderer/Corbis; **p. 70**, Lee Celano/ *The New York Times*/Redux; **p. 74** (left), Rob Grabowski/ Retna Ltd.; **p. 74** (right), Tibor Bozi/Corbis; **p. 76** (left), © IFC Films/Courtesy Everett Collection; **p. 76** (right), © 20th Century Fox Film Corp. All rights reserved. Courtesy: Everett Collection; **p. 78**, BlueMoon Stock/ Alamy; **p. 82**, AP/Wide World Photos; **p. 84**, Photo by Jack Kurtz/ZUMA Press. © 2005 by Jack Kurtz; **p. 85**, Spencer Grant/ZUMA Press.

Chapter 5
pp. 88–89, Ebet Roberts/Redferns/Getty Images; **p. 93**, Library of Congress; **p. 94**, Mick Hutson/Redferns/ Getty Images; **p. 97**, Paul Hoeffler/Redferns/Getty Images; **p. 100**, Bettmann/Corbis; **p. 102**, John Cohen/ Getty Images; **p. 104**, Lynn Goldsmith/Corbis; **p. 106**, Jan Woitas/epa/Corbis; **p. 109**, AP/Wide World Photos.

Chapter 6
pp. 110–111, Claudette Barius/© HBO/Courtesy: Everett Collection; **p. 112**, Fox Searchlight/Photofest; **p. 114**, Kristin Murphy/WireImage/Getty Images; **p. 117**, Michael Germana/Everett Collection; **p. 119**, China Photos/ Getty Images; **p. 120**, Courtesy Everett Collection; **p. 121**, Robert Voets/© CBS/Courtesy: Everett Collection; **p. 122** (left), © Sony Pictures/Courtesy Everett Collection; **p. 122** (right), © Columbia Pictures/ Courtesy Everett Collection; **p. 125**, Photo by Hasbro, Inc. via Getty Images; **p. 128** (left), Kelsey McNeal/© ABC/Courtesy: Everett Collection; **p. 128** (right), Monty Brinton/CBS/Landov.

Chapter 7
pp. 132–133, The Kobal Collection/20th Century Fox/ Paramount/Wallace, Merie W.; **p. 136**, Kevin Dietsch/ UPI/Landov; **p. 137**, Hulton Archive/Getty Images; **p. 140**, Ruth Fremson/*The New York Times*; **p. 144**, Michel Arnaud/Beateworks/Corbis; **p. 146**, Jeff Vespa/ WireImage/Getty Images; **p. 150**, Joan Marcus.

Chapter 8
pp. 152–153, Pictorial Press Ltd./Alamy; **p. 157**, Universal/ Everett Collection; **p. 159**, Jeaneen Lund; **p. 161**, Pictorial Press Ltd./Alamy; **p. 164**, Courtesy Everett Collection; **p. 167**, Timothy A. Clary/AFP/Getty Images; **p. 170**, Franz-Marc Frei/Corbis; **p. 172**, Barry Schultz/ Sunshine/Retna Ltd.

Chapter 9
pp. 174–175, Kye R. Lee/*Dallas Morning News*/Corbis; **p. 178**, Courtesy of Michael Graves Design Group; **p. 180**, Richard Cummins/Corbis; **p. 183**, Starr Restaurants; **p. 186**, Mark Mainz/Getty Images; **p. 189**, Reed Saxon/AP; **p. 192**, David Katzenstein/Corbis; **p. 193**, Hiroko Masuike for *The New York Times*.

Chapter 10
pp. 194–195, Eric Risberg/AP Photo; **p. 198**, Reuters/ Shannon Stapleton/Landov; **p. 200**, Joel Ryan/PA Photos/Landov; **p. 202**, Ge Jin, © 2008; **p. 206**, AP Photos; **p. 209**, John Moore/Getty Images; **p. 211**, TriStar Pictures/Courtesy Everett Collection; **p. 213**, Bob King/ AP/Wide World Photos.

Index